THE SECOND AMERICAN PARTY SYSTEM

PARTY FORMATION IN THE JACKSONIAN ERA

Publication of this book was sponsored by the American Association for State and Local History, Nashville, Tennessee, under its continuing program to promote a better understanding for our national heritage at a local level. It is the recipient of the Association's Manuscript Award for 1964.

The Second American Party System

PARTY FORMATION
IN THE JACKSONIAN ERA

By

RICHARD P. MC CORMICK

THE UNIVERSITY OF NORTH CAROLINA PRESS · CHAPEL HILL

To
KATCH, JOHN, AND DOT

Acknowledgments

The pleasantest task of an author, with the drudgery of research and writing behind him, is to express his appreciation of the indispensable assistance he has received in the course of his labors. Because of the nature of this study, I owe an especially large debt of gratitude to the authors of the scores of monographs on the political history of individual states. My heavy reliance on this scholarship is inadequately suggested by the references in my bibliography. I am also greatly obliged for services that exceeded every reasonable expectation to the staffs of the Rutgers University Library, the New York Public Library, the Library of Congress, the University of North Carolina Library, the Cambridge University Library, and the state archival agencies in Massachusetts, Connecticut, New Jersey, Maryland, Virginia, North Carolina, Kentucky, Tennessee, and Georgia.

Among the many individuals who aided me, my special thanks are due to Carl E. Prince, who served as my research assistant for a year and compiled the election data upon the analysis of which so much of this investigation depended. My mentor, Roy F. Nichols, was constant in his interest and encouragement. He, together with John A. Munroe, Harry R. Stevens, and Alvin K. Lynn gave helpful suggestions based on their reading of the manuscript. The students in my seminar over the past dozen years contributed more than they realized by their probing essays and by their tolerance of my musings.

My studies were facilitated by a generous grant from the Social Science Research Council and by assistance from the

Rutgers Research Council. For the ideal environment in which most of my writing was done I am eternally grateful to the Master and Fellows of Jesus College, Cambridge. I am duly appreciative of the sponsorship of the publication of this book by the American Association for State and Local History.

In any assessment of my obligations, I must dutifully acknowledge that the greatest of all is to my wife, who by her many sacrifices as well as by her unstinting helpfulness has filled the role of the ideal academic spouse.

RICHARD P. McCORMICK

New Brunswick
New Jersey

CONTENTS

———•◦•———

CHAPTER I

INTRODUCTION

The purpose of this study is to investigate the formation of the second American party system. The first American party system, which had its origins late in Washington's presidency, entered upon a stage of arrested development after 1800, and by 1820 it had all but disintegrated. In 1824, essentially as a result of the revival of the contest for the presidency, there began a new era of party formation. At different times between 1824 and 1836, parties identified by their stands on the presidential question were formed in state after state. By 1840, when the new parties had attained an equilibrium of forces nationally, politics in every state was conducted on a two-party basis. A methodical investigation of when, how, and under what circumstances party formation occurred in each state, together with a description and assessment of the nature of party organizations and the response of the electorates to party appeals should afford important insights into parties and politics in the Jackson period.

Historical investigations of American political parties have usually been concerned with providing answers to two broad questions. What doctrines, ideologies, or programs did each party espouse? What interests, classes, or sections were most strongly represented in the composition of each party? We have wanted to know what the Federalists and the Democratic-Republicans "stood for." We have sought to distinguish Whigs

3

from Democrats in terms of the socio-economic bases of the two parties. Without at this time endeavoring to account for this preoccupation with the questions of doctrine and composition, I would merely suggest that this time-honored approach to the study of parties is not only limiting but may also be deceptive. Surely the political phenomena that we deal with under the category of parties are exceedingly complex and subtle. They vary over periods of time and from place to place. They present us with hosts of bewildering problems. Attempts to describe and analyze them may properly involve us with questions other than those of ideology and constituencies. Moreover, inquiries exclusively directed toward defining the differences between parties will be deficient in describing the common attributes of the parties that made up any particular party system. This study will be concerned, then, not with the formation of a single party, nor with the qualities that distinguished Democrats from Whigs, but rather with the emergence of a new two-party system.

Because my perspective on American parties is admittedly unconventional, and may well be confusing or disappointing to those who perceive parties only in terms of doctrines or constituent groups, some brief explanation of my own approach would seem to be in order. Basically, I share with Professor Maurice Duverger the understanding that American parties are above all electoral machines, engaged in nominating and electing candidates, rather than, as Edmund Burke put it, being "a body of men united for promoting by their joint endeavours the national interest upon some particular principle in which they are all agreed. . . ." I find myself in agreement with Professor Duverger, too, in his insistence that parties must be studied systematically in terms of their structures and that the structures of parties are profoundly affected by the constitutional and legal environment within which they evolve. I have therefore devoted what to some may appear to be a considerable amount of attention to the matter of party structure and to constitutional forms in examining the process of party formation.

The crucial importance of the relationship between the structure that parties assume and the constitutional environment would seem to be obvious, but it has commonly been slighted. There were, generally speaking, no political parties before 1789. Within a decade, parties had come into existence. Although we may relate their origins to the conflict between Jeffersonians and Hamiltonians or to the controversy over the Jay Treaty, we must acknowledge that comparable conflicts and controversies before 1789 had not produced parties. It would seem to be incontrovertible that it was the new constitutional environment, brought into effect by the adoption of the federal Constitution, that created the essential conditions for the emergence of parties. Moreover, the structures of these parties were to be directly influenced by the form of the Constitution. There may be many reasons why American parties differ profoundly in structure from parties in other nations, but any analysis of such differences could well begin with the difference in constitutional forms.

The influence of the constitutional and legal environment on party structures is evident at the state level as well. In the period with which this study is concerned, there was a remarkable range of constitutional diversity from state to state. Massachusetts, New York, Virginia, and Illinois, for example, represented four different types of constitutions, and party structures within those states varied accordingly. Later, as state constitutions tended to become more uniform, party structures were to become less differentiated.

Because this study deals with a particular party system and is confined solely to the period of party formation, it can not, of course, result in generalizations about the nature of parties in other eras; neither can it be regarded as descriptive of parties after they have reached the stage of maturity. These qualifications are essential, for they imply my conviction that each of the three party systems that has existed in the United States since the 1790's must be viewed as a distinctive entity, differing so fundamentally from one another as to constitute separate models.

This is not the place to enter into a detailed discussion of the differences among the three party systems, but abundant evidence exists to make it clear that the circumstances under which parties formed in the 1790's, the 1830's, and the 1850's were highly dissimilar. What may have been true with respect to the role of certain factors in one instance would not necessarily apply to all. The second party system, as I see it, was a very special kind of party system. It was unique in its origins, in its national comprehensiveness and balance, and in the fatal flaws that brought about its early disruption. This, again, would seem to be a generally acceptable proposition, but it must be acknowledged that students of American parties have been prone to see the history of parties as a continuum or to ascribe to parties at all times similar attributes. Any generalizations about American political parties may have to be qualified in terms of the particular party system under consideration and the particular stage of development of that party system.

Studies of American parties have most commonly been conceived within one or another of two frameworks. Some scholars have endeavored to treat parties as national entities and have accordingly looked to activities in Congress, in the national party conventions, or in presidential campaigns to find evidence on which generalizations about parties might be based. Others, recognizing the federalized nature of American parties, have chosen to concentrate on the investigation of party development within a single state. Both perspectives are useful and valid, but both have serious and obvious limitations. Employment of the national perspective can lead to gross distortions of certain factors operative on party development and can result in a deceptively oversimplified picture of party behavior. Similarly, descriptions of parties within a single state are open to the criticism that although they may negate,

modify, or confirm the generalizations that have been set forth
by nationally oriented studies of parties, they leave us in doubt
as to whether the state under consideration is to be viewed as
exceptional or typical.

There is an alternative perspective from which to study
the formation of the second American party system. The
most rewarding approach, I believe, is to attempt to investigate party developments in all of the states simultaneously.
I would suggest that if there were but five states in the Union,
instead of several times that number, we should all have concluded long since to study parties in this manner. But the
difficulty is that with such a large number of political communities, the task of making an analytical and comparative
study of all of them is so formidable as to be discouraging.
Having attempted it, I am more than ever aware of how
formidable is such an undertaking. It is no simple matter for
one scholar to attempt to familiarize himself with details of
party formation in each of twenty-three states to the extent, at
least, that some meaningful and reliable comparisons, contrasts, and generalizations can be made about party behavior.
Nevertheless, I am fully persuaded that such an approach to
the study of parties is essential.

What I have tried to do, therefore, is to ask a series of
identical questions relevant to the emergence and development
of parties in each of the states that had been admitted to the
Union before 1824, exclusive of South Carolina.[1] The questions were framed partly with the consideration in mind that
it should be possible to answer them in fairly concrete terms.
More importantly, they were designed to get at definite, though

1. South Carolina has been excluded from this survey for two reasons. Because there were no state-wide elections for any office earlier than 1860, many
of the analyses of electoral data that have been made with respect to other
states are not feasible in the case of South Carolina. Also, in part as a result
of the peculiar electoral-constitutional system, as well as the extraordinary
influence of John C. Calhoun, the conduct of poiltics in South Carolina was
so distinctive as to be markedly different from any other state. Interesting as
South Carolina was as a special case, I have not deemed it necessary to include
the state in this comprehensive treatment of party formation.

limited, problems related to the formation and operation of parties in the states. It was necessary that the questions be identical and specific in order that the answers might be comparable. I did not wish merely to present brief, unstructured summaries of the history of parties in each of the states but rather to organize information about party formation in such a way as to facilitate a comparative study of the problem.

One set of questions concerned the constitutional and legal environment within which elections were conducted. Who was eligible to vote? What was the method of voting? What was the voting unit? When were state and national elections held? What were the units of representation in the state legislature? How was the governor chosen? When were local officials made elective by popular vote? What was the method of electing congressmen and presidential electors? In addition, some attempt was made to identify special or peculiar influences—economic, sectional, ethnic, cultural, or traditional —that apparently operated to produce distinctive political behavior.

A second set of questions was intended to reveal how politics was conducted before 1824. What was the party situation? What devices of management and nomination were employed? What was the style of campaigning? Were elections being contested on a party basis in the years 1820 to 1824? How extensive was voter participation in both state and presidential elections? The answers to these two sets of questions provided the background essential to an understanding of the formation of parties subsequent to 1824.

The third group of questions dealt with the formation and development of parties subsequent to 1824. When, after 1824, were parties formed to contest national elections? When did they contest state elections? When did the new parties become similarly aligned for the purposes of contesting both state and national elections? What circumstances best explain the emergence of parties at a particular time? What was the nature of party organization? When did the device of the state convention make its appearance? When did the parties acquire an elaborate structure of organization at all levels of government? When did campaigns become "popular" in style? What was the condition of party balance or imbalance between 1824 and 1852? What was the extent of voter participation in state and presidential elections?

To most of these questions quite specific answers can be given. They are factual or descriptive. Some of the questions, however, depend on the definitions given to particular terms or involve elements of judgment. For example, it is relatively simple to date the first use of the state convention in each state or to measure voter participation. But descriptions of "party situations," or determinations of when "party formation" can be said to have taken place, present some problems. Even more difficult to establish are the answers to queries regarding the "special influences" that affected political behavior or the "circumstances" that explain the timing of party formation.

It would seem to be desirable to set forth some working definitions of the terms "party," "party situation," and "party formation." Because a party may possess certain attributes when it is in the process of formation and other attributes when it reaches maturity, the obvious difficulties involved in defining the term are compounded. Furthermore, parties assume various forms depending on a number of conditions that vary from state to state. Rather than attempting at this point a definition of what a party *is*, I shall merely set forth those conditions I have taken to be indicative of the existence of a party or parties. Where I have found that votes cast in an election were concentrated behind a slate of candidates nominated by some agency, formal or informal, and when such evidence of leadership and voter cohesion was manifested in successive elections I have concluded that a party existed. The minimum requisites of a party, then, would be leadership and voter identification with that leadership and with the candidates put forward by the leaders. Additionally, the party might have a name, an elaborate organization, a relationship with parties in other states pledged to the same candidates and purposes, and even a program or statement of beliefs and principles.

Several different types of party situations can be distinguished. There was, first of all, the "no party" situation, which prevailed in all states before parties were formed and which existed in some states after the disintegration of the first party system. In this situation voters identified themselves with the candidates as individuals, voting followed no discernible or consistent pattern, and there was no disciplined relationship between a leadership group and either candidates or voters. There might, however, be some informal management of politics by juntos or factions. Loose coalitions of influential personages might be formed to support candidates for office or a powerful junto might dominate the actions of a majority in the legislature, for example, but this type of management I have not deemed to constitute a party. In a very large number of states down to 1836, politics was indeed conducted on a "no party" basis, and it would be important to know in more detail than is now possible how this kind of politics operated.

A second recognizable category is the "one-party" situation, which prevailed in most of the southern states until late in Jackson's administration and was observable at various times in many other states as well. Typical of this situation was a rudimentary party apparatus that provided leadership at the state level, chiefly for the purpose of securing agreement on a single slate of presidential electors. Where virtually all leaders, candidates, and voters professed the same party allegiance, contests for offices other than the presidency might be waged on the basis of personalities or between factions. A special type of one-party situation existed in certain New England states after 1817, where despite the "retirement" of the Federalists from politics the Republicans felt it necessary to attempt to retain the elaborate party organization that they had constructed when interparty competition was intense.

A third situation is what I have described as the "dual party" system.   In this case, politicians and voters assumed one set of party identities when contesting state elections and quite a different set of identities when contesting congressional and presidential elections.   In effect, there was one party system for national politics and another for state politics.   This situation was not uncommon in the newer states of the West, although it was not restricted to that region.   The dual party system was usually short-lived; in time the intense interest and the pressures generated by the contests for the presidency became dominant in determining party alignments.   A distinguishable variety of the dual-party situation existed in certain states, notably New York, Georgia, and Kentucky.   In those states at particular periods what can best be termed "state-oriented" parties developed and waged vigorous contests for supremacy within the state.   But these contests bore no direct relation to national politics and the opposing parties might even support the same presidential candidate.

The classic situation, which actually did not become prevalent until after 1834, was the two-party situation.   In this case two parties—each with a structure of leadership and a mass of voters that responded to partisan appeals—contested elections at all levels of government and exhibited approximately the same alignments in both state and national elections.   Such two-party situations can for purposes of analysis be classified somewhat arbitrarily as balanced or unbalanced, competitive or non-competitive, depending on whether the majority party customarily received less than, or more than 60 per cent of the total vote cast.   They can also be categorized, with considerably less precision, on the basis of the elaborateness of the organizational structures of the two parties.

Finally, there were some instances of multiparty situations. These were remarkably few earlier than 1840; aside from insignificant exceptions the Antimasonic party was involved in each such situation. Multipartyism was always of brief duration and its effects were usually moderated by more or less successful efforts directed toward producing a fusion of the Antimasons with one of the "major" parties. Given the fluid character of American politics in the decade of the 1820's, the relative rarity of multiparty situations is striking and testifies to the strength of the forces in the American political system that militated against third parties.

In considering the condition of parties in the states during the period covered by this study, then, I have considered it appropriate, and even necessary, to distinguish among several types of party situations rather than to try to use a single concept of "party" that would have to be so abstract or general as to be all but meaningless. Although I have identified five major types of party situations, it would be more nearly correct to observe that each state, especially down to 1836, must be treated as a special case. I am persuaded, however, that the categories I have employed do not result in serious distortions of actual conditions, and they do facilitate meaningful descriptions of political behavior.

In organizing this state-by-state analysis of party formation, I have grouped the states into four regions. This arrangement is not arbitrary. It proceeded from the discovery that within each region—New England, the Middle States, the South, and the Newer West—there were strong similarities, deriving from explainable factors, and that each region differed notably from every other with respect to its patterns of party development and general political behavior. Grouping the states in this way made it feasible to draw detailed comparisons of the process of party formation within each region and also to discern contrasts among regions. If this study possesses any virtues, they derive from the opportunities that this comparative approach has offered for relating what might otherwise be regarded as unique incidents to comparable incidents in every other state in order to secure some sound basis for making generalizations about party formation.

The restricted scope of this inquiry should be obvious. I have asked a limited number of fairly specific questions about a particular dimension of parties. Consequently, my answers can not purport to add up to a comprehensive account of party formation. There are other aspects of party than those upon which I have focused. It would be necessary in any comprehensive study to examine in detail the manifestations of party behavior in state legislatures and in Congress. I have made some investigation of the development of the national party convention, but this subject, together with other related matters involving leadership and management of parties at the national level, I have had to regard as tangential to my primary concern with party formation in the states. And, as previously stated, I have not sought the answers to the traditional questions of what parties stood for and what classes or interests they represented.

It is the major thesis of this study that the second American party system had its origins in the successive contests for the presidency between 1824 and 1840. It did not emerge from cleavages within Congress, nor from any polarization of attitudes on specific public issues, nor did it represent merely the revival in new form of pre-existing party alignments. The second party system did not spring into existence at any one time. Rather, new party alignments appeared at different times from region to region. The most influential factor determining when alignments appeared within a particular region was the regional identifications of the presidential candidates. As changes occurred in the personnel involved in the contest for the presidency, corresponding changes took place in regional party alignments. New England, for example, was politically monolithic in support of John Quincy Adams, but when Clay was substituted for Adams, a two-party situation resulted. The South was monolithic behind Jackson, but when he was replaced by Van Buren, the South divided into two parties.

Somewhat ironically, in view of the strong regional consciousness manifested by the electorate, the net effect of the successive contests between various candidates was to produce a party system that by 1840 was remarkably free of regional bias. The two new parties were balanced and competitive in every region. For a very brief period—between 1840 and 1852 —the nation, for the only time in its history, had two parties that were both truly national in scope. But this curiously contrived party system was, in a very special sense, "artificial," for it could survive only if the regional feelings that had so largely shaped its being were obliterated. Such feelings did not subside, the second American party system broke down in the 1850's, and the third party system—with its decided regional bias—was then formed.

This exceedingly general statement of my central thesis can be supplemented by a series of detailed propositions.

1. The second American party system can be conceptualized as a distinctive party system, differing in the circumstances of its origins and in many general characteristics from earlier and later party systems.

2. The second party system did not form at one point in time; its formation took place over a period of approximately sixteen years. New party alignments appeared first in the Middle States, next in New England, then in the Old South, and finally in the new states of the West and South.

3. Party formation was most directly conditioned not by divisions in Congress nor by explicit doctrinal issues but rather by the contest for the presidency.

4. The sequence of party formation from region to region can best be explained in terms of the regional identifications of the presidential candidates.

5. Under the second party system, the two-party style of politics was for the first time extended to the South and the West.

6. The second party system was peculiar in that it produced balanced parties in every region and in nearly every state. There were no "one-party" regions, as there had been before 1824 and were to be after 1854.

7. This "balanced" character of the second party system, produced by the particular circumstances associated with its formation, made it an "artificial" party system. It could survive only by avoiding regionally divisive issues.

8. The second party system was characterized by similar alignments of voters in both state and national elections in every state. Previously, a wide variety of party situations—"one-party," "no-party," and "dual-party," as well as "two-party"—had maintained.

9. The most crucial development in the extension of the second party system was the abrupt emergence of a two-party South between 1832 and 1834. This development owed much to the substitution of Van Buren, a northerner, for Jackson as the prospective Democratic candidate in 1836.

10. In particular northern states, where the contests for the presidency did not, for local reasons, stimulate the formation of balanced parties oriented toward the major presidential candidates (especially between 1827 and 1834), the Antimasons flourished.

11. Party structures differed in form from region to region depending upon the local constitutional and legal environments. In general, however, the convention plan of party organization and management gradually replaced the caucus and earlier informal devices.

12. The new type of institutionalized parties that developed, with their elaborate organizations and corps of managers and activists, were something more than mere media for expressing the will of the electorate. They possessed interest of their own; they were active—rather than neutral—factors in the political process.

13. The second party system brought into general acceptance a new campaign style that was popular and "dramatic." This style can properly be regarded as a significant form of American cultural expression. It added to American politics a "dramatic" function that transcended concern with govern-

ment, issues, or candidates and afforded a generalized emotional experience.

14. The rate at which voters participated in elections was directly related to the closeness of interparty competition rather than to the presumed charismatic effect of candidates or the urgency of particular issues.

15. Because parties do not form, but rather are formed by leaders, the fortunes of particular parties in the formative period were greatly affected by the capacity of individual party leaders.

The materials used in preparing this study, as well as the manner in which those materials have been organized, have made it inexpedient for me to follow the usual canons of historical documentation. To a considerable extent my information on the course of party development in each state has been drawn from a wide array of familiar secondary works, although in numerous instances I have had to consult contemporary newspapers and similar sources to obtain the answers to specific questions. In addition, the analysis of election statistics, upon which I have relied very heavily in dealing with almost every aspect of party formation, is based upon an extensive collection of data that I have compiled and arranged to suit the particular needs of my investigation. In these circumstances it would have been exceedingly cumbersome to provide detailed citations for every statement, and I have not done so.

Instead, I have sought to reduce my documentation to a minimum and have prepared a detailed bibliography so arranged as to indicate clearly the sources that I have consulted for each state. In a separate listing I have given the sources from which I obtained my election statistics for each state. In general, I have supplied citations in the text only when the statements made are not readily verifiable in the secondary accounts, or where the incident referred to was especially crucial to party formation, or where material has been quoted directly.

———•———

CHAPTER II

THE FIRST AMERICAN
PARTY SYSTEM

———•———

The relationship between what I have chosen to call the first and the second American party systems requires some explanation. The parties that developed within the states and throughout the nation after 1824 were new parties. They did not have their origins in the same types of circumstances that had produced the first party system, they reflected the fact that significant alterations had taken place since 1820 in the environment of politics, and they differed in many characteristic respects from the early parties. There are, at present, divergent interpretations of the history of political parties, and because this study derives in part from my conception of what happened, I feel obliged to try to state very briefly my general understanding of the course of party development down to 1824.

Before the establishment of the new government under the federal Constitution, politics in the several states was conducted on a non-party basis. Throughout the colonial period, despite the vitality of representative institutions in all of the colonies, it has not yet been established that parties, in any acceptable sense of that term, can be said to have existed. Something approaching party politics can be detected in Rhode Island, Connecticut, New York, and Pennsylvania at certain periods, but the formations were either vague or transitory and bore little resemblance to the parties of the early federal era.

19

The movement for independence gave rise to the elaborate organization of what might be considered a "Whig" party, but once the issue of allegiance—or independence—had been settled, this party became identical with the state, and the opposition, which had never possessed a comparable organization, was identified with treason.   Meanwhile, under the new state constitutions, with their modest provisions for an expanded electorate and for new categories of elected officials, politics was conducted much as before.   Candidates were self-nominated, or were put forward by "friends," and voters responded as individuals rather than in terms of any party identities.

Political interest generally was centered on contests for seats in the legislatures or on the claims of rival candidates for local offices.   The township and the county—rather than the state—constituted the arena of electoral politics, and at those levels politics could be managed informally by the candidates themselves or by loose cliques of influential citizens.   Within the legislatures groupings often existed, based on sectional, economic, or other factors, and there were leadership juntos that exerted a powerful influence on the course of legislation, on appointments, and perhaps on the selection of favored candidates in gubernatorial elections.   But even in such states as New York and Pennsylvania, where factional groupings are most discernible, parties had not yet appeared.

The form of government instituted under the federal Constitution added new dimensions to American politics and stimulated the formation of political parties within the states and throughout the nation.   The provisions that were made for choosing the president were to give a national scope to politics and encourage cooperation among political leaders in the several states in behalf of particular candidates.   In quite a different way, the creation of a House of Representatives elected from the states by popular vote served to relate state politics to national politics.   Whereas in 1790 parties had not been formed in any state, by 1800 in most of the states politics was being conducted on a party basis.

How these early parties emerged and what they represented remain subjects of controversy. My own view would be that a cleavage first developed within the administration, that is, within the circle closest to the president; that in due course a comparable cleavage manifested itself in Congress; that the formation of these congressional factions encouraged the building of parties in the states; and that the successive contests for the presidency in 1796 and 1800 contributed further to focus and heighten party feelings. The first American party system is distinguishable from the second in that parties seem to have formed within Congress before they formed in the states and before the contest for the presidency became the dominant consideration. The studies of Dauer, Charles, and Cunningham are all in general agreement on the fact that by 1795 the members of Congress had become aligned in two opposing groups, each with recognizable leaders, consistent positions on public issues, and—at least in the case of the Republicans—a mechanism, the caucus, for managing party affairs. These "interior-type parties," to use the terminology of M. Duverger, did not reflect pre-existing party alignments in the states nor were they created directly in response to the exigencies of presidential politics.

After parties had become delineated in Congress, a stimulus was given to the formation of similar party alignments in the states. But in 1796 a new factor was introduced into the situation with the contest for the presidency between Jefferson and Adams. Their candidacies served to dramatize the partisan cleavage that was emerging and to extend party strife beyond the bounds of the congressional districts to encompass an entire state. Although it is quite impossible to differentiate them at this time, it would appear that two very different national influences now became operative in party formation, the one emanating from the interior-type congressional parties and the other from the contest over the presidency.

Party formation proceeded rapidly during Adams' administration, nurtured by spectacular clashes over foreign policy as well as by intense controversy over domestic issues. As party lines became drawn ever more sharply, party leaders both within Congress and in the states viewed the issues of the day from a new perspective, that of party advantage. They also became increasingly engrossed, as 1800 approached, with mobilizing their forces for the presidential election. The area of party politics was broadened to include not only the struggle for control of Congress and the presidency but also contests at other levels of government. National alignments established a framework for conducting party politics within the states, and even within counties and townships.

By 1800, or shortly thereafter, two-party situations are observable in most of the states. These parties had to perform a variety of functions, depending in large part on the character of the constitutional and legal framework within which they operated. In general, they competed in the election of congressmen, presidential electors, governors, members of state legislatures, and other officials. But their functions, and their organizational structures, varied according to whether governors and presidential electors were chosen by the legislature or by popular vote, whether congressmen were elected from districts or from the state at large, whether the county was the major electoral unit or whether there were many different electoral units, and whether the balance between the parties was close or uneven.

The Republicans soon established themselves as the dominant party. Although the Federalists retained control of most of the New England states until after the War of 1812, they were confronted by a formidable opposition even in that region. Their position in the Middle States was weak, except in Delaware and Maryland, and they were unable to maintain their enclaves in the states of the Old South or to acquire a foothold in the newer states of the West. The presidential elections of 1804 and 1808 resulted in lopsided victories for the Republicans and demonstrated that they were in a dominant or competitive position in every state except Connecticut.

The Federalists were quite ineffectual outside New England and certain of the Middle States. The War of 1812, and the events leading up to it, occasioned a reversal in the declining fortunes of the Federalists. They increased their dominance in New England, won impressive triumphs in Maryland, Delaware, and New Jersey, and even threatened the control of the faction-ridden Republicans in New York. Rallying behind De Witt Clinton of New York in 1812, they nearly achieved victory. Had Pennsylvania not remained faithful to Madison, he would have been defeated in his bid for re-election. But this resurgence was short-lived, and it did not extend to the South or to the West. By 1817 the Federalists had lost all of the Middle States, except Delaware, and all the New England states, except Massachusetts. Indeed, after 1819 the only New England state in which the Federalists continued to compete on a state-wide basis with their opponents was Massachusetts, which finally succumbed to Republican control in 1823.

As parties formed within each state, more or less elaborate machinery was developed, chiefly for the purpose of securing agreement on candidates. It was recognized very early that if a party did not concentrate its entire vote behind a single candidate for each office it would dissipate its strength and risk defeat. The elaborateness of the party apparatus varied and was generally related to the intensity of party competition. Where the Federalists were non-existent or weak, as in Tennessee or North Carolina, little or no formal machinery was required to insure a Republican victory. But throughout most of New England and the Middle States, where the parties were often closely balanced, parties became highly organized at all levels of government.

It is probably significant that in most states the management of party affairs at the state level was ostensibly assumed by the caucus, made up of party members in the legislature and, in most instances, co-opted party leaders. New Jersey and Delaware were exceptional in that they pioneered in the use of the delegate state convention, and in Maryland, where there

were no state-wide elections, there was apparently no formal
machinery for managing state party affairs. Elsewhere, from
Massachusetts to North Carolina, the legislative caucus held
sway.

In New England, where the caucus type of party management was most highly developed and was used by both parties,
nominations were made for state-wide elective offices and, in
addition, a central committee was appointed to exercise
supervision over local party committees. The result was a
centralized, well-disciplined party apparatus. In New York
and Pennsylvania, and probably Ohio as well, the caucus was a
regular feature of party machinery but it did not wield so great
an influence as it did in New England. In Virginia and North
Carolina, because Federalist opposition was weak and the state
was not an important unit of electoral activity, the caucus had
very limited functions. Kentucky, Tennessee, and Georgia
were so overwhelmingly Republican in sentiment that they
developed little in the way of formal party machinery.

Below the state level, where some device was needed to
make nominations for congressmen, members of the state
legislature, and county officials, there was extensive use of
delegate conventions. By around 1810 such conventions were
commonly employed throughout New England and the Middle States and also in Ohio and, on rare occasions, in Kentucky.
Elsewhere in the South and West such party management as
there was in the counties and congressional districts was informal. The convention machinery, which was very complex
in those states that had several different types of electoral units,
was devised and used almost exclusively for the purpose of
securing agreement on party candidates. It was not contrived
for the purpose of formulating party policy. The legislative
caucus, on the other hand, might concern itself with party
policy and customarily adopted an address that served as a party
platform.

It would be extremely important to be able to evaluate
the degree to which both caucuses and conventions were sub-

servient to party leaders and were "used" to lend a kind of sanction to decisions previously determined by the leaders. Were the caucuses and conventions genuine decision-making bodies, or were they, rather, cosmetic devices designed to give a color of popular authority to the leaders' decisions? Was the Virginia Junto—or the Essex Junto—the agent of the caucus or its master? Such questions have been the subject of little investigation and would doubtless be difficult to answer, but they are crucial to any understanding of the nature and operation of parties.

The construction of a party apparatus was not the exclusive work of the Republicans, as has so often been suggested. On the contrary, the Federalists in a number of states vied with the Republicans in building elaborate party mechanisms. In New England, Republicans and Federalists employed essentially the same kind of party machinery. Elsewhere, conspicuously in Delaware and Maryland, the Federalists employed party machinery with as much energy and success as their rivals. Although the Federalists generally did not have an aversion to organizing, they were disposed—especially in New England—to favor a secret type of apparatus and were less inclined than were the Republicans to embrace the delegate-convention system.

Zealous as the Federalists were in developing party machinery in those states where they were strong enough to compete with the Republicans, they lacked effective organization at the national level. The Republicans used the device of the congressional caucus to secure agreement on candidates for the presidency and vice-presidency. The caucus had come into existence in 1796, and in 1800 it was convened secretly to endorse Aaron Burr as Jefferson's running mate. Subsequently it met openly every four years to perform its nominating function. The Federalists made similar use of the caucus in 1800, and they may have held some kind of secret caucus in 1804, but thereafter they abandoned the device, presumably because their congressional forces were so numerically weak and geographically concentrated as to give little authority to their pronouncements. In 1808 and 1812 Federalist leaders met in "convention" in New York City for the purpose of concerting their forces in the presidential campaigns, but by 1816 they had abandoned any hope of mounting an effective opposition in national politics.

The failure of the Federalists to sustain themselves as a national party brought about the decline and eventual disintegration of the first American party system. Many explanations of the unsuccessful career of the party could be advanced. It could be argued that they lacked effective leadership, that they espoused unpopular policies, that they were too strongly identified with the Northeast, and that they represented the outmoded survival of aristocratic traditions in an increasingly democratic society. There is certainly merit in all of these contentions. But in an admittedly narrow political context, the failure of the Federalists could be attributed to the fact that they did not appreciate the importance of the contest for the presidency in the American party system and did not fully exploit the potentialities of that event. Except in 1812, they virtually permitted the presidency to go to the Republicans by default; they made no determined, imaginative, or far-ranging efforts on behalf of their poorly selected candidates.

The Republicans, once they had won the presidency and dominance in Congress, obviously possesed many advantages over their rivals. In their efforts to achieve power, they had been stimulated to organize an offensive against the Federalists and had created the rudiments of party machinery and a strong *esprit de corps* among their adherents. The congressional caucus, the leadership assumed by the president, the availability of federal patronage, and the relationships that were established among prominent party figures all operated to strengthen and perpetuate the party. Of decided importance, too, was the availability of the successive members of the "Virginia dynasty"—Jefferson, Madison, and Monroe—whose prestige was sufficiently great to forestall the kind of crippling conflict over the succession that was to ruin the party in 1824. The early formation of the Virginia-New York alliance, despite the occasional restiveness of the junior partner, gave the party a strong base in the Middle States and by moderating its sectional character conferred on the Republicans a national appeal that the Federalists could not match.

Indeed, the party ultimately became the victim of its success. As the Federalists weakened, both at the national level and within individual states, the Republicans found it increasingly difficult to maintain the fiction that unity and discipline were essential to the party. Unity was destroyed by factionalism, partisan zeal subsided, party machinery fell into disuse, and even party identification came to have little meaning.

A cursory survey of the condition of parties in the states before the presidential election of 1824 reveals the extent to which the first American party system had disintegrated. There were fourteen states, exclusive of South Carolina, in which at some time politics had been organized on the basis of competition between Republican and Federalist parties. In only five of these—Maine, Massachusetts, New Jersey, Delaware, and Maryland—were elections still being contested in terms of the old party designations. In seven other states—Vermont, New Hampshire, Connecticut, Rhode Island, Pennsylvania, Virginia, and North Carolina—the Federalists had either "retired" from electoral combat or had become so weakened through loss of members or fusion with Republican factions as to leave the Republicans virtually unchallenged. Only in New Hampshire and Pennsylvania were there major contests in elections, and these were between rival factions within the old Republican party. Elsewhere, elections were dull affairs that gave unopposed victories to Republican candidates, except when local personal rivalries aroused voter interest. Two other states—New York and Ohio—can be treated as special cases. In New York after 1820 the Bucktails and the Clintonians represented a distinctive type of party formation that had no counterpart elsewhere. In Ohio few vestiges of partisanship survived; even the Republican party had all but lost its identity and politics was conducted essentially on a personal basis.

There were nine states in which politics had never really been organized on the basis of the old party distinctions. In seven of these—Indiana, Illinois, Tennessee, Missouri, Alabama, Mississippi, and Louisiana—elections featured contests among personalities, local factions, and ethnic or sectional groupings rather than parties, although all of these states expressed a nominal Republican allegiance in presidential elections. Here, again, two other states presented special situations. In Georgia the curious alignment that pitted the Troup party against the Clark party bore no relationship to national parties and was so loose and informal in organizational structure as to constitute a kind of quasi-party. Kentucky offered a unique instance of state-oriented parties arising out of the agitation of a specific issue, the "relief" legislation that followed the Panic of 1819, and its Old Court and New Court parties endured until 1826. Most of the "no-party" states, as they may be vaguely designated, were not to experience genuine party formations until late in the Jackson era. They form an interesting category, among other reasons, because they illustrate how politics could be conducted over a long period of years on a no-party basis.

The first American party system had been influenced by the constitutional and legal environment that prevailed during its formative years. By 1824, when we can begin to observe the formation of the second American party system, that environment had altered, and the party system was to reflect these new conditions. Most important of all was the gradual change that had taken place in the method of choosing presidential electors. In 1800 electors were chosen by the legislatures in ten states; in only two states were they chosen by popular vote of the state at large. By 1824 only six states still clung to the legislative choice, and after 1832 South Carolina was the only state that did not choose electors by popular vote from the state at large.

The significance of this change in the method of conducting presidential elections has been too little appreciated. The general adoption of the popular, state-wide voting procedure gave a popular dimension to the presidential contest, created or enhanced the need for state party machinery, weakened the political authority of legislative caucuses, occasioned the development of national party conventions, and made the presidential election the dramatic focal point of American politics. What most differentiated the Jackson elections from those in which Jefferson was involved was this change in the method of choosing electors.

Between 1800 and 1824, too, suffrage qualifications were liberalized in several states—notably Connecticut, New York, New Jersey, and Maryland—with the result that nearly all adult white males were eligible to vote by 1824 in presidential elections, except in Rhode Island, Virginia, and Louisiana. Voting was also facilitated by refinements in election machinery. In most states polling units—or election districts—were reduced in area in order to enable voters to exercise their franchise with a minimum of inconvenience. *Viva voce* voting, with its lack of secrecy and its cumbersomeness where long slates of officials had to be elected, was steadily replaced by the ballot, and—indeed—by the printed ballot. As state constitutions were revised, more and more offices were made elective, instead of appointive. The custom of holding state elections at different times from presidential elections persisted, however, and before 1832 only New York held both elections on the same day.

Whereas the first American party system had been effectively limited to fourteen states—in four of which the Republicans quickly achieved lopsided dominance—the second American party system would embrace twenty-three states by 1835. In the sense, then, of geographic and sectional extension, the party system acquired a new dimension, and the difficulties inherent in operating national parties was compounded. One of the remarkable achievements of the second party system was to be the extension of party politics to these newer states.

In many other respects, the political environment had altered between the age of Jefferson and the age of Jackson. As long as politics could be managed informally, without the agency of elaborate party apparatus, those who were recognized at the time as "the gentry" wielded decisive influence. But the role of the gentry declined when politics was organized on a party basis. The management of the party type of politics required considerable manpower, demanded the expenditure of large amounts of time on routine or trivial matters, called for talents that were by no means restricted to the gentry, and offered tangible rewards in the form of patronage and prestige to attract men from many ranks and callings. For increasing numbers of men, politics, or more specifically the operation of party machinery, was to become a vocation.

The new politics was also to reflect the revolution that was under way in communication and transportation. The vast multiplication of newspapers and magazines facilitated the transmission of news of politics, and the intense zeal of partisan editors was a potent factor in molding and heightening party spirit. The steamboats, canals, and ultimately the railroads enlarged the dimensions of the political community, making it feasible to hold state and national party conventions, stage "monster" rallies, conduct extensive campaign tours, and generally to manage politics on a grand scale.

The new brand of politics was to differ from the old, then, in part because of these changes in the environment. Politics was not to be conducted under the same conditions in 1830 as in 1800. The sum effect of new conditions was to give an increasingly popular tone to politics. Campaigns and elections assumed the aspect of folk festivals. Candidates and voters indulged themselves in a moving, engrossing, and satisfying dramatic experience. As many foreign observers astutely noted, politics in the United States filled a need that was met in many European nations by the pomp, ceremony, and pageantry of the great established churches. The opportunity to participate in spectacular election contests gave the humble citizen a sense of identification that was intensely important to him. No account of American politics can ignore this "dramatic" appeal, although we have scarcely begun to appreciate its peculiar force and its powerful consequences.

The second American party system derived in part from the experience acquired during the era of the first party system, in part from the changes occasioned by the altered environment of politics, and in part from the imagination and zeal of the leaders who were to give a new form to the party system. The transition from the old to the new system occurred at different times and under particular circumstances in each state, but throughout the nation as a whole the major influence on the development of parties was to be the contest for the presidency. With these general considerations in view, we can proceed to examine the course of party formation in the New England states, and subsequently in the Middle States, the South, and the New West.

CHAPTER III

PARTY FORMATION IN NEW ENGLAND

N ew England in 1824 was a politically mature region that had acquired considerable experience in conducting its politics on a two-party basis during the era of the first American party system. Although each state exhibited peculiar features, they were all shaped by common cultural and constitutional traditions and conformed to similar patterns in government and politics. Indeed, no region was more homogeneous in its political behavior than was New England in the early nineteenth century.

The cultural inheritance of New England, the influence of which has been strongly emphasized by all who have studied the region, can be variously interpreted. But surely one of its effects was a highly developed regional consciousness, which was to manifest itself in political attitudes and practices. This regional consciousness was operative on political parties both before and after 1824. As much as any other combination of factors, it explains the distinctive political behavior of New England.

In more concrete terms, the conduct of politics was profoundly affected by constitutional provisions that made the state—rather than any of its political subdivisions—the most important unit of politics. Because many officials were elected annually from the state at large and because the county was of negligible importance in the electoral system, party manage-

35

ment at the state level was greatly facilitated. In all of the New England states, therefore, centralized control of parties through caucuses and central committees was a conspicuous feature of politics from the early years of Jefferson's administration.

In no other region were Federalists and Republicans so thoroughly organized over such a long period to compete with one another for supremacy. Interparty competition continued to be intense in most states until 1817, or later. Even after the Federalists had been vanquished, and—in a manner peculiar to New England—had retired from electoral combat, old party distinctions survived, and the Republicans preserved both their identity and their party apparatus. Party formation after 1824 in New England must be understood in terms of this common background.

The revival of the contest for the presidency did not at once stimulate the formation of a new two-party system because the region was overwhelmingly committed to its native son, John Quincy Adams, in 1824. Not until 1827, when there was the prospect that Adams might be defeated in his bid for re-election, did opposition leaders venture to organize feeble Jacksonian parties in several states. By 1829, with Adams eliminated from the national scene, the Jacksonians had acquired considerable strength everywhere, and a new party system was emerging. The eruption of the Antimasonic movement blurred alignments for a time in certain states, but in general the redefinition of party loyalties that took place between 1827 and 1832 was to endure for the succeeding two decades.

MASSACHUSETTS

Massachusetts, unlike most states in 1824, possessed a still vigorous two-party system that had been in operation for more

than a quarter of a century. When the voters went to the polls
in April to cast their ballots in the gubernatorial election,
they divided their suffrages between two candidates bearing
Federalist and Republican labels. A year later, however, the
familiar pattern began to alter. Old party distinctions lost
their meaning as, for a brief period, support for the native son,
John Quincy Adams, seemingly overbore all other considerations. Then, with the approach of the presidential election of
1828, partisan divisions again manifested themselves in both
state and national politics and new party formations emerged.

The old party system that was to break down in 1824 had
begun to take form in the first year of John Adams' presidency.
Despite the aversion of the citizens of Massachusetts to overt
partisan "interference" in the free choice of elective officials,
party organization was well advanced by 1800 and had gained
such a degree of public acceptance by 1804 that it was no
longer necessary to hide party activity behind a thin veil of
secrecy. Both parties acknowledged the use of elaborate apparatus for nominating candidates, managing campaigns, and
conducting party affairs, and the voters in turn assumed
partisan identities. Perhaps the most remarkable feature of
this early party system was its stability. Federalists and Republicans alike, using similar techniques for centralizing party
management, were extraordinarily successful in maintaining
party unity and avoiding the factional discord that characterized parties in certain of the Middle States. Too, they remained well balanced and competitive almost from their inception down to 1824, a condition that was common to but
one other state—Delaware.

The constitutional and legal framework within which elections were conducted in Massachusetts influenced the structure
of party organization. Although the constitution of 1780 pre-
scribed a small property qualification for voting, which was
transformed into a taxpaying qualification in 1821, it would
appear that in practice only a very small minority of adult
males were actually disfranchised. State elections were held

annually, and paper ballots—which, after 1830, might be printed—were used. With the town as the voting unit, the governor, lieutenant-governor, and senators were elected in April and the representatives in May, until 1831, when the state elections were shifted to November. The town was the constituency for representatives. Senators were elected initially from counties, but after 1812 (except from 1814-1816) were chosen from districts made up of one or more counties. Representatives were apportioned roughly on the basis of population and senators ostensibly on the basis of taxes paid. Congressmen were always elected under the district system, but the method of choosing presidential electors was subject to frequent changes until 1824, when the practice of state-wide elections on a general ticket was adopted. Although not peculiar to that state, Massachusetts election laws were unusual in the requirement that successful candidates must receive an absolute majority of the total vote cast.

Under this system of representation and election the town and the state were the most vital arenas of political activity. The county, the senatorial district, and the congressional district were secondary units that had somehow to be accommodated within the party structures. The fact that there was no competing focus of political power intermediate between the town and the state explains in part, at least, the remarkable authority wielded by party institutions at the state level in Massachusetts, as well as elsewhere in New England.

The management of party affairs at the state level was—in both parties—a function of the legislative caucus, or, more properly, the mixed legislative caucus. First used by the Federalists in 1800 to nominate their candidate for governor, the same mechanism was soon copied by the Republicans and was employed by both parties with great effectiveness throughout their existence. Often referred to in official party propaganda as a "Grand Convention of citizens from all parts of the Commonwealth," the caucus was in fact composed of party members within the legislature and an indeterminate number of party stalwarts who were co-opted to attend.

The Federalist caucus customarily met in February, during the legislative session, to nominate candidates for governor and lieutenant-governor and to draft an "address" to the voters. In addition it appointed a Central Committee, which appointed county committees, and these in turn appointed town committees. The Central Committee, made up of seven men from Boston and vicinity, not necessarily members of the legislature, issued political directives in the form of circular letters before election campaigns and generally determined party strategy. The county committees sponsored mass meetings at which the names of candidates for the senate would be presented and ratified, and the town committees functioned similarly with respect to the nomination of representatives.

The Republican caucus was closely patterned after the Federalist model.[1] At the level of the counties, senatorial districts, and congressional districts, however, the Republicans as early as 1808 were using what were referred to as conventions of delegates—rather than mass meetings—to nominate senators and congressmen. There is also some evidence to indicate that within the Republican party, party committees below the state level were elected, rather than appointed.

That both parties were under highly centralized direction is evident from their handiwork. What is far from clear, though, is the relationship between the Central Committee and the caucus. Whether the controlling influence of the state parties was in fact the caucus, or whether the caucus was largely controlled by the Central Committee—the membership of which changed little over the years—is a question worthy of further investigation.

There were definite conventions that regulated the style

1. Federalist party machinery is described in Samuel Eliot Morrison, *The Life and Letters of Harrison Gray Otis, Federalist, 1765-1848*, (2 vols.; Boston and New York, 1913), especially I, 286 ff. For early references to the Republican organization, see the (Boston) *Independent Chronicle*, Mar. 1, 1804, Feb. 9, 20, 1809, Feb. 15, 1810; *Boston Patriot*, Mar. 31, 1810.

of politics in Massachusetts. Elections were relatively orderly affairs, conducted with decorum, and corruption was all but non-existent. Personal solicitation of votes by candidates was regarded as improper, and there was no "stump speaking" or theatrical campaigning before 1840. Voters were appealed to through "addresses" and letters in the newspapers, through broadsides and pamphlets, and through personal solicitation by party committees in each town. Party members were inspired to action in town caucuses, county mass meetings or conventions, and by printed circular letters from the Central Committee. Federalists made effective use of the Washington Benevolent Societies to stimulate party enthusiasm while Republicans indulged themselves in celebrations of the Fourth of July and the anniversary of Jefferson's accession to the presidency. The conduct of politics, in brief, reflected the distinctive character of Massachusetts society and might properly be studied as a form of cultural expression as well as an aspect of government.

The stability, durability, and balance of the parties in Massachusetts was, by contrast with other states, most extraordinary. From 1800, when the parties became competitive, through 1824, the state elections were usually closely contested, and in most years the victorious candidate won by a margin of less than 10 per cent of the total vote. Never did a third-party candidate enter the lists, nor was there ever more than a scattering of votes for independent candidates for the governorship. The Federalists retained their dominance until 1807, when James Sullivan became the first Republican governor. The Republicans won the governorship again in 1808, 1810, and 1811, but could not score another victory until 1823. The only clear-cut Republican triumph in a presidential election was in 1804, when electors-at-large pledged to Jefferson were chosen by popular vote. Despite the vicissitudes of the party elsewhere, and despite the hopeless position of the party in national politics, the Federalists remained the dominant party in Massachusetts until 1823. Even then, they lost the gubernatorial elections of 1823 and 1824 by relatively small margins.

Although party competition was sustained and party organization was highly developed, voter interest in politics, as measured by participation in elections, was in general surprisingly low. Voter participation in gubernatorial elections, expressed in terms of the percentage of adult white males voting, rose from 30.8 per cent in 1800 to 41.8 per cent in 1804. It then climbed steadily to a peak of 67.4 per cent in 1812, which was to be the highest rate of voter participation in any state-wide election in Massachusetts through 1860. Participation remained near the 60 per cent level until 1817, when it began to decline, reaching a low of 40.6 per cent in 1822. In 1823 there was a revival, which brought the figure above the 50 per cent mark, and in 1824, 57 per cent of the adult white males participated in the election that was in fact to be the last for the old party system. In presidential elections, when electors were chosen by popular vote, participation tended to be at an even lower level than in state elections, except in 1804. Why the Massachusetts voter seemingly was apathetic about going to the polls I do not know, but this apathy was to continue to characterize the state in the decades after 1824 as well.

With the revival of the contest for the presidency in 1824, Massachusetts politics entered a distinctly new era. Old party distinctions had ceased to have any meaning by 1828, and two new parties, primarily oriented toward national politics but exhibiting as well the effects of local circumstances and personal rivalries, were forming. But the most important single factor bearing upon party formation in Massachusetts—and indeed throughout New England—was the candidacy of a native son, John Quincy Adams, in 1824 and 1828. As a sectional favorite, his strength was so great as to inhibit the formation of a genuine opposition party until near the end of his troubled administration.

In the presidential election of 1824, conducted for the

first time with electors chosen at large by popular vote, Adams received five-sixths of the votes cast. Fewer than 30 per cent of the estimated electorate went to the polls, in contrast to the 57 per cent that had turned out for the gubernatorial election in April. Adams had the support of the leadership of the Republican party; most Federalists, recalling Adams' "apostasy" from the party in 1808, probably remained aloof from the election. An unpledged opposition slate of electors attracted its small support from a diverse array of Crawford-ites, Calhounites, die-hard Federalists, and disgruntled Republicans. The low voter turnout may have been attributable to the one-sided nature of the contest or to the lack of compelling enthusiasm for any of the candidates, or both.

The election itself was not the signal for a reorganization of parties. Before the gubernatorial election of 1825, the old parties caucused as in the past, although the Federalist agreed to support the Republican nominee for governor, Levi Lincoln, who was all but unanimously elected. A similar attempt to end old conflicts was made in 1826, but dissident Federalist factions sponsored irregular candidates, who collectively polled nearly one-third of the total vote. In 1827 there was again only scattered opposition to the re-election of Lincoln, representing neither the continuance of old party loyalties nor the emergence of a new opposition party. Although relative harmony reigned at the state level, the Federalist and Republican parties retained their organizations, in spite of fusion movements in many areas and the irrelevance of such divisions to national politics. But in 1827 the Federalists ran their last candidates for office; a year later there was no Federalist party.

The most practical political question of the period was whether the old Republican party, which had now become in reality the Adams party, would remain "exclusive" or would permit former Federalists to "amalgamate." Both policies had supporters within the party leadership, and the issue was not determined until 1829. The first clear sign that amalgamation was under way came in 1827 with the election of Daniel

Webster to the United States Senate by a predominantly Republican legislature. But early in 1828, separate caucuses were held by the "Republican members" of the legislature and the members "friendly to the national and state administrations" to renominate Lincoln for governor. By June 11, 1828, when the Administration-Republican members of the legislature met to choose an electoral ticket pledged to Adams and Rush, they also named a Central Committee, made up of former Federalists as well as Republicans.[2]

Still the issue of "amalgamation," as well as the future structure of the Administration-Republican (or National Republican) party, remained unsettled. On February 12, 1829, the "members of the legislature friendly to the present [Lincoln] State administration" met in the New Court House in Boston under the chairmanship of Robert Rantoul to renominate Lincoln for governor and to consider "what measures it is expedient to take for maintaining our party, and giving it organization and efficiency in the ensuing elections." After an adjournment, the session reconvened on February 16 and approved an "address" recommending a political organization throughout the state, on "liberal and national principles, which should not go to the exclusion of plain straight-forward republicans of any denomination." Thus was the National Republican party, as it must now be called, brought into existence. Although it called for unity of sentiment, as well as "liberal principles," the address did not specify what principles should be espoused.[3]

Vague though it was about principles, the new party caucus was explicit on the subject of organization. A Central Committee of nine men was chosen. Then the members present from each county nominated a man to be county chairman, and these nominees were elected by the full caucus. The county chairmen, at the request of the Central Committee,

2. *Hingham Gazette*, Mar. 14, June 20, 1828.
3. There are full accounts of these caucuses in the (Boston) *Columbian Continel*, Feb. 21, Mar. 14, 18, 25, 1829.

were to call county conventions—made up of delegates from the towns—for the purpose of electing county committees. They were also to correspond with the Central Committee on all matters affecting the interests of the party. In this manner a centralized type of party organization, much like that in existence before 1824, was ordained. Too, the new organization contemplated that, in keeping with long tradition, the legislative caucus of the party would annually make nominations for state offices, reconstitute the Central Committee, and appoint county chairmen.

One Republican faction endeavored to preserve the old party on an "exclusivist" basis. Meeting—perhaps significantly —in the Old Court House, with Benjamin F. Varnum as chairman and Horace Mann as secretary, a group of Republican legislators endorsed the nomination of Lincoln for governor but chose their own Central Committee and stated their abhorrence of amalgamation. In the ensuing state election these "Exclusivists," as they were termed, endeavored to run candidates for the legislature, but the movement produced slight results and appears to have been abandoned after the election. Despite subsequent vicissitudes, the new party that was formally launched on February 16, 1829, was to endure for a generation, first under the name of National Republican and later under the Whig label. At its core, the party represented a continuance of the old Republican party, but after 1824—and especially after 1827—it received accretions of strength from former Federalists and suffered losses to the emergent Democratic and Antimasonic parties.

Organized support for Andrew Jackson was slow to develop in Massachusetts. His name scarcely figured in the election of 1824, and it was not until 1827 that preliminary steps were taken to organize a pro-Jackson party by two very diverse elements. David Henshaw (Boston wholesale druggist, proprietor of the *Statesman,* and ambitious political manager) together with Marcus Morton (former Republican Congressman from Western Massachusetts and lieutenant-governor before ascending to the supreme bench of the state) constituted the leadership of what was to emerge as the dominant Jacksonian faction. Henshaw favored Crawford in 1824, shifted to support of Adams in 1826, and in 1827 turned to Jackson. It is not apparent that he admired the general or his policies, but he was, like Morton, enamoured of Calhoun and susceptible to his influence. He also appears to have wished to play a larger role in politics than that allotted him by the Administration-Republican party. A second faction, headed by the ultra-Federalist, Theodore Lyman, Jr., and with the *Jackson Republican* as its organ, supported Jackson out of detestation for Adams, but by 1829 this odd ally had been out-maneuvered by the energetic and astute Henshaw, who was recognized by the Jackson administration as the head of the party in Massachusetts.

Henshaw and his *Statesman* faction began their organizational activities on behalf of Jackson with a dinner on January 8, 1828, the anniversary of the general's victory at New Orleans. In the April election, Marcus Morton was the unwilling candidate of the faction for governor, receiving little more than a token vote. "Judge Morton was not regularly nominated," explained the *Statesman*, "and there was not the least concert or arrangement to procure support or draw out strength." But the Henshaw organ predicted that there would be concerted efforts put forth in the presidential contest.[4] In preparation for that contest, a Jackson Republican "Convention," composed of members of the legislature friendly to Jackson and "delegates" from Boston and nearby towns, met in the State House on June 10, 1828.[5] An electoral ticket, headed by Henshaw, was adopted, and a Central Committee of nine members was appointed, which was authorized to prepare and publish an address. Over the succeeding few months, feeble attempts were made to stimulate party organization at the levels

4. *Boston Statesman*, June 3, 7, 1828.

5. The convention was reported in the *Boston Statesman*, July 12, 1828, and in the (Concord) *New Hampshire Patriot*, July 21, 1828.

of the counties and towns, but the movement was not widespread. When the presidential election was held, the Jackson ticket polled only one-sixth of the total vote cast; that the electorate was indifferent to the contest is indicated by the low turnout of approximately one voter in four. Despite this dismal showing, the Jackson-Democratic party had in fact made its debut.

Fortified with an appointment as collector of the Port of Boston, and with patronage for his henchmen, Henshaw displayed only moderate zeal for building the strength of the party of which he was to be the "boss" for a decade. In 1829, Marcus Morton, even though he was not formally a candidate and no genuine party exertion was made in his behalf, polled almost the same number of votes that Jackson had received in 1828. In 1830, however, the Jacksonian members of the legislature caucused in February, nominated Morton for the governorship, and adopted an address and resolutions dealing with state issues. Conventions were held in several counties to name senatorial candidates, and later in the year congressional district conventions presented Jacksonian candidates for Congress. As a result of these organizational efforts, Morton more than doubled the number of votes he had received in 1829, although he had less than half as many as the victorious Lincoln. Morton was again the nominee of the caucus in 1831, but his vote fell below that of the previous year.

Doubtless with an eye to the presidential election of 1832, but also because a change in the constitution made necessary a second gubernatorial election in November, 1831, the Jacksonian members of the legislature decided on June 9, 1831, that it was expedient "to organize the Republican party in this Commonwealth" and issued a call for a state convention, to be held in Worcester on September 1.[6] Each county was to

6. *Boston Statesman*, June 25, 1831. For the report on the Worcester convention see *ibid.*, Sept. 10, 1831. The Jackson Central Committee named the county chairmen, who in turn appointed the township chairmen. Henshaw,

send delegates equal in number to its representation in the General Assembly. The Worcester convention, attended by over two hundred delegates, nominated Morton for governor, appointed two delegates-at-large to attend the Democratic National Convention, and directed that conventions should be held in each congressional district at the call of the Central Committee to choose district delegates to the National Convention. Morton again went down to defeat, this time running third to Lincoln and the Antimasonic candidate.

By 1829, then, the old parties had been replaced by new ones, which contested on an extremely uneven basis both state and national elections. They did not represent the continuation of old allegiances under new names; they were new parties. The National Republicans owed their dominance largely to the fact that they were able to merge the ablest leadership elements in the older parties, initially on the popular issue of support for John Quincy Adams. Their opponents, lacking a popular program and led by figures who commanded little respect and who lacked both zeal and capacity, were doomed to remain for a decade in a position of weakness. Both parties were tightly controlled by their leaders, operating through a Central Committee ostensibly named by the legislature caucus, and both were content to conduct politics in the traditional restrained, conservative manner. Popular interest in the new political order was negligible. No election between 1825 and 1830 brought as many as 30 per cent of the adult white males to the polls.

Scarcely had a new two-party system emerged when the Antimasonic enthusiasm assumed political form and complicated the scene. The first rumblings of the movement were felt in Bristol County in 1828, and by 1829 it had spread sufficiently to produce the state's first political convention, held in Faneuil Hall in December to form a party organization. By 1831 the party felt strong enough to enter the November

---

with his extensive patronage as collector of the Port of Boston, functioned at least down to 1835 as the boss of the party.

gubernatorial contest behind Samuel Lathrop, nominated by a state convention in May. Lathrop ran second to Lincoln and was again the party's candidate in 1832. In that year he fell below Lincoln and Morton in the poll, although the Wirt electoral ticket took second place in the presidential voting. In 1833, after devious maneuvers designed to unite the National Republicans and the Antimasons behind a single candidate had foundered, the redoubtable John Quincy Adams, running as an Antimasonic candidate for governor, polled the highest vote the party was ever to secure, but he fell far short of victory. By 1834 the party had begun to crumble, and the disintegration was hastened by the decision in 1835 to support the Whig candidate for governor, the Democratic candidate for lieutenant-governor, and Van Buren for the presidency. By 1836 the party had ceased to be a factor of consequence, and the two-party system was restored.

The Antimasons did succeed in bringing to the polls men to whom the major parties had little appeal. Voter participation rose markedly after 1830, rising to over 45 per cent of the estimated electorate in 1834. When the party fell apart, these new voters apparently retained their political interest, and the major portion of them seem to have moved into the Democratic ranks. Too, the Antimasons may have had the effect of inducing the major parties to exhibit increased concern about the reform measures that were being agitated at the time. Neither the Whigs nor the Democrats were disposed to offer substantial concessions to the Antimasons, however, with the result that there was no "amalgamation," such as was to occur in certain other states. Basically, the Antimasonic party, like the Workingmen's party—which flourished briefly in the same years—reflected popular discontent or frustration with the two major parties.

After 1835 the Democrats steadily narrowed the margin that separated them from their opponents. In 1836 Van Buren received 45 per cent of the popular vote, the strongest showing made by any Democratic presidential candidate until after the Civil War. Marcus Morton, the perennial candidate for governor, increased his vote from around fifteen thousand in 1833 to over fifty-one thousand in 1839, when he finally won an election. The Whig vote, meanwhile, had remained relatively stable. The Democrats obviously profited more than the Whigs from the demise of the Antimasons. Too, the party leaders were compelled to make concessions both to a "Workingmen" faction and a western "Country" faction, with the result that the image of the party as a spokesman for the "common man" was strengthened. In 1838 George Bancroft replaced Henshaw both as collector of the Port of Boston and as the party leader, and under his guidance the party was reorganized on "reform" principles and reached its peak effectiveness. As the parties became more competitive, voter participation rose to a new high of 66 per cent in the 1840 elections.

The formal structure of the major parties underwent little change. Although both Whigs and Democrats resorted on occasion to the use of state conventions, especially in preparation for presidential elections, the caucus and the Central Committee were retained as the prime agencies of state party management.[7] Campaign practices remained relatively sedate, until the election of 1840, with its enormous mass meetings, popular oratory, and generally festive atmosphere, broke down the traditional reserve. It was, indeed, with the election of 1840 that the new order of politics that had its inception in the revival of the contest for the presidency sixteen years earlier finally reached maturity.

7. The National Republicans held their first state convention at Worcester, October 11-12, 1832. *Journal of the Proceedings of the* [Massachusetts] *National Republican Convention ... Worcester, October 11, 1832* (Boston, 1832). The Whigs held state conventions in 1833, 1836, 1840, and regularly after 1843. In the intervening years nominations were made by mixed conventions, made up of Whig members of the legislature together with delegates from towns not represented by Whigs in the legislature. For reports of the mixed conventions, see *Boston Courier*, Mar. 28, 1836; Mar. 20, 1837; Mar. 4, 1839; Mar. 1, 1841.

MAINE

Maine, until its separation from Massachusetts in 1820, had conducted its politics largely within the framework fixed by its parent. As in Massachusetts proper, Federalists and Democratic-Republicans contested for political office year after year. Old party distinctions lingered on into the period of statehood and were discernible even after 1824. But as the Adams administration drew to a close, Maine, like Massachusetts, went through the throes of political reorganization, out of which emerged two new and durable parties. The precise circumstances of party formation in Maine, however, and the relative strength of the contending parties, reflected peculiar local conditions.

The government of Maine was in general patterned after that of Massachusetts. State elections were held annually on the second Monday in September to choose a governor and members of the legislature. Senators were elected from districts made up of one or more counties; representatives had the towns as their constituencies. Adult male citizens enjoyed the suffrage. Voting was by ballot, and an absolute majority of the total vote was required for the election of governor and senators. Sheriffs, judges, and registers of probate were elected by each county. Congressmen were elected by districts, and, before the adoption of the general-ticket system in 1832, presidential electors were chosen on the district basis, with two electors-at-large.

Techniques of party organization in Maine earlier than 1820 were, of course, an extension of those employed in Massachusetts. Capitalizing on discontent with tangled land titles, the Democratic-Republicans had become the majority party by 1803. In subsequent years they acquired a lopsided preponderance over their Federalist rivals, who nevertheless remained in the field, sustained by their Massachusetts brethren.

When separation from Massachusetts threatened to place the Maine Federalists in the position of a hopeless—and, even worse, office-less minority—they negotiated a remarkable agreement with their Republican opponents. In return for lending their assistance to the movement for statehood, they were promised a quota of offices proportionate to their party's strength, which was calculated to be one half that of their adversaries. This pledge was honorably respected until 1828, when its apparent violation contributed an important ingredient to the conditions influencing the reorganization of parties.

Fortified by the assurance of jobs, the Federalsits retained their identity down to 1828. They ran a gubernatorial candidate in 1821 and 1822, who was overwhelmingly defeated, and thereafter contented themselves with contesting lesser offices in areas where they had some possibility of success. They do not appear to have established the elaborate apparatus for managing state party affairs that the Massachusetts Federalists had, but they were charged, probably accurately, with maintaining a secret organization. The Republicans had set up a state machine, emanating from their legislative caucus, and, as they had done at least since 1810, continued to make effective use of delegate conventions to nominate state senators, congressmen, and presidential electors.[8]

As the presidential election of 1824 approached, internal divisions in the Republican party manifested themselves. The ruling junto within the party—Chandler, Holmes, King, Preble, and Ware—sought to align the party behind Crawford, whom they regarded as the "legitimate" successor to Madison. But in a discordant party caucus in January, 1823, the junto was unable to prevail, and the majority decision was to support the sectional favorite, John Quincy Adams. In the ensuing campaign, despite the opposition of the influential Portland *Argus*, the Adams forces scored a three-to-one victory. Both factions in the contest insisted upon calling themselves Demo-

8. (Boston) *Independent Chronicle*, Feb. 10, 1810; *Boston Patriot*, Mar. 31, 1810.

cratic-Republicans, and after the election, although factional fights persisted, the old party was assumed to be still intact. Both factions united in the legislative caucus to support the same gubernatorial candidate from 1824 through 1828, and the nominee was elected without opposition.

The *Argus*, however, and the old junto, were soon critical of President Adams, and in March, 1827, the paper came out openly against his re-election. In the ensuing months, the two opposing Republican factions were at work organizing the Adams and Jackson parties, later to be called the National Republicans and the Democrats. The pro-Adams forces held an expanded mixed legislative caucus on January 23, 1828, reportedly with a thousand partisans in attendance, to organize for the presidential contest. This demonstration was soon followed by conventions in each congressional district to choose electors. The Jackson forces were similarly engaged.[9] In the September state election, although the governorship was not contested, opposing tickets were run for the legislature and for Congress. The presidential election in November brought another victory for Adams, but this time by only a three-to-two margin.

In 1829, Governor Enoch Lincoln, who had remained neutral on the "presidential question" and who had been unanimously elected in the previous three years, declined the invitation of the caucus to stand for another term. The National Republicans in the legislature then nominated J. G. Hunton; the Jacksonians announced plans to hold a state convention—the first in Maine—at Augusta on June 10. Each town was invited to send delegates equal to twice the number of its representatives in the legislature and some 241 actually

9. (Portland) *American Patriot*, Jan. 19, 26, Apr.-July, 1828. The Adams electoral ticket was generally referred to as the "People's Ticket." The (Augusta) *Kennebec Journal*, July 11, 1828, published a long list of the leaders of the Jackson party, county by county, pointing out that most were either Federalists or holders of patronage posts. There were active "Young Men's" organizations at work in the presidential canvass. (Portland) *American Patriot*, Sept. 13, 1828. There were "Young Men's" organizations active in New York in 1828 also.

attended.   Samuel E. Smith, who possessed the advantage of having supported Adams in 1828, was made the party's nominee, and an address that avoided reference to national questions was adopted.[10]

The major issue in the campaign grew out of the charge that the state administration had "proscribed" all but loyal supporters of Adams in making appointments to state offices. On the eve of the election a group of Federalists, headed by James Bridge, published a circular which declared that the political agreement that had been negotiated a decade before had been violated and that violence over the presidential question had revived political proscription.   For this reason, and because they asserted that he was superior in ability to Hunton, they announced their support of Smith.   The *Argus*, while it made the most of the proscription issue and welcomed the support of Bridge and his associates, nevertheless persisted in denouncing the opposition as Federalists; it shrewdly avoided making Jackson the central figure in the campaign.[11]   In an election that produced the largest turnout of voters by far since Maine had achieved statehood, Smith was elected by a margin of less than 1 per cent of the total vote.   In no previous gubernatorial election had more than 40 per cent of the eligible voters participated; now over 55 per cent went to the polls. A year later, in 1830, with Smith and Hunton again the opponents, the voter turnout soared to 67 per cent, and Smith was again the winner.

The Jacksonians had now established their ascendancy. From that date down to 1854, when another major reorganization of parties was to occur, the Democrats lost only two gubernatorial elections, in 1837 and 1840, and they suffered defeat in a presidential contest only in 1840. In general, Maine was as heavily Democratic as Massachusetts was Whig.   Voter participation reached an all-time high of 83 per cent in 1838,

10. (Portland) *Eastern Argus,* May-June, 1829; (Boston) *Columbian Centinel,* Mar. 14, 1829.

11. (Portland) *Eastern Argus,* May 1-28, Sept. 4, 1829; (Augusta) *Kennebec Journal,* Sept. 4, 1829.

when the Democrats recaptured the governorship, and exceeded 80 per cent in the 1840 presidential election. Thereafter, as the Whigs grew relatively weaker, participation declined to a low of 47 per cent in 1847.

The conduct of politics in Maine was less sedate, more popular, than in Massachusetts. As early as 1828, "Young Men's" organizations were active campaign auxiliaries, and large-scale state political gatherings—initiated by the Adams Republicans in 1828—became common. Both parties used the state convention more or less regularly after 1832 to make nominations for state-wide offices, and by 1840 these conclaves were attended by several thousand delegates and auditors.[12] The two party system, at least until after 1840, was relatively undisturbed by third-party complications, although the Antimasons presented poorly supported candidates for governor in 1833 and 1834.

The crucial year of party reorganization in Maine was 1828. Until then, the overwhelmingly dominant Democratic-Republican party had remained nominally intact, despite the strains of internal factionalism. But the split that occurred in the 1828 presidential election was to be decisive. With the state election of 1829 the Democrats, fortified by a substantial accession of Federalist support and skillfully led by the old junto, were nearly equal in strength to their rivals. The two new parties had become established. The existence of a competitive two-party situation, something that Maine had not previously experienced, brought with it a popularization of politics and high voter participation.

NEW HAMPSHIRE

New Hampshire, in common with its New England neighbors, early developed a vigorous system of two-party politics,

12. Niles' *Register*, XLIV, 424; LIV, 290; LVIII; 228, 276, 403; (Washington) *National Intelligencer*, Aug. 9, 1834.

vestiges of which were still apparent in 1824. Again, however, the epic contest for the presidency in 1828 was made the occasion for a reorganization of parties. Soon New Hampshire was distinguished as the banner Democratic state in the North, if not in the nation. Probably in no other state in the region was politics practiced so zealously or the art of party management raised to such a peak of perfection.

The New Hampshire constitution was in most respects patterned after that of Massachusetts, but certain features of its system of elections were to have a profound effect on political strategy and organization. Elections were held annually in March for the choice of governor and members of the legislature. Printed ballots were used from an early date, and adult male inhabitants were eligible to vote. Representatives were elected from the towns; councillors and senators from districts. The county was a unit for electing a register of deeds and a treasurer. Presidential electors, except in 1800, were elected on a general ticket by popular vote, and members of Congress were invariably chosen down to 1846 not from districts but on a general ticket.

In New Hampshire, then, the *state* was an especially important unit of politics, for not only the governor but congressmen and presidential electors as well were chosen from the state at large. This circumstance made state-wide devices for party management most essential. Too, the system produced a "winner take all" brand of politics.

Party divisions had made their appearance in New Hampshire by 1796 and by 1803 the dominant Federalists were being seriously challenged by the Republicans. In preparation for the 1804 elections there was held in Concord on December 28, 1803, a "General Convention of the Republican members of the general court . . . and a large number of respectable citizens from the distant parts of the state." This mixed legislative caucus, apparently the first to be held in the state, was called for the purpose of "adopting such measures as should appear best calculated to promote *union* and *harmony* among the

Republicans." John Langdon was nominated for governor, together with five candidates for councillor, twelve for the senate, and treasurers and registers of deeds for each county. Six persons from each county were named to a "Grand Committee of Elections and Correspondence" whose main function was to "get out the vote" for the party ticket. The remarkable feature of this caucus is that it made nominations not only for statewide office, but also for districts and counties.[13] Throughout its history, the Republican caucus continued to nominate candidates for governor, councillors, congressmen, and presidential electors, and, at least down to 1816, for senators. County candidates were nominated after 1810 by county delegate conventions and senators by district conventions after 1816. At the town level, where representatives were nominated, there was also a vigorous caucus-committee apparatus.

The Federalists as early as 1799 had employed the caucus to make nominations and determine policy, but they were slow to create a comprehensive campaign apparatus. Aroused by the challenge presented by the Republicans, William Plumer met secretly with five other Federalist leaders in Concord on July 4, 1804, and launched a network of party committees. With Plumer as state chairman, each of his five associates undertook to establish county committees, which in turn appointed "agents" for each town. The town agents were to name lieutenants for every school district. Plumer himself wrote and published a rousing address to the electorate. Thus mobilized, the Federalists won a major victory in the August congressional election. Plumer's secret network was not efficiently maintained, in part because the Federalists were rent

13. (Walpole) *Political Observatory,* Feb. 4, Apr. 7, 1804; (Boston) *Independent Chronicle,* Feb. 23, 1804. During the session of the legislature in June, 1804, the Republican caucus met again to nominate candidates for Congress and presidential electors. (Walpole) *Political Observatory,* Aug. 4, 1804. In 1816 the caucus recommended that state senators be nominated by delegate conventions, convened in each district. There is evidence, however, that even after this date senators were nominated by the caucus and that the district conventions might ratify or reject the nominations. (Concord) *New Hampshire Patriot,* Mar. 2, 1819.

with factionalism, but his general plan of a secret, centralized apparatus was the model for subsequent campaign efforts.[14]

The Republicans elected their first governor in 1805 in a contest that brought nearly 70 per cent of the eligible electorate to the polls. In the three succeeding elections, the Federalists virtually retired from the field, but in 1809 they surprised their opponents by turning out in force and winning the governorship. They were also victorious in 1813, 1814, and 1815. From 1809 through 1817, every state election was bitterly fought. Under the stimulus of close party competition and intensive organization, more than 70 per cent of the electorate customarily went to the polls, and in 1814 participation exceeded 80 per cent. After 1817, the Federalists, weakened by internal divisions, could no longer mount an effective opposition in state elections, and they soon left the field to the Republicans. The collapse of the Federalists engendered internal factionalism within the Republican party. In 1823 Levi Woodbury was elected to the governorship, with Federalist support, over the "regular" nominee. For the next three years the legislative caucus made no nominations for the governorship and factional rivalry threatened to disrupt the party.

In June, 1826, internal discord was ostensibly replaced by harmony when the Republican caucus was revived and General Benjamin Pierce was nominated as the party's gubernatorial candidate. Isaac Hill, the aggressive editor of the *New Hampshire Patriot*, who had been virtually alone in expressing a preference for Crawford in 1824, insisted that the old party must remain united in the face of Federalist attempts to create dissension. Unity could be preserved, he argued, "only by a willingness to tolerate a difference of opinion as to the man who shall be next Executive Chief of the Union. Indeed, if we suffer a difference on this question to divide us, we are at the mercy of our ancient political enemy. . . ."[15] General Pierce

14. Lynn W. Turner, *William Plumer of New Hampshire, 1759-1850* (Chapel Hill, 1962), 144-45; (Walpole) *Political Observatory*, Apr. 7, July 26, Aug. 18, 1804.

15. (Concord) *New Hampshire Patriot*, Feb. 19, 1827.

took a neutral position on the "presidential question," and the party's congressional ticket included both Adams and Jackson supporters. Although there were factional conflicts within some counties, the old party machine creaked to victory behind Pierce over scattered opposition.

It had obviously been Hill's strategy to defer a showdown on the issue of the presidency in the hope that he could build up sufficient support for Jackson within the Republican party to carry the state in 1828. Not until after the state election in March, 1827, did Hill hoist the Jackson banner.[16] His declaration, which cost him the loss of the state printing, was the signal for the formation of two new parties. When the legislature convened in June, preparations began for contesting the state, congressional, and presidential elections to be held in 1828 on the new issue of loyalty to Adams or to Jackson. This issue had not arisen in 1824, when, in the lowest turnout of voters in the state's history, Adams had met with no opposition. It had been suppressed for three years, in the interest of preserving the old Republican party, but now it could no longer be avoided.

On June 14, 1827, the leading supporters of Adams, including Senator Samuel Bell, former Governor David L. Morrill, and Congressmen Ichabod Bartlett and Thomas Whipple, convened a meeting of "friends of the National Administration" at the Court House in Concord, to launch what was to become the Adams, or National Republican, party.[17] Next, an attempt was made by the Adams men to have the legislature adopt a resolution approving the policies of the Adams administration, but the legislators, resentful of the attempt to make them commit themselves, tabled the resolution. Hill, meanwhile, filled every issue of his paper with scathing attacks on what he called the "Amalgamation party" and with appeals to all Republicans

16. *Ibid.*, May 14, 1827.

17. *Ibid.*, June 19, 1827. Hill charged that this meeting was inspired by forces outside the state, apparently referring to Daniel Webster. William Plumer, a devoted friend of Adams, was also a leader of his cause in New Hampshire.

to mobilize behind Jackson. Later in June, both factions held caucuses to nominate candidates. General Pierce was put forward by the Jacksonians; his opponent was John Bell, brother of Senator Samuel Bell.

In the election, held in March, 1828, the newly mobilized parties contested town, county, and district offices, as well as the governorship. With two-thirds of the eligible voters participating, the Adams party scored a victory, winning both the governorship and control of the legislature. The high voter turnout signified that the former Federalists, who had remained away from the polls for several years, were now exercising their franchise, but whether they gave the preponderance of their support to Adams or to Jackson is not clear.

No sooner had the state election ended than preparations were made for the presidential election. A meeting of Jacksonians in Dover on April 5 proposed that a state convention should be held at Concord in June, with each town to have delegates equal to its representation in the legislature. Other Jacksonian meetings elsewhere in the state applauded this recommendation, and soon meetings were being held to choose delegates. The convention, the first ever held in New Hampshire, was probably called because the Jacksonians were in a minority in the legislature and consequently many towns would not have been represented in a legislative caucus.

On June 11 nearly two hundred delegates from the eight counties of the state convened for a two-day session.[18] The convention was remarkable for the elaborateness of its organization, doubtless the product of Isaac Hill's fertile mind. The delegates elected a president, William Badger, a secretary, and two assistant secretaries. A credentials committee was then appointed, together with a committee on business. The latter committee recommended that the convention should nominate eight electors, with each county selecting one; that six congress-

18. *Ibid.*, Apr. 14, 21, June 9, 16, 1828; *Proceedings and Address of the New Hampshire Republican State Convention* ... [Concord, 1828]. The legislature was in session at the time, and many of the legislators served as delegates.

men should be nominated, one each by the delegates of six hypothetical districts; and that a gubernatorial candidate for the election to be held in March, 1829, should be nominated by ballot. The committee also recommended that there should be a committee of ten to prepare resolutions, a similar committee to frame an address, and a committee on ways and means to defray the expenses of the convention and the printing of the proceedings. These recommendations were adopted, General Pierce was nominated as the gubernatorial candidate with 160 votes out of a total of 188, and candidates were named for Congress and electors. Before adjourning the delegates adopted a set of resolutions applauding Jackson and created a ten-member committee of correspondence, headed by Isaac Hill. The Adams party, adhering to traditional procedures, held a mixed legislative caucus, with delegates present from towns not represented in the legislature by Adams men. Bell was renominated for governor and slates of candidates for elector and for Congress were adopted.

Despite Hill's brilliant efforts, regional loyalty to Adams was sufficiently strong to occasion a second defeat for the Jackson party. More than three-fourths of the electorate voted, again indicating the presence of former Federalists at the polls, and Adams received 53 per cent of the vote. Largely because of the intensity of the party competition, New Hampshire's voter turnout was the highest in the nation.

The defeat of Adams in the national election, however, forecast disaster for his party in New Hampshire. In the state elections in March, 1829, the Jacksonians swept the field, electing Pierce to the governorship, along with a full congressional slate, four of the five councillors, and a heavy majority in the legislature. Hill's strategy in this campaign was to appeal to those Republicans who had temporarily separated from the grand old party to return to the field; he did not make loyalty to Jackson the crucial issue.

For nearly a decade the Democrats carried every election, often against little more than token opposition. Hill was elected to the Senate in 1830 and at the end of his term there was three times elected to the governorship. Samuel Dinsmoor and William Badger, who had aided Hill in forming the Jackson party, were also rewarded with terms as governor. Jackson carried the state by a sizable margin in 1832, and again New Hampshire—with nearly 75 per cent of its eligibles voting—led the nation in voter turnout. Unable to win any state offices, or congressional seats, under New Hampshire's "all or nothing" system of politics, the Whigs languished and—like the Federalists of an earlier day—virtually retired from the field. Accordingly, voter participation fell to a low point of 37 per cent by 1837. In 1838 the Whigs emerged from their lethargy, and for the next few years made energetic, but unsuccessful, efforts to challenge the dominant Democrats. After 1840, politics in New Hampshire was complicated by the rise of the Free Soil party, and in 1846 the Democrats for the first time failed to win the governorship. But the machine that Hill and his associates built in 1827 had operated with extraordinary efficiency.

Hill was the peerless leader of the party during the years of its greatest success. From his office in Concord, known as the "Dictator's Palace," he skillfully guided the actions of the party caucus, which in turn enforced iron discipline on the party in the legislature. The party continued for some years after 1829 to use the legislative caucus to nominate candidates for state-wide office and in 1830 for the first time to appoint a Central Committee of four Concord men and a General Committee of Correspondence of one from each county.[19] Not until after 1835 did the state convention succeed the caucus as the customary device for making nominations to state-wide offices by both parties.[20]

Party formation in New Hampshire, then, resulted from

19. (Concord) *New Hampshire Patriot,* July 5, 1830. In 1831, because the incumbent governor received a federal judicial appointment after the legislature had adjourned for the year, a state convention was held to nominate a new candidate. *Ibid.,* Nov. 15, 29, 1830, Jan. 22, 1831.

20. Niles' *Register,* XLVIII, 310; LII, 386; LIV, 273, 289.

the division of the Republican party in 1827 over the issue of presidential succession. Behind the break, however, lay factional rivalries within the party that had become acute by 1823. The Hill faction, mobilizing behind Jackson after the 1827 state election, suffered a defeat in 1828, but once Adams had ceased to be a factor in national politics, they obtained an ascendancy in the state that was almost impregnable. The new parties were the result of a split in the old Republican party, but it must be presumed that former Federalist voters were attracted to the polls and entered the ranks of both parties. The alignment of parties that emerged in 1828 was a durable one. The Jacksonians maintained their identity and became the Democratic party; the Adams party endured under the labels of National Republican and Whig. Neither party, as of the time of its origin in 1828, could be defined in terms of a distinctive set of policies. It would rather seem that the "presidential question" was used by rival leadership cliques in New Hampshire—as well as in Maine and Massachusetts—in their efforts to gain political dominance in the state.

CONNECTICUT

Connecticut, at least down to 1830, had an exceedingly peculiar system of politics because the nature of its constitution made it all but impossible for a two-party system to function. Until it suffered its first—and final—defeat in 1817, the Federalist party had easily beaten off the challenge of the feeble Republican minority. For the next dozen years the Toleration-Republican party held power by as decisive a margin as the party that it had displaced. Thus, although Connecticut entered the era of new party formations with a tradition of party competition that dated from 1800, it was a unique and vastly unbalanced kind of competition. After

1830 changes in the constitution were a major factor in facilitating the emergence of two competitive parties that had their origins in the factional division that occurred within the Republican party in 1828 over the presidential question.

Connecticut retained its ancient charter of 1662 until a new constitution was adopted in 1818. Elections were held annually in April for a governor, lieutenant-governor, treasurer, and secretary, and for a twelve member Council of Assistants elected from the state at large. Members of the lower house were elected semi-annually in April and September from the towns, and at the latter election a unique kind of primary was also held to nominate candidates for the council and also for members of Congress every other year. Congressmen were elected from the state at large down to 1840. Presidential electors were chosen by the legislature until 1820, when they became elective by popular vote from the state at large. The state, then, was a unit for electing the executive, the council, congressmen, and electors. Elections were conducted by ballot, but the procedure was extremely cumbersome because there were separate ballots to be voted for each office until a printed, single ballot was introduced in 1836. Voters had to be freemen and possess a modest amount of property, a requirement that of itself did not seriously restrict the franchise. But the procedure for the admission of freemen, coupled with the notorious "Stand-Up Law" of 1801 and the non-secret character of the method of casting ballots for members of the council all contributed to discourage voting, especially by non-Federalists.

The council was the all-important center of governmental and political authority. In practice it controlled the extensive state patronage, initiated most legislation, and enjoyed great prestige. Partly because of the nature of the system by which its members were nominated and elected, it was remote from popular control, underwent little change in personnel from year to year, and functioned as a respected oligarchy. Moreover, the method of election virtually guaranteed that all members of the council would be of the same political party. Consequently in Connecticut the minority party had virtually no office, appointive or elective, that it could hope to win except township officers and representatives.

When partisanship first manifested itself in Connecticut around 1800 the political "establishment" was overwhelmingly committed to Federalism; it was against this formidable, strongly entrenched group that the Republicans had to contend. The center of Republican activity in the state was New Haven, where a small group of leaders, including Abraham Bishop, Gideon Granger, Pierpont Edwards, and Asa Spalding, worked valiantly to build the party. Before 1803, and perhaps as early as 1798, this group arranged informal caucuses at which candidates were agreed upon; after that date the mixed legislative caucus was used. The Federalists, similarly, developed an organization after 1800, the key element of which was the mixed caucus. In both parties, management of party affairs was highly centralized. A committee, chosen by the caucus, appointed county and town party officials. While the Republicans resorted to mass meetings and observances of July 4 and March 4—the anniversary of Jefferson's inauguration—to whip up popular sentiment, the Federalists relied on the strong influence wielded by the Congregationalist clergy and their masses of appointed office-holders to maintain the supremacy of the party.

Republican strength grew steadily until 1806, when the party's gubernatorial candidate received over 40 per cent of the vote in an election that brought nearly 42 per cent of the electorate to the polls. This was the peak of voter participation between 1800 and 1817. By 1812 the party had been reduced to a remnant, and it experienced no revival until the end of the War of 1812. Then a long-smoldering religious issue caught fire and brought about the downfall of the Federalists. The Episcopalians, traditionally the staunch allies of the Congregationalists in the Federalist party, had become increasingly dissatisfied with the preferred position enjoyed by the Congregationalist establishment. Accordingly, in February, 1816, Episcopalian leaders met with Republican politicians and worked out an agreement to form a "Toleration" party, pledged to the separation of church and state and constitutional reform. Oliver Wolcott and Jonathan Ingersoll, both former Federalists, were nominated for governor and lieutenant-governor on the Toleration ticket and were defeated by a narrow margin in 1816. The following year they were victorious, and in 1818 the Federalists did not even place a candidate in the field.

The Toleration-Republican party redeemed its campaign promises by sponsoring a constitutional convention. The new frame of government, in addition to securing religious disestablishment, provided for taxpayer suffrage and annual elections in April for all state officials. With the religious issue settled and with the Federalists in retirement, Connecticut after 1820 had virtually a one-party system. The Republicans, as they may loosely be called, continued to use the caucus apparatus for making nominations for state-wide offices, although party discipline was weak and numerous independent candidates entered the field, especially in congressional elections. There was a brief neo-Federalist revival in the elections of 1825 and 1826, but it was quite ineffectual and soon expired. The absence of party excitement was reflected at the polls; voter participation in gubernatorial elections in the decade after 1820 rarely exceeded 20 per cent and in 1824 reached an all-time low of 12 per cent.

The presidential election of 1824 did not disturb the political tranquility of Connecticut. Only 15 per cent of the eligibles voted, and the Adams ticket prevailed over an unpledged slate—which was supported by adherents of Crawford and Clay—by a margin of almost four to one. Political affairs remained calm until 1828, when two issues arose that were to shatter the old Republican party and necessitate new techniques of party organization.

Sentiment had been growing in the state for the election of

members of the upper house from districts. In the April, 1828, state election, proponents of this reform organized a "Union" party, which defeated the regular caucus slate of senatorial candidates and captured the lower house as well. This group then put through an amendment to the constitution making senators elective by districts, effective in 1830. The new electoral arrangement was to prove to be a fatal blow to the old caucus system and to the "winner take all" brand of politics that had prevailed in Connecticut. To the extent that the upper house, controlled by a single party, had been the keystone of the political and governmental order, the whole edifice was seriously shaken.

Meanwhile a second factor of discord in the form of agitation of the presidential question disturbed the political scene. Among the numerous factions in the crumbling Republican party, one, led by J. M. Niles, publisher of the Hartford *Times*, and including also Henry and Thomas Seymour and Henry W. Edwards, undertook to organize support for Jackson. The "regular" caucus of the Republican party in May, 1828, nominated an electoral slate pledged to Adams. Niles and his cohorts, in part because they had little support in the legislature, countered with a call for a state convention, which met in Middletown on August 7, 1828.[21] After electing a president and two secretaries, the convention adopted the recommendation of a committee on business which proposed that eight electors should be named, one by the delegates from each of the eight counties; that a central committee of correspondence of five members and county committees of three members

21. (New Haven) *Connecticut Journal*, Aug. 12, 1828; *Address to the People of Connecticut Adopted at the* [Jackson] *State Convention* ... [Hartford, 1828]. This convention was not the first of its kind held in the state. In August, 1812, the Republicans held a convention at Hartford in an effort to revive the party. Norman L. Stamps, "Political Parties in Connecticut, 1789-1818," (Ph.D. diss., Yale University, 1952), 204 *et. seq.* Much earlier, on March 25, 1766, and March 30, 1774, contending factions in Connecticut had held colony-wide conventions at which nominations were made for the governorship and other offices. Oscar Zeichner, *Connecticut's Years of Controversy, 1750-1776* (Chapel Hill, 1949).

should be appointed; and that a second convention should be held in January 8, 1829, to name a ticket for the state election. Other committees were appointed to prepare resolutions and draft an address. The convention then proceeded to adopt an electoral ticket pledged to Jackson and chose a central committee headed by J. M. Niles. In the ensuing election, which brought only 27 per cent of the electorate to the polls, the newly formed Jackson party polled less than one quarter of the votes cast.

The split in the old Republican party that occurred during the presidential election could not be healed. In 1828 such pro-Jackson men as Niles and Edwards had been placed on the "regular" caucus ticket of nominees for the Senate. But in 1829 the caucus, dominated by Adams men, "proscribed" all Jacksonians. The latter, meanwhile, had convened in Middletown as scheduled in January, 1829, and had named their own senatorial slate, headed by Niles. They did not offer a candidate for the governorship; not until 1833 did they feel sufficiently strong to offer such a challenge to their adversaries. The Adams wing of the old Republican party, adopting the label of "Independent" in a frank appeal for Federalist support, won the state election, despite a strong showing by the Jacksonians. Encouraged by their performance, the Jacksonians decided to hold a third state convention at Hartford on May 13, 1829, to undertake a thorough organization of the party and make special preparations for contesting senate seats under the new district plan.

At this Hartford meeting, which was actually a mixed caucus rather than a delegate convention, it was agreed that "Democratic Electors" should meet in their respective towns on the first Monday in January to elect twice as many delegates as the town had representatives in the general assembly. These delegates would then meet in the newly created senatorial districts on the second Monday in January to nominate candidates for the senate. On the first Wednesday in February all the delegates would assemble at a state convention in Middletown to nominate candidates for state offices.[22]   This plan of organization, which introduced the convention system on a lasting basis in Connecticut politics, worked to good effect in the 1830 elections.   Although the Jacksonians did not contest the governorship, they did offer candidates for lieutenant-governor and secretary, and their senatorial candidates were generally successful over divided opposition.

The National Republicans saw the virtues of the tactics employed by the Democrats, and in September and November, 1830, they, too, held state conventions for the purpose of perfecting their organization and announcing their support for Henry Clay.   Subsequently, they were to use district and state conventions regularly to nominate candidates.[23]   The Antimasons, who made their appearance in Connecticut in 1829, also held two state conventions in 1830 and entered a ticket in 1831 state election.   Thus, partly as a result of the change in the method of electing senators and in part as a consequence of the new currents set in motion by the revival of the contest over the presidency, the old political order broke down.   New parties, formed essentially around factions of the old Republican party, had by 1830 introduced a new order that was to endure in its major outlines for a generation.

Jackson remained something of a handicap to the Democratic party in the land of steady habits.   In 1832 the National Republicans carried the state for Clay; Jackson polled about one-third of the total vote and Wirt one-tenth.   In 1833, however, the Democrats for the first time nominated a gubernatorial candidate, Henry W. Edwards, and when no candidate received a majority, Edwards was elected by the legislature. The Antimasons, who consistently polled less than one quarter of the votes in state elections, retired from the field after 1834, and thereafter the Democrats and Whigs, nearly equal in strength, battled for control, with frequent shifts in domi-

22. Hartford Times, Mar. 23, Apr. 20, June 15, Dec. 14, 1829; New Haven Advertiser, Feb. 9, 1830.
23. Jarvis M. Morse, A Neglected Period of Connecticut's History, 1818-1850 (New Haven, 1933), 106; Niles' Register, XXXIX, 94; XL, 127, 279-80.

nance. Voter participation after 1836 was consistently above 60 per cent, reaching a peak of 76 per cent in the presidential election of 1844. For some reason that is not apparent, voter participation in presidential elections was invariably higher than in state elections, and frequently by a considerable margin. Only in Connecticut did this condition prevail. The new style of politics reached maturity in 1844, when both parties belatedly succumbed to the popular type campaign, complete with stump speeches and torchlight processions, that had swept most of the nation by 1840.

VERMONT

Vermont during the era of the first party system had two vigorous political parties that competed for dominance for nearly two decades. But after 1828, as new parties came into existence nationally, Vermont politics did not fit readily into a two-party pattern. Instead, for most of the years down to the eve of the Civil War, there were three parties in the field. In brief, the issues that so evenly divided the nation in the Jackson era did not encompass or reflect the concerns that were most urgently felt in Vermont. Or, to put it differently, Vermont was such an atypical state that its politics could not be adjusted to a national norm. In the sense that it did not develop two durable and balanced parties it can be characterized as a "disoriented" state.

The structure of government in Vermont bore many resemblances to that of other New England states, but its constitution also evidenced substantial borrowing from Pennsylvania. At the state election held annually on the first Tuesday in September, a governor, deputy governor, treasurer, and twelve councillors were elected from the state at large and representatives were chosen from the towns. Voting was by ballot; and there were no property or taxpaying restrictions on the franchise. As in the first Pennsylvania constitution, full legislative power was vested in the house of representatives. The governor and council could suggest revisions of bills and could exercise a suspensary veto on legislation, but the upper house did not enjoy co-ordinate status with the lower house. All civil, military, and judicial appointments were made by the legislature, including county judges, sheriffs, and justices of the peace. A majority of the total vote cast was required for the election of the state's executive officers and for members of Congress. Presidential electors were chosen by the legislature until 1828, when they became elective by popular vote from the state at large. Congressmen were usually elected from districts, although on occasion they were chosen from the state at large. In 1828 the constitution was amended to require that the voters be citizens, and in 1836 the council was replaced by a senate of thirty members apportioned among the several counties. It will be apparent that, as elsewhere in New England generally, the town and the state were the major units of political organization prior to 1836. Consequently Vermont was to develop at an early date powerful agencies for state-wide political management, comparable to those of her neighbors.

Party cleavages appeared in Vermont before 1797, although until the death of the respected and popular Thomas Chittenden in that year there was no contest over the governorship. In 1797 a Federalist, Isaac Tichenor, was elected governor by the legislature when no candidate received a majority of the popular vote. By the legislative session of 1798 party spirit had reached such a height that the dominant Federalists introduced a policy of proscribing members of the opposition party when making appointments to office. The Republicans secured a majority in the legislature in 1801, but not until 1807 were they able to unseat Tichenor. The Federalists recaptured the governorship in 1808, and in 1813 and 1814 their candidate was elected by the legislature when the popular vote failed to produce a choice. After 1814 Federalist strength declined rapidly, and from 1818 through 1828 the Republican gubernatorial candidate faced no organized party opposition. For about a decade, beginning in 1806, the two parties were very evenly balanced, elections were fiercely contested, and voter participation frequently exceeded 70 per cent of the eligibles, reaching a high point of 80 per cent in 1812.

Both parties used the legislative caucus to make nominations for state-wide offices, determine legislative policy and appointments, and manage party affairs. The Federalist machinery was, as in New Hampshire, kept shrouded in secrecy, but the existence of the Republican caucus was revealed in 1805, although it had probably come into existence much earlier.[24] Meeting at the end of the legislative session, usually in November, the Republican caucus would name candidates for governor, lieutenant-governor, and councillors and appoint party committees. Even after the demise of the Federalists, the Republican caucus continued to function and it was seemingly the authoritative voice of a united party until 1828.

The presidential election of 1824 occasioned no excitement in Vermont. A slate of electors pledged to Adams was elected by the legislature with few dissenting voices. As party competition languished, interest in elections waned, and no state election in the decade after 1818 attracted as many as 30 per cent of the electorate to the polls.

This decade of apathy ended in 1828, when the urgency of the presidential question and the eruption of Antimasonry shattered the political calm. Looking forward to the presidential election, which was to be conducted by popular vote for the first time in Vermont, the Republican caucus in November, 1827, had nominated an Adams electoral ticket. Jacksonian sentiment was slow in organizing, but on June 27, 1828, a "numerous and respectable meeting" of Jackson supporters was held at the State House in Montpelier in response to no-

24. For an unusually revealing description of the Republican caucus, see the "Rutland Letters" in the (Windsor) *Post Boy*, beginning June 11, 1805.

tices that had previously been inserted in three newspapers.
A convention to consider amendments to the state constitution
was then in session, and that event may have determined the
timing of the meeting. Under the chairmanship of Ezra
Meech, one of the largest landowners and wealthiest farmers
in the state and a former member of Congress, this informal
convention named a Jackson electoral ticket and adopted the
customary address and resolutions. No nominations were
made for state offices.[25] The state election in September, which
was not contested, brought fewer than 30 per cent of the
voters to the polls, but for the presidential contest in November, participation rose to over 55 per cent. Adams received
more than three quarters of the popular vote.

The cleavage produced within the old Republican party
by the conflict over the presidential question persisted. On
July 15, 1829, the Jacksonians held a state convention at Montpelier, with delegates attending from each county, and nominated candidates for governor and lieutenant-governor to oppose the nominees of the National Republican caucus.[26] Badly defeated in 1829, the Democrats sought to perfect their
organization for the 1830 elections. At a state convention in
Montpelier on July 7 and 8, again under the chairmanship of
Ezra Meech, the assembled delegates nominated Meech for
governor, appointed a central corresponding committee of
three members and corresponding committees for each county.
Conventions were also held in the congressional districts to
nominate candidates for Congress.[27] Thereafter it was the
usual practice for the party to use delegate conventions in
making all nominations. The National Republicans, victorious in 1829 and 1830, adhered to the legislative caucus until

25. (Concord) *New Hampshire Patriot*, July 7, 1828.
26. *American Annual Register*, 1827-29, I, 17; (Middlebury) *National Standard*, Aug. 11, 1829.
27. (Middlebury) *National Standard*, June 1, 22, July 13, 1830. After the
election, which resulted in another defeat for the Democrats, the party was
reorganized at a mixed legislative caucus on November 5, 1830. A new central
committee and new county committees were appointed. *Ibid.*, Nov. 16, 1830.

1831, when they held their first state convention in June.[28] Both parties were well organized by 1830, but neither was able to withstand the challenge of Antimasonry.

In no state except Pennsylvania did Antimasonry acquire the political dominance it achieved in Vermont. Marshalled by the adroit "Randolph Triumvirate"—Martin Flint, Leffeus Egerton, and Calvin Blodgett—and guided on occasion by emissaries from New York, the movement had a powerful appeal to the religious minded Vermonters. The frenzy first assumed political form in 1828, when an Antimasonic candidate ran well in the fifth congressional district. The enthusiasm spread, and on August 5, 1829, a state convention was held in Montpelier at which the party was organized to contest state elections, and candidates were named for governor, lieutenant-governor, and councillors. The party ran second to the National Republicans in 1829, but in 1830 it had sufficient support to force the gubernatorial election into the legislature.

By 1831, the Antimasons were the most numerous party in the state, with the National Republicans second and the Democrats a poor third. William A. Palmer won the governorship and was re-elected on three successive occasions, although only in 1833 did he received a majority of the popular vote. The party from the outset possessed a thorough, highly centralized organization. At the first state convention a central state committee and county committees of vigilance, with power to appoint sub-committees in towns and school districts, had been set up. This pattern of organization was maintained throughout the life of the party.[29]

After the presidential election of 1832, in which the Antimasons again led the field, the National Republicans and the Democrats formulated plans for uniting their strength. In July, 1833, the two parties held their state conventions simul-

28. *Ibid.*, Nov. 16, 1830; Niles' *Register*, XXIX, 234.

29. (Middlebury) *National Standard*, Aug. 11, 25, 1829; (Brattleboro) *Vermont Phoenix*, Mar. 4, 1836.

taneously in Montpelier and agreed on a "Union Ticket." The Democrats were to have the governor and four councillors; the National Republicans were allotted the lieutenant-governor, treasurer, and eight councillors. A letter from the National Republicans to the gubernatorial nominee, Ezra Meech, observed that party feelings had become calm after the presidential election and stated that while they could not unite with those whose motto was proscription, they could join with a party "whose opinions on the great and leading interests of our country agree with ours."[30] The Antimasons easily defeated this odd coalition, and in 1834 there were again three distinct tickets in the field. By 1835, there were signs of an approaching merger of Whigs and Antimasons, for the disheartened Whigs failed to make an official nomination for the governorship. Strongly influencing the course of events locally was the approaching presidential election, which offered no prospects for success nationally to the Antimasons.

The fusion of Whigs and Antimasons was consumated early in 1836. Whig members of a state constitutional convention met together in January and made plans for a state convention at which all who were opposed to "Executive Tyranny" would be welcomed, "without distinction of party names." On February 24 the Whig convention was held, simultaneously with the Antimasonic convention. After the Antimasons had agreed on a state ticket and a slate of electors pledged to Harrison and Granger, the Whigs adopted the same nominees. Each party, however, retained its own organization. After the state election, which brought victory to the coalition, leaders of the two parties met in October and November and set about creating a unified party. This work was completed by July 12, 1837, when the Whig State Convention met at Montpelier. The Antimasons had vanished as a separate party, but such former Antimasonic leaders as Milton Brown and C. L. Knapp were appointed to the Whig state committee, and the guberna-

30. Niles' *Register*, XLIV, 348.

torial nominee of the convention was Silas H. Jennison, an Antimason.[31]

As long as the Antimasons had remained on the scene, there was obviously considerable shifting of individual party loyalties. National Republican strength declined from a high of 14,325 in 1829 to a low of 10,159 in 1834. When the Whigs and Antimasons merged in 1836, many of the latter, accepting the designation of "Jack Masons," aligned with the Democrats. Early in 1837 a conference of Democratic and Jacksonian-Antimasonic politicians agreed to unite in issuing a call for the next state convention, signifying the merger of one Antimasonic faction with the Democrats.[32] The three-party contest after 1829 had the effect of greatly increasing voter participation. Whereas fewer than 30 per cent of the electorate had voted in the 1820's, more than half went to the polls after 1830. The Antimasons undoubtedly attracted the major portion of these "new" voters, but by 1837 the chief beneficiary of the enlarged electorate was the Democratic party.

The two-party competition that prevailed for several years after 1837 brought out even larger numbers of voters. Although the Whigs invariably prevailed, the Democrats usually polled around 45 per cent of the vote, and they could expect to elect not only a sizable number of representatives from the towns but also some Congressmen and—after 1836—several senators from Democratic counties. Voter participation accordingly rose well above 60 per cent and reached an all-time peak of nearly 82 per cent in the gubernatorial election of 1840. Both parties retained and expanded the convention system, which operated at the levels of the county, congressional district, and the state, together with an extensive network of party committees. By 1840, campaign techniques had become popularized; fifteen thousand persons were reported to have attended the Whig state convention in Burlington in

31. (Brattleboro) *Vermont Phoenix*, Jan. 23, Feb. 5, Oct. 28, Nov. 5, 1836, July 21, 1837.
32. *Ibid.*, June 16, 1837.

June.[33] Thus, belatedly, the new two-party system that had been forecast by the breakup of the old Republican party in 1828, became a reality. It was not, however, to endure, for after 1841 the Free Soil party was to emerge and grow steadily in strength and to pose a continual threat to the unity of the major parties.

RHODE ISLAND

Rhode Island politics corresponded superficially to the New England pattern, but in that curiously "otherwise minded" state politics had, in fact, become a fascinating kind of game played in accordance with a peculiar and ancient set of rules. The game had originated early in the eighteenth century and had become ritualized by the 1750's, when the classic contests between the Ward and the Hopkins factions convulsed the tiny colony. After independence some new features were added, but the game continued to be played much as in the past. The indigenous parties, which rarely concerned themselves with issues or ideologies, adjusted themselves loosely to the national alignments in the period of the first party system, and after 1828 a similar vague adjustment was made to the second party system. But because of the odd code that prevailed in Rhode Island, partisanship had neither the same meaning nor the same consequences that it had elsewhere.

The constitutional framework within which politics was conducted was provided until 1842 by the venerable charter of 1663, as interpreted and modified by custom and legislative enactments. The most significant feature of the government established under this charter was that the crucial electoral arena was the colony—later the state—as a unit. Annually in

33. Niles' *Register*, LVIII, 307.

April the qualified voters chose a governor, deputy governor, treasurer, secretary, attorney, and ten members of the upper house on a colony-wide basis. Semiannually, in April and August, members of the lower house were elected from the towns. Thus there existed an obvious inducement to form colony-wide parties in order to carry a full slate of general officers. Moreover, as in Connecticut, New Hampshire, and Vermont, the victor in the general election held an unusually commanding position. After 1790 the importance of the state as an election unit was further enhanced because congressmen were invariably chosen at large until 1843, and presidential electors were popularly elected from 1800 in the same manner. The congressional elections were customarily held in August and the presidential vote in mid-November.

Voting privileges were confined after 1762 to adult males who had been admitted to freemanship in a town and who owned real property valued at $134. In 1822 voting was restricted to whites. In the nineteenth century the suffrage qualifications probably barred about half of the adult white males from voting. Elections were conducted in the towns, and a form of printed ballot—known locally as a "prox"—was used. Each voter was required to sign his prox, with the result that no secrecy was preserved. When the legislature convened in May all of the proxes for the several offices were counted and the results were made known. If a candidate failed to secure a majority of the total vote cast for a particular office, a choice was usually made by the legislature.

The main object of politics in Rhode Island was to secure a majority of the joint meeting of the legislature in order to obtain the hosts of public offices at the disposal of that body. Virtually all offices in the state were appointive by the legislature on an annual basis. These annual prizes included the three seats on the Supreme Court, five common pleas judges for each of the five counties, five Supreme Court clerkships, five clerkships of the courts of common pleas, five sheriffs, public notaries for each county and justices of the peace for each town, numerous militia officers, and such miscellaneous officials as inspectors of ferries and inspectors of scythe stones. Frequent changes in the political complexion of the legislature was the rule in Rhode Island and, correspondingly, there was a frequent turnover among the appointive officials. Oddly enough, the treasurer, secretary, and attorney general— and even the governor in some periods—were regarded as somehow being above or outside the political game, and these officials usually enjoyed long tenure in office. The jobs that were the prizes of the political victors were important for the prestige and the emoluments that they conferred. But, in addition, it was in accord with the rules of the game for the appointed judicial officers to render decisions biased in favor of their fellow partisans.

The party contests featured wholesale corruption and astonishing coalitions and shifts in allegiance. There were the usual ingenious practices for fraudulently qualifying voters, usually on the basis of spurious deeds to land. Even more imaginative, though, was the technique of bribing electors of the opposite persuasion to stay away from the polls. In the Rhode Island game party loyalties were flexible, with the result that influential leaders changed sides frequently, and in particular circumstances the warring factions would agree to support the same candidates for specified offices. Although the political scene often appeared incomprehensible—or distressingly opportunistic and mercenary—to outside observers, it had long since become familiar and obvious to Rhode Island's inhabitants.

The mobilization of parties for the annual contest for offices was of ancient origin. No colony, it would seem, was more precocious than Rhode Island in organizing its politics on a party basis. There were rival proxes for general officers, backed by vigorous factions that were prepared to resort to any means of achieving victory, several decades before the revolution. Between 1757 and 1770, when Samuel Ward and Stephen Hopkins led their respective parties in a series of bitterly fought contests, the techniques of party management attained a remarkable level of maturity. Despite the high suffrage qualifications, and the expenditure of huge campaign funds to bribe voters not to vote, there were occasions when nearly half of the adult white males cast their proxes. After Ward's defeat in 1770, and his subsequent retirement from the political arena, party strife subsided, and relative harmony reigned throughout the revolutionary era. But in 1786 discord over the paper money issue contributed to the revival of party strife, with a "Country" party pitted against what was known as the "Minority" party. In 1790 the "Minority" secured its first victory as the proponents of the Federal Constitution.

After 1790 political divisions in Rhode Island assumed some resemblance to the emerging national alignments. However, as a result of one of those truces peculiar to that state's politics Arthur Fenner held the governorship without opposition from 1790 until his death in 1805. Fenner came to be regarded as a Republican, but he was not an active partisan. Rhode Island's congressmen down to 1800 were usually identified as Federalists and in the presidential elections through 1812, except in 1804, Federalist electors were chosen. After Fenner's death a split occurred in the Republican ranks, and in 1807 a Union prox, headed by James Fenner and supported by most of the Federalists and one Republican faction, was victorious.

Traditional party lines were restored in 1811 when the Federalists supported William Jones against Fenner, now heading a reunited Republican party. Jones won, and in the three succeeding years the Federalists reigned supreme. Republican strength revived after the War of 1812, and in 1817 Nehemiah Knight led the Republican prox to victory. Thereafter Federalist opposition dwindled. Except in 1821 the Republicans were not even challenged by an opposition prox, although the Federalists continued to run candidates for the lower house. In 1824 James Fenner returned to the governorship and encountered negligible opposition until after 1829, when the suspicion that he was sympathetic to Jackson made him a central figure in the conflict between the newly emerging parties.

Party management in Rhode Island, as in the other New England states, was centered in the legislative caucus. Because the legislature met frequently and enjoyed extensive powers and because such an obvious need existed for perfecting party arrangements on a state-wide basis, the caucus was a convenient instrument. It is not clear when the caucus began to assume such functions, but there is evidence that at least as early as 1790 both the "Country" and the "Minority" parties caucused to agree on the proxes of general officers to be supported in the April election. From an early date, too, these nominating caucuses included not only party members in the legislature but also non-legislators. By 1807 the Republicans had adopted the practice of requesting towns that were represented in the legislature by Federalists to elect delegates to attend the caucus, and by 1815 it was apparently the practice to request all towns to send delegates to what was called a "convention," with the understanding that the towns might name their members in the legislature. The Federalists adopted similar arrangements to insure that every town would be represented in the annual mixed caucus or convention. Meeting soon after the legislature convened in mid-January, the conventions nominated full slates of general officers, as well as senators. In years when congressmen were to be elected, a convention would be held, usually during the legislative session in June, to make nominations, and in presidential years the conventions would meet in October to name candidates for electors.

In addition to the caucus-convention, the party machinery included pre-convention meetings in the towns to choose delegates and pre-election meetings to perfect campaign plans. On election day "drag committees," as they were called, worked energetically to bring voters to the polls. When a crucial contest was in prospect, both parties would seek to augment their

strength by "propounding" new freeman or by making fraudulent conveyances of land to freemen who lacked the requisite
property qualification. Meanwhile, the party presses indulged
in the usual charges and counter-charges and, in keeping with
ancient tradition, deplored the efforts of their adversaries to
keep alive party strife.

Voter participation was normally at a very low level because of the restrictions on the suffrage and the devious arrangements that were made from time to time to lessen party
competition. Before 1810 it was exceptional if more than a
quarter of the adult white males voted. But in 1811 and 1812,
when Republicans and Federalists engaged in all-out contests
for supremacy, voting soared to unprecedented heights. The
Republicans were bolstered by recently organized Tammany
Societies and the Federalists in turn had their Washington
Benevolent Societies. With political excitement running high,
a vote equivalent to 47 per cent of the adult white male population was cast in the April, 1811, state election, and a year
later the proportion approximated 50 per cent. This level of
participation was not exeeded in a state election until 1843,
although it was approached in 1817 and 1818, when the Federalists made their final efforts to withstand Republican challenges. After 1818 participation fell off sharply; only once
earlier than 1830 did it rise above 20 per cent.

The political scene was remarkably tranquil in 1824. The
Federalists had ceased to contest the election of general officers, although they continued to elect members of the lower
house of the legislature. The Republicans, however, maintained their party apparatus, meeting annually in convention
to put forth their prox. The presidential election of 1824
occasioned little interest and no controversy. On October 26
a convention of the "friends of Adams" met in Providence
and nominated four electors. On the following day the regular Republican convention was held and the same four electors
were endorsed.[34] In the ensuing election, in which 12 per

34. Niles' *Register*, XXVII, 148.

cent of the adult white males participated, there were only scattering votes against the Adams ticket.

For the next few years Rhode Island remained a one-party state, wholeheartedly loyal to President Adams and to Governor James Fenner. Signs of discord first appeared before the state election in 1828. On January 15 and 18 an "Administration Convention," made up of members of the legislature and other citizens friendly to Adams, nominated a full state ticket. On January 16 the regular Republican convention, composed of delegates and legislators, convened as usual and agreed upon a slate that was identical with that adopted by the "Administration Convention" except for three of the ten senatorial nominations. The three men in question were assumed to be supporters of Jackson, and those who defended this "regular" prox took the position that state politics should be kept separate from the presidential question. Somewhat surprisingly, two of the three exceptional senators on the "regular" prox were elected.[35]

This preliminary trial, however, did not represent an accurate forecast of the relative strength of the Adams and Jackson supporters. In preparation for the presidential canvass, both the "friends of the National Administration" and the "friends of Jackson" held meetings in Providence late in October to nominate electors. Significantly, neither of these meetings purported to act in the name of the Republican party, and no regular Republican convention was held.[36] Once again the Adams ticket registered an easy victory, garnering three-fourths of the vote in an election in which 18 per cent of the adult white males participated.

The breach that had been created by the presidential question in 1828 widened into a complete breakdown of the old Republican party in 1829. When the customary notice was issued to the towns early in January, 1829, to choose delegates to the annual Republican state convention, separate meetings

35. (Providence) *American & Gazette*, Jan. 18–May 13, 1828.
36. *Ibid.*, Oct. 31, Nov. 4, 1828; *Newport Mercury*, Nov. 1, 15, 1828.

were held in many towns to appoint "Jackson" delegates or "Adams" delegates. The editor of the staunchly Republican Providence *Patriot and Columbian Phenix* deplored the impending schism. "The Republicans of this state generally, and with very few exceptions," he opined, "are willing, nay desirous, of reorganizing the party—but they will not do so, under the appelation of "Jackson Republicans," "Adams Republicans," or any other cognomen—but simply Republicans."[37]

This prognostication was in error. On January 14 and 15, with the legislature in session, two separate caucus-conventions were held, representing the Adams and Jackson wings of the old Republican party, each with some accretions of erstwhile Federalists. Both conventions nominated the same general officers, including Governor Fenner, but each named distinct slates of senatorial candidates. The Jacksonian convention, which labelled its slate "The Landholders Republican Prox," adopted a lengthy address in which it extolled the president-elect but conceded that the sentiments it represented were as yet espoused by a minority in Rhode Island.[38] Despite this pessimistic forecast, the Jacksonian prox was elected in its entirety by a narrow but decisive margin. It was this state election that brought an end to the old Republican party and produced a new party alignment in Rhode Island.

The new parties soon extended the area of combat to include the state's two congressional seats and the general officers. Each party put forth candidates, nominated by the traditional type conventions, in the congressional election held in August, 1829, and the "Opposition" Republicans, backing the two incumbent representatives, won a lopsided victory over the Jacksonians. When the two conventions met in January, 1830, they once again nominated the same general officers but advanced opposing lists of senators. However, Governor

37. Jan. 10, 1829.
38. (Providence) *Patriot and Columbian Phenix,* Jan. 28, 1829. The *Patriot* maintained a discreet neutrality throughout the campaign and then joined the Jackson cause.

Fenner, long regarded as a neutral, had recently indicated that his sympathies lay with Jackson, and numerous "Opposition" leaders had opposed his inclusion on their prox. Accordingly, at a subsequent meeting in January, the "Opposition" replaced both Fenner and his lieutenant-governor with candidates of their own persuasion. Doubtless aided by the popularity of Governor Fenner, the Jacksonians succeeded in carrying all but two members on their prox.[39]

For several years after 1830 neither party was able to secure and hold a commanding position with respect to its rival. The National Republicans won the state election in 1831, unseating even Governor Fenner. In 1832 the election was complicated by the presence in the field of an Antimasonic prox, headed by the millionaire, William Sprague. The Antimasons had first organized in March, 1830, but in the election of that year and again in 1831 they had endorsed the "Opposition" prox.[40] Now, with their own slate of candidates, they secured sufficient votes to prevent any candidate from acquiring the requisite majority. Subsequently the Antimasons threw their support generally to the Democrats, and John Brown Francis was elected to the governorship in 1833 and held that office against strong opposition until 1838 when Sprague, now running as a Whig, accomplished his defeat. The National Republicans carried the state for Clay in 1832, winning nearly 57 per cent of the total vote, but in 1836 the Democrats by a smaller margin won behind Van Buren. After 1838 the Whigs held the ascendancy until party lines were temporarily disrupted by the turmoils that preceded and followed the Dorr War.

It is not apparent that the emergence of the new two-party system after 1829 resulted in any profound alterations in the traditional methods of conducting politics in Rhode Island. The caucus-convention continued to be utilized by both parties to make nominations for state-wide offices. Party machinery remained quite simple. The newspapers, at least, do not dis-

39. *Ibid.*, Dec. 12–May 8, 1830.
40. *Ibid.*, Mar. 27, 1830, Jan. 1, Apr. 13, 23, 1831.

close the existence of any state central committees, county committees, or town committees, but the fact that calls were issued for state conventions, for meetings to elect delegates to those conventions, and for pre-election meetings to mobilize party strength at the polls may imply that some kind of party structure existed.[41] Voter participation between 1830 and 1840 rarely exceeded 30 per cent in state elections, but this rate was nearly twice as high as in the previous decade. Control of the legislature, and consequently control of state patronage, was the chief concern of both parties. Probably for this reason voting in state elections down to 1840 was at a higher level than in presidential elections.

Party strength in elections tended to be extremely erratic. For example, although the Jacksonians were victorious in the state elections of 1829, 1830, and 1831, they were badly beaten in the congressional election of 1829 and did not even enter the contest in 1831. Similarly, the Whigs offered no opposition to Governor Francis in 1837, but in 1838 they rebounded to win the governorship. Equally erratic was the behavior of outstanding political figures. William Sprague ran for the governorship in 1832 as an Antimason, was elected to Congress in 1835 as a Democrat, and became a Whig governor in 1838. John Brown Francis, after serving several terms as a Democratic governor, was subsequently elected to the Senate as a Whig. Dutee J. Pearce, a member of Congress, shifted his allegiance in 1833 from the Whig to the Democratic party. The redoubtable Thomas Dorr was a Whig in 1835, a Constitutionalist in 1837, and a Democrat in 1839. The persistence of old patterns of behavior is also evident in the constant charges of electoral corruption, in the recurring pleas for an end to party strife, and in the slight attention given to issues in campaigns.

It does not appear that the Jackson party in Rhode Island was controlled or led by a single man, such as Hill in New

41. (Providence) *Republican Herald*, Feb. 6, Mar. 26, June 11, 25, Sept. 10, Nov. 5, 12, 1836.

Hampshire or Henshaw in Massachusetts. Instead, those prominent in the councils of the party varied somewhat from year to year, a fact which makes it difficult to identify with any assurance the actual leadership core. This circumstance may account for the erratic course of parties and the abrupt shifts in party allegiance. It is also difficult to generalize about the distinctions between the two parties, although in a loose way the Jacksonians were the "country" party and the Whigs were the "city" party.

Although it was the presidential question that provided the occasion for a new alignment of parties after 1828, there is little to suggest that explicit national issues were involved in the rupture of the old Republican party. Rather, the revival of the contest for the presidency created a situation in which political leaders could identify with opposing presidential candidates and thus give a new definition to parties. As was the case throughout New England, the formation of new parties was delayed until the defeat of Adams left New England without a favorite son, thus encouraging certain leaders to come out strongly for Jackson. But the newly formed parties continued to be state-oriented to an unusual degree, and they continued to play the game of politics according to the peculiar Rhode Island rules.

CONCLUSIONS

New England had experienced two decades of party contests during the period of the first American party system. Well organized and competitive Federalist and Republican parties had emerged in each state by 1804, or earlier, and politics was conducted on a two-party basis until around 1817, when—except in Massachusetts—the Federalists declined in strength and were unable to challenge Republican supremacy in state-wide elections. When the Federalists collapsed, they did not amalgamate with their erstwhile opponents. Instead they tended to retire from politics, leaders and followers alike, and leave the field exclusively to the Republicans. Consequently, even after the demise of the Federalists, there was not a return to the no-party politics of the pre-1796 period but rather a persistence of political identities and the retention by the Republicans of their organization, however weakened by factional discord, and their control of offices and power.

Party organization was highly developed and characterized by the centralization of control in a state committee and a mixed legislative caucus. The character of party organization was largely determined by the unusual importance of the state as an election unit. Because the executive officers in all states —as well as members of the upper house, congressmen, and presidential electors in some—were chosen annually by the voters of the state at large, the parties required some device for mobilizing support behind a slate of candidates. The requirement, peculiar to New England, that candidates for major offices must receive a majority—rather than a mere plurality— of the vote cast, gave added urgency to the need for strong party management. The legislative caucus, usually augmented by co-opted or delegated party members, met that need.

Where there was occasion for making nominations at levels intermediate between the state and the town, such as the county, senatorial district, or congressional district, delegate conventions were used. The general practice of investing the central committee with the power to appoint county committees, coupled with the fact that the county was unimportant as an election unit, enhanced the power of the managing group at the state level. The caucus apparatus was widely employed not only to nominate candidates and constitute party committees but also to fix legislative policy and distribute patronage.

Because in some states the majority party might make a clean sweep of all offices, except seats in the lower house, the minority party faced a dismal prospect. This circumstance may explain the abrupt collapse of the Federalists, especially in New Hampshire, Connecticut, and Vermont, once they could no longer compete successfully in state-wide elections. The effect of this "winner take all" type of politics had weakened by the 1830's as offices that were formerly elective from the state at large were made elective by counties or districts. This change both lessened the strength of centralized party control and enhanced the ability of a minority party to sustain itself.

The vigor of political life in New England while the first party system flourished is attested to by the high proportions of the eligible voters that turned out for elections. In Massachusetts, Maine, New Hampshire, and Vermont, where there were no substantial restrictions on the suffrage, from three-fifths to as many as four-fifths of the adult white males might go to the polls. Indeed, the peaks of voter participation recorded in those states before 1815 were to be exceeded slightly, if at all, after 1828. In every state, however, as party competition declined and Federalists retired, voter participation fell, and in the early 1820's only about a quarter of those eligible to vote were stimulated to cast their ballots. Vigorous though the parties were, and intense in their efforts to mobilize voters, campaign practices remained sedate, untheatrical, and relatively free from corrupt or demagogic practices.

The presidential election of 1824 had little observable effect on the New England political scene. In most states there were individual Republican leaders who were partial to Crawford, Calhoun, or Clay, but the bulk of the "regular" organization was firmly committed to John Quincy Adams, who encountered no real opposition in the election. So one-sided was the contest that only one voter in five in New England was inspired to go to the polls. The proscribed Federalists, still in retirement, seem to have exerted little or no influence. In the succeeding state elections after 1824, the Republicans maintained their identity and their unity and behaved as though the minor discord occasioned by the presidential question in 1824 represented mere differences of opinion within the Republican family.

When, in 1827 and 1828, supporters of Jackson revealed themselves and began to organize for the presidential contest, the division that occurred was essentially a split in the old Republican party. In some states, notably New Hampshire, Massachusetts, and Maine, the emergent Jacksonians can be identified as factions that had previously manifested themselves within the party, and the Jackson cause provided them with a new rallying cry in their warfare against the opposing party faction. It would be difficult to contend that the leaders of the Jackson faction were motivated by zealous enthusiasm for Old Hickory or for the policies that he might be presumed to favor; most of them had admired Calhoun or Crawford in 1824, and ideology played little discernible part in their campaign strategy in 1828.

The size, ability, and influence of the Jackson leadership core varied from state to state. It was numerous and potent in New Hampshire and Maine, small and feeble in other states. It was to be the objective of the leaders to secure a substantial following in order that they might compete with the Adams party for elective and appointive offices, state and federal, and for the power and prestige that rewarded political strength. To this end they applied their talents for organization and propaganda.

By 1828 there were Jackson tickets in the field in every state, challenging that dominant faction of the old Republican party which had become aligned behind Adams. The new party divisions appeared first in the state elections in New Hampshire, Maine, and—in a very slight degree—Massachusetts in 1828, before the presidential election. The Jacksonians did not contest state elections in Vermont, Connecticut, and Rhode Island until 1829. In the presidential contest they failed to win a single state. They came close in New Hampshire, ran well in Maine, and were overwhelmed in the other four states by a three-to-one margin, or better. Except in New Hampshire, where three-fourths of the electorate voted, participation was well below the average of the pre-1815 years, although in every state except Massachusetts the turnout was greater than in 1824. The party alignments that were formed in 1828 were new; they did not represent a continuance of old cleavages. They were also durable, and they were operative thereafter in both state and national elections. The old Republican party, which had survived through the "era of good feelings" and the early contentious years of the Adams administration, foundered in 1828, and both the Adams and Jackson factions could rightfully claim to be the true heirs of Jefferson.

The crucial importance of the presidential election of 1828 in the history of party formation in New England requires some special emphasis. In no other region did old party identities persist so long; nowhere else did the Republican party so long maintain its unity and sense of exclusiveness. In certain other states, conspicuously New York and Pennsylvania, new state-oriented parties—Bucktails and Clintonians, Family and Independent—arose after 1816. Where the Federalists had never been strong, as in North Carolina, Tennessee, or Ohio, what was in fact a kind of no-party politics came to prevail. But in New England, in part because the Federalist threat existed until well after 1815 and because of the strong and highly centralized character of party machinery, the Republicans did not succumb entirely to internal factionalism nor were new parties formed around state issues.

Why, then, did the split come in 1828? The answer is to be sought in the attitudes and calculations of rival leadership groups within the old Republican party. So overwhelming was the support for Adams as a sectional favorite in 1824 that the party remained united behind him in 1824; it would have been foolhardy to attempt to rally a party behind an opposition banner. But by 1828 there was the prospect of a Jackson victory nationally and beyond that the elimination of Adams as a central figure in national politics. Dissident Republicans, therefore, could take the calculated risk of organizing a Jackson party with some hope of ultimate success. Conversely, as will be seen, it was imprudent in southern and western states to organize anti-Jackson parties until 1834, for similar reasons.

The new party was badly beaten in New England in 1828, but with the removal of Adams as a factor it soon made large gains. The Democratic advance between 1828 and 1832, in my opinion, was less a tribute to Jackson's magnetism as a candidate than a reflection of the indifference of the National Republicans to Clay, who did not have Adams' sectional appeal. The fact that parties formed in 1828, at a time, surely, when ideological distinctions were as yet unformulated, reinforces the view that political calculation by factional leaders inspired the reorganization of parties. The new alignments, at least in their initial phase, derived from the opportunity for maneuver provided by the revival of the contest for the presidency rather than from a polarization of the electorate around opposing views of public policy.

The breakup of the old party created the opportunity for the former Federalists to assume new identities and thus return to the political field. The course followed by the Federalist leaders varied from state to state. In Maine, for example, there was a publicized union of Federalists and Jacksonian Republicans in September, 1829. In Massachusetts, although a small Federalist remnant supported Jackson in 1828, the bulk of the party leadership was successfully amalgamated with the Adams wing of the Republican party in a series of maneuvers that culminated in the organization of the National Republican party in February, 1829. The New Hampshire supporters of Adams, at least in 1828, also included a strong Federalist contingent. Elsewhere the issue of amalgamation was not extensively discussed, and it would require considerable detailed investigation to trace the course of individual Federalist leaders.

At the level of the electorate it becomes difficult to gen-

eralize about the new allegiances assumed by the voters because, among other complexities, voter participation remained
generally low and—in certain states—the Antimasons disrupted
the simple two-party pattern. That is, most Federalists and a
sizable proportion of Republicans had ceased to vote regularly
during the 1820's, chiefly because of the absence of party competition. When voters began to return to the polls after 1827,
they returned slowly. Not until 1836 or 1840 did voting in
most states reach the pre-1815 level. Whether the individuals
who voted in 1828 were the same individuals who had voted,
say, in 1816, would again be a problem that could be resolved
only by the most tedious and detailed kind of research.

Originating in every state as an opposition party, the Jacksonians faced an uphill struggle in their efforts to secure
dominance over their adversaries. In state elections they
registered their first triumphs in New Hampshire and Rhode
Island in 1829 and in Maine in 1830. Both New Hampshire
and Maine were to remain under Democratic control until
the party upheaval of the 1850's. In Connecticut the two
parties had become closely balanced by 1833, when the Democrats first secured the governorship, and for the next two decades there were frequent shifts in control. Massachusetts
Democrats were hopelessly outnumbered until after the collapse of the Antimasons in 1835, when they began to gain
ground. They won the governorship in 1839 and 1842, but
the state normally produced a heavy Whig majority. Vermont
was the impregnable stronghold of the Antimasons to 1836
and of the Whigs thereafter.

Except for Connecticut, where there was close party competition after 1833, and Maine, where there were occasional
Whig victories, the New England states tended to be politically
unbalanced by comparison with the rest of the nation. In
presidential elections, the average margins between the percentages of the votes obtained by the candidates of the major
parties in the New England states was seventeen points in 1836,

fifteen points in 1840, and fifteen points in 1844.[42] The average margins for all of the states in the same years were eleven, eleven, and nine. The section, quite obviously, was not politically homogeneous. New Hampshire was one of the two or three most heavily Democratic states in the nation while its neighbor, Vermont, ranked equally high on the list of staunch Whig states. Massachusetts and Rhode Island were predominantly Whig, but Maine was regarded as a Democratic stronghold and Connecticut was generally to be found in the "doubtful" category.

Despite the differing political complexions of the New England states, they tended to move in the same political direction in presidential elections. Every state was more Democratic in 1832 than in 1828. In 1836, Democratic strength rose again in every state, reaching the highest point it was to attain until 1852. In 1840 there was a falling off of Democratic votes in every state, followed by a resurgence in every state in 1844. There was a mixed reaction in 1848, but in 1852 there was again a unanimous movement in the Democratic direction. Indeed, it could be argued that New England's behavior in presidential elections was more strongly influenced by the sectional ties of the candidates than by any other factor. Clay ran poorly in 1832 and 1844; Van Buren ran well in 1836, as did Pierce in 1852. New England, in brief, manifested a preference for northern candidates.

The structure of party organization in New England was distinctive. Everywhere, except in Rhode Island, the legislative caucus was used to make state-wide nominations, elect a central committee, and in many states to enforce party discipline in legislative matters and appointments. It was also the common practice for the central committee to appoint county committees. Nominations for offices below the state level were

42. The "average margin" figure is a simple index of the degree of party dominance. It is obtained by calculating the percentage of the vote obtained by each major party and subtracting to obtain the difference. For example, if in a particular state the Democrats obtained 58 per cent of the vote and the Whigs 42 per cent, the margin in that state would be sixteen points.

made by delegate conventions. This general pattern was still adhered to in 1828 by the dominant or Adams faction of the old Republican party. The state convention made its appearance in 1828, when the Jacksonians in New Hampshire and Connecticut used the mechanism to prepare for the presidential election. The Jacksonians also introduced the state convention in Maine and Vermont in 1829 and in Massachusetts in 1831. The apparent preference of the Jacksonians for the convention, as opposed to the caucus, should not lead to the conclusion that a desire to democratize party procedures was originally involved. The main reason for the shift to the convention is to be found in the simple fact that in 1828 there were so very few Jacksonians in the state legislatures that a caucus could hardly be a feasible or authoritative device for making nominations or instituting an extensive party apparatus. It was this same consideration that motivated the Antimasons to resort to the use of the state convention when they emerged in each state.

The introduction of the state convention into New England politics in 1828 did not bring about the abrupt demise of the old caucus system. In Massachusetts, for example, although Democrats, Antimasons, and Whigs all employed the state convention occasionally after 1828, the two major parties placed more frequent reliance on the caucus, at least down to 1840. Similarly, Hill's New Hampshire Jacksonians pioneered in using the state convention, but once the party had been established in power it reverted to the caucus system for several years. Elsewhere the convention was firmly established in Connecticut after 1830, in Vermont after 1831, and in Maine after 1832. Rhode Island had its peculiar variety of mixed convention as early as 1815 and seems to have shifted to the regular convention around 1835. There was also a persistence in New England of the highly centralized party structure. At least in Massachusetts, New Hampshire, and Vermont, the traditional practice of authorizing the central committee to appoint county committees was followed in the 1830's. At the same time, however, delegate conventions in the counties and districts were held to make nominations for other than state-wide offices.

Ultimately, of course, the caucus was generally abandoned in favor of the state convention, but precisely what this change implied is a subject that has scarcely been investigated. The common assumption would seem to be that it represented a democratization of party management. Conventions, however, could be manipulated and controlled by a small leadership group as readily as could the caucus. It is quite possible that the chief function of the convention was a cosmetic one. That is, it was designed to give the appearance of placing nominations, the formulation of party platforms, and the choice of party officials in the hands of duly elected delegates. In actuality, however, it could be employed to give a kind of popular sanction to the decisions made and enforced by the party leadership. It did, at least, represent a concession to the democratic tendencies of the times; it did create the impression that the people, through their delegates, were being allowed to participate in managing party affairs.

In the same vein, the conduct of campaigns in New England also altered. By 1840 the ancient taboos against demagogic appeals and theatricalism were breaking down. Politics increasingly assumed what I shall call a dramatic function. It provided the voter with an exciting experience, with the opportunity to identify himself with great issues and personalities. This aspect of politics was less highly developed in New England than in certain other sections, perhaps because there were competing crusades of a moral or religious character which could absorb emotional energies, but it was yet another sign that the old order of politics was passing.

The re-establishment of a two-party system after 1828 was delayed and complicated in some states by the eruption of Antimasonry. The Antimasons were the strongest party in Vermont from 1831 to 1835; rivalled the Democrats in Massachusetts in the same years; and polled a respectable minority

in Connecticut. There are many approaches to an explanation of the varying appeal of Antimasonry from state to state.
One starting point would be a recognition of the fact that except in New Hampshire fewer than 30 per cent of the eligible
electorate was voting in the years before 1828 in New England,
and in Connecticut participation fell below 20 per cent. The
revival of party competition in 1828 produced sharp increases
at once in New Hampshire and Maine, which may suggest that
in those states the party leaders succeeded in making the new
alignments seem vital and appealing to the voters. Elsewhere,
the response was less positive, and a very sizable segment of the
electorate remained indifferent to the new parties.

There was, then, a vacuum into which the Antimasons
could move. Or, to employ a different metaphor, there were
vast numbers of the politically unchurched waiting to receive
the word. Doubtless Vermont, for cultural reasons, offered a
peculiarly attractive field for the Antimasonic missionaries.
But one must also be impressed with the exceptionally skilled
leadership and the thoroughly competent organization that
the party possessed in that state. Largely as the result of the
vigor and capacity displayed by the Antimasonic politicians,
voter participation was stimulated and by 1832 three men out
of five went to the polls. Similar opportunities presented
themselves in Massachusetts and Connecticut, but in those
states the electorate remained relatively apathetic. Voter participation in Massachusetts had reached only 40 per cent by
1833; in Connecticut in the same year it was at 30 per cent.

Not only the Antimasons, but the major parties as well,
were unable to rouse the voters in these two states, and the
Antimasons may be credited with major responsibility for inducing voters to return to the polls. Upon the demise of the
party, the Democrats seem generally to have inherited more of
the Antimasonic vote than the Whigs, despite the fact that in
Vermont and Massachusetts the bulk of the Antimasonic leaders united with the Whigs.

One of the most intriguing problems that strikes the student of New England politics in the Jackson era is the extraordinary contrast between the strength of the Jacksonians in New Hampshire and their weakness in Vermont. Why should these neighboring states have diverged so widely in their political allegiance? New Hampshire in 1836 was the most heavily Democratic state in the nation; Vermont produced the most lopsided Whig majority. The problem is all the more perplexing because before 1824 and after 1856 the two states exhibited similar political tendencies. We do not have adequate studies of either of these states for the period on which we might base explanations of their contrasting behavior. I should suggest, however, that in addition to any explanations in terms of social, economic, or cultural differences, due weight should be accorded to the factor of political leadership.

Isaac Hill and his associates were unusually gifted politicians, and surely much of the credit for the remarkable strength of the Democracy in New Hampshire must be ascribed to their genius. Ezra Meech in Vermont, on the other hand— or David Henshaw in Massachusetts—can be set down as poor political leaders. There must obviously be limits to which political leadership can advance a party in a particular state, but those limits are flexible, and, given the loose character of American political parties, they allow considerable scope for the exercise of political talents. Parties are made by leaders, and leaders such as Isaac Hill—or George Bancroft in Massachusetts—could vastly enhance the prospects of their parties. In New England, because of the tradition of highly centralized parties, and perhaps, too, because of the relatively low voter participation and restrained campaign techniques, it may be that the factor of leadership was even more influential than in other areas.

Finally, the most readily measurable effect of the recreation of a two-party system in New England after 1828 was the rise in voter interest as evidenced by participation in state and presidential elections. As party competition increased, voters returned to the polls, and in 1840 from two-thirds to more than four-fifths of the adult white males participated in the presidential election, except in Rhode Island. Voter participation in New England, however, remained conspicuously below the national average and in most states was not significantly different from the levels that had been achieved between 1807 and 1817, when the first party system had flourished. With respect to presidential elections between 1824 and 1848, two New England states exceeded the national average voter participation in 1832 and 1840, one state was above the average in 1824, 1828, and 1844, and no states attained the national average in 1836 or 1848.

New England as a whole ranked behind every other section in voter participation in presidential elections. This condition was not unrelated to the fact, previously discussed, that in the New England states parties tended to be less evenly balanced than in other sections. As a general rule, where one party held a considerable margin over its opponent, the voting tended to be light. But this generalization does not fully explain New England's political behavior. Voting reached a peak in 1840 and then fell off markedly in each of the three succeeding presidential elections, despite the fact that party balance did not alter greatly. A similar decline occurred throughout the nation, but the descent was more rapid in New England than elsewhere. It may well be that New England never entirely accommodated itself to the second party system and found the parties and their candidates less and less appealing after 1840 in terms of the issues and concerns that mattered to the region.

In most of the New England states voter participation was slow in returning to the levels that had been attained during the era of the first party system. Maine surpassed its previous high in the 1830 gubernatorial election (67.3 per cent), Connecticut in the 1835 gubernatorial election (59.1 per cent), New Hampshire in the 1838 gubernatorial election (81.8 per cent), and Rhode Island in the 1843 gubernatorial election (56.3 per cent). Massachusetts never did surpass, before 1860, its record voter participation of 67.4 per cent registered in 1812. Vermont, Massachusetts, and Rhode Island never recorded as high participation in a presidential election before 1860 as they had attained in state elections before 1820. Not until around 1840 did voting in New England in general equal or surpass former standards. In the presidential election of 1840, voter participation was, on the average, twenty percentage points higher than it had been in 1832. Jackson's contests with Adams and Clay did not bring unprecedented numbers of voters to the polls, but the spectacular Log Cabin campaign established new highs.

In comparing voter participation in state and national elections, it becomes evident that, except in Connecticut, voting in state elections tended to equal or surpass voting in presidential elections. Massachusetts, Maine, Vermont, and Rhode Island all achieved their maximum votes in gubernatorial elections. Considering the forty-two gubernatorial elections held in the six states in the same years as the presidential elections from 1824 through 1848, the gubernatorial vote was higher than the presidential in twenty-two instances. State politics, then, tended to hold equal interest with presidential politics in New England, except in Connecticut, where the presidential vote invariably exceeded the gubernatorial vote.

CHAPTER IV

PARTY FORMATION
IN THE
MIDDLE STATES

The Middle States, quite obviously, do not lend themselves so readily to generalizations as New England. They differed greatly in size, population, and demographic characteristics as well as in their social, economic, and constitutional profiles. Each exhibited in its political behavior some markedly distinctive features not common to the others. Yet they may properly be grouped together in one broad category for purposes of analysis, for they shared certain traits that make them clearly distinguishable not only from the New England states but also from those of the South and the West. Most conspicuously, they tended to be closely divided between two parties and to adapt more rapidly to the second party system than the states in any other region.

There were competitive Federalist and Republican parties in all of the Middle States by 1800, but the subsequent course of politics varied from state to state. Except in Delaware, the Republicans rapidly gained the ascendancy, although they were commonly plagued by internal dissension, especially in New York and Pennsylvania. Party management was on the whole weaker at the state level than in New England, and there was no uniform pattern of party organization. More than in any other region, avidity for patronage and other spoils of office constituted a major theme of Middle States politics.

In part, surely, because there was no regional favorite in

103

the race, the Middle States were divided in sentiment in 1824; Crawford, Adams, and Jackson all secured electoral votes there. After 1824, as the contest narrowed down to one between the supporters of Adams and of Jackson, there was sufficient enthusiasm for both men to produce a fairly even alignment of parties, except in Pennsylvania. Consequently, a new two-party system had emerged by 1828, although the complication of Antimasonry influenced alignments in New York and Pennsylvania for several years. But it is evident that new party alignments formed first in the Middle States and that in broad outlines those alignments persisted in most states until the collapse of the second party system in the 1850's.

Perhaps because the Middle States stand between the sectional extremes of New England and the South, they were consistently in the category of "doubtful" states. The intensity of interparty competition in turn occasioned extremely elaborate party machinery, operated by shrewd professionals, and a high rate of voter participation. A region by the process of subtraction, lacking the highly developed self-consciousness of New England or the South, the Middle States held the balance of political power in the nation.

NEW YORK

In contrast to the relatively simple style of politics that characterized New England, New York politics baffled contemporary observers, as well as later students, by their extraordinary complexity. Bewildering shifts in the party allegiance of prominent politicians, violent factional strife, intense preoccupation with the spoils of office—these were but the more obvious features of the political scene. The peculiar nature of New York politics is not difficult to explain. Inherited from the colonial period was a semi-feudal land system, which pro-

duced a small number of powerful, landed families who vied
with one another for political dominance.   The constitution
of the state, with its complicated and conservative suffrage provisions and its omnipotent Council of Appointment, further
differentiated New York from its neighbors.   The heterogeneity of the state and its rapid growth in population were also
factors that made for a singularly involved and dynamic brand
of politics.   In time, or more precisely, by 1822, the operative
effect of the first two influences had become negligible, although patterns of behavior formed in the earlier period
lingered on.   Diversity and growth, however, continued to
pose challenges.

Much might be made of the aristocratic background of
New York politics.   In the colonial period New York politics
bore the closest resemblance to English politics of any colony.
Here were great landed magnates lording it over their tenants,
unabashed use of corruption and intimidation, severely restricted suffrage privileges, pocket boroughs, and even "government" influence in the form of huge land grants and sine-
cures.   The DeLanceys, the Livingstons, and their connections,
fought one another for lucrative place and privilege, as well as
for prestige, while the role of the yeoman was essentially restricted to choosing which set of aristocrats to support.   The
revolution reduced the dimensions of the aristocracy and
brought new men to the fore, but, as Dixon Ryan Fox demonstrated, aristocratic influences in politics persisted for half a
century after the break with England.   Much of New York
politics, then, down to the Jackson era, is to be understood in
terms of alliances and counter alliances, to say nothing of
broken alliances, among great families.

The constitution of 1777, designedly one of the least democratic of the state constitutions, helped perpetuate aristocratic
tendencies and, by its provisions respecting patronage, enhanced the venality of New York politics.   Drafted by conservatives, the most influential of whom were John Jay,
Gouverneur Morris, and Robert R. Livingston, it created a

government that was remarkable for its remoteness from popular control. Two classes of voters were created. Only those
men who owned freeholds valued at £100 were eligible to
vote for governor, lieutenant-governor, and state senator.
Those who had freeholds worth £20 or rented tenements with
a yearly value of forty shillings might vote for assemblymen,
and consequently for members of Congress. Under these
provisions, only about 40 per cent of adult white males were
eligible to vote for governor; an additional 30 per cent could
vote for assemblymen. This left nearly one-third of the men
with no voting privileges.[1] The governor and lieutenant-
governor were elected for three-year terms. The assembly,
made up initially of seventy members apportioned among the
counties, was elected annually. The senators, twenty-four in
number, were chosen for four-year terms and were apportioned among four districts.[2]

The constitution vested a veto power over legislation in a
Council of Revision, made up of the governor, chancellor, and
judges of the supreme court. The judges, appointed for good
behavior and deeply involved in politics, exercised their veto
over one hundred times, and the council could be over-ridden
only by a two-thirds vote of the legislature. The appointing
power was entrusted to a Council of Appointment, consisting
of the governor and four senators, one from each district,
chosen by the assembly. This body ultimately had some fifteen
thousand jobs to distribute, including over eight thousand
military appointments and nearly seven thousand civil offices.
In the latter category were judges, justices of the peace, court
clerks, public notaries, commissioners of deeds, public auctioneers, district attorneys, sheriffs, coroners, county treasurers,
and mayors and clerks of cities. It was this tempting mass of
patronage that was to bring the "spoils system" to New York

1. Richard P. McCormick, "Suffrage Classes and Party Alignments: A Study
in Voter Behavior," *Mississippi Valley Historical Review*, XLVI (December,
1959), 397-410.

2. In 1801 the number of senators was increased to 32, and the lower house
was to have a minimum of 100 and a maximum of 150 members.

at an early date and that was to give a distinctive cast to parties and factional politics.

State elections were held annually in April for a period of three days. Voting was by ballot after 1787 and the polling unit after 1778 was the township. Because of the dual suffrage provision, the voting procedure was relatively complicated and separate ballot boxes were used for different offices. Congressmen were usually elected in November on the district basis. Presidential electors were chosen by the legislature through 1824. Thus the county was the unit for electing assemblymen, the senatorial district for state senators, the congressional district for congressmen, and the state for governor, lieutenant-governor, and presidential electors. At each of these levels, then, the party had to create agencies for securing agreement on nominations.

The swirling currents of party politics in New York from 1789 to 1817 are so turbulent, and have been so skillfully described in detail by Jabez D. Hammond and Dixon Ryan Fox, that only the broadest characterizations are called for here. Political divisions made their appearance during the controversy over the ratification of the federal Constitution and then found expression in the state election of 1789, when Governor George Clinton encountered strong opposition from the Federalist candidate, Robert Yates. With Clinton's retirement in 1795, the Federalists succeeded in electing John Jay to the governorship, and he was re-elected in 1798; the only Federalist ever to secure that office. Despite factional divisions, and a resurgence of the Federalists between 1810 and 1816, the Republicans retained the governorship from 1801 until 1817, with Daniel D. Tompkins as the incumbent after 1807.

The strength of the opposing parties after 1801 remained remarkably stable. In those gubernatorial elections that were fought on a party basis, as was the case in 1801, 1810, 1813, and 1816, the Federalist vote varied only between 46 per cent and 48 per cent of the total vote cast. Too, the heavy vote in these elections seems to indicate that virtually all—90 per cent and over—of those who were legally eligible to vote for governor actually voted. This rate of participation is so extraordinary as to suggest the probability that many who were not properly qualified must have voted. It is also interesting to observe that with the governor elected by £100 freeholders and the assembly elected by men of lesser estates, the Republicans could win the governorship and the Federalists could at the same time—in 1813, for example—elect a majority to the assembly.[3]

The political scene in New York rarely exhibited the simple outline of straight-forward two-party conflict. Both major parties, and particularly the Republicans, were afflicted by bitter rivalries among competing leadership groups. The Clinton and Livingston families, with their numerous relations and dependents, sometimes in alliance but often in opposition, wielded great influence within the Republican party. But other leaders, such as Aaron Burr, Morgan Lewis, and Daniel D. Tompkins could at various times command large followings and make their bids for power. Changes in allegiance from one faction to another, and even from one party to another, were a frequent occurrence. Burr was a leading Republican in 1801 and the Federalist-backed candidate for governor in 1804. Morgan Lewis, a Livingston connection, enjoyed Clintonian support when he was elected governor as a Republican in 1804, but in 1807—a rupture having taken place in the Clinton-Livingston alliance—he opposed the "regular" Republican candidate, Daniel D. Tompkins. The maneuvering of the Tammany braves in these years was equally devious. When the Republicans fell out, as they did conspicuously in 1804 and 1807, a large segment of the Federalist party entered into alliance with the minority Republican faction. No party organization, it seemed, was sufficiently strong to impose discipline upon the rival family and factional groups contending for domination of the Republican party at the state level.

The beginnings of party apparatus in New York go back at least to 1789, when Federalist leaders met in New York City to

3. McCormick, "Suffrage Classes," *passim.*

nominate Robert Yates for governor and appoint a committee of correspondence to manage the campaign. Even earlier, there are instances of political meetings at the township level to nominate assembly candidates. In 1795 the Federalists used a legislative caucus to place John Jay in nomination for the governorship, and the Republicans adopted the same device in 1801 to nominate George Clinton. Thereafter the caucus, occasionally with non-legislators in attendance, became the accepted method of making nominations for state-wide office and remained in use until 1824.

At other levels the delegate convention gradually assumed form. The township primaries in the early years appointed corresponding committees to meet in appropriate electoral units and agree on candidates for assembly and Congress. By 1811, when the correspondence system had given way to delegate conventions, the legislative caucus relinquished to district conventions the nomination of state senators. The authority of the caucus, however, and the independence of local and district conventions, was seriously impaired by the enormous power vested in the Council of Appointment.

It was in 1801, following the return of George Clinton to the governorship after six years of Federalist dominance, that the political potentialities of the council were first exploited for obvious party purposes. De Witt Clinton, nephew of the governor and destined to be a disruptive force in New York politics for a generation, influenced the council to remove political enemies and appoint loyal supporters, large numbers of them members of the Clinton and Livingston families. The practice persisted, and in 1807 Morgan Lewis carried it to new extremes when he had the council sweep the Clintonians out, including the removal of De Witt Clinton as mayor of New York City. It was soon apparent that whoever controlled the council could, by dispensing thousands of offices, exert strong influence on the caucus and also on the composition of the local conventions. Most observers were agreed by 1821 that the council was the root of much of the political turmoil that convulsed parties in the state. Because the council was sub-servient, for various reasons, to individuals such as De Witt Clinton, Ambrose Spencer, or Morgan Lewis, rather than to the party caucus, it was used less to build a unified party than to enhance one or another faction, thus exacerbating intra-party feuds.

Dissension within the Republican ranks was also fomented, according to Hammond, by the Virginia partner of the insecure Virginia–New York alliance. According to this plausible theory, it was the deliberate policy of the Virginians to weaken the New York Republicans in order to ensure the Virginian succession to the presidency. Certainly there was restiveness among New York Republicans in 1808, 1812, and 1816 as a consequence of the secondary role allotted to them. But there were abundant local causes of discord, regardless of the machinations of the Virginia Junto.

New York politics began to assume new form following the election of De Witt Clinton to the governorship in 1817, and the transformation was carried forward by the drastic revision of the state constitution in 1821. The circumstances that led to Clinton's elevation to the governorship are illustra-tive of the oscillations in his career. In 1815 he had—for the second time—been removed from the New York City mayoral-ty, and his political prospects were bleak. When Tompkins defeated Rufus King for the governorship in 1816, the Re-publican party was seemingly united and Clinton was a figure of little influence. But Tompkins resigned the governorship in 1817 to become vice-president, and this development created an opportunity for Clinton and his friends.

Of crucial importance in the revival of Clinton's interest was the alliance that he formed with Judge Ambrose Spencer, who was acknowledged to have paramount influence at that time over the Council of Appointment. Spencer, a former enemy of Clinton's, had become apprehensive of the rising power of Martin Van Buren and Tompkins in the party, and he saw an opportunity to retain his pre-eminence by joining forces with Clinton. Perceiving that if the nomination of Tompkins' successor was made in the usual fashion by the legislative caucus, the Van Buren forces would prevail, the Clintonians shrewdly proposed that the party should hold a mixed convention, to be made up of Republican members of the legislature together with elected delegates from those counties that were represented in the legislature by Federalists. The plan was adopted, and when the convention met, the Clintonians had a majority. Clinton was nominated over the opposition of Tammany and the Van Buren faction.[4] The Federalists offered no opposition candidate, and Clinton was all but unanimously elected. His vote, however, was little more than half as large as that which had been cast in 1816.

As soon as Clinton had been installed in the governorship, there was friction between his followers and those led by Van Buren, now becoming known as the Bucktails. The Bucktails secured control of the Council of Appointment in 1818 and began to use that body in the traditional way, to the detriment of the Clintonians. By 1819 the split had widened. The Republicans caucused as usual to agree on a candidate for speaker of the assembly, but subsequently the Clintonians refused to be bound by the caucus decision. Later in the session there was another caucus to decide upon a candidate for Senator, but it broke up into Clintonian and Bucktail factions. This was, strictly speaking, the last caucus of the old Republican party in New York.

Thereafter Clintonians and Bucktails, each claiming to be the legitimate Republicans, functioned as opposing political parties. In the state election in 1819 the two parties ran opposing slates of candidates for the legislature. In 1820 the Bucktail caucus nominated Tompkins for governor and the Clintonians, at a public meeting in Albany, rallied behind De

4. Niles' *Register*, XII, 96. For political developments in this period I have relied heavily on Jabez D. Hammond, *The History of Political Parties in the State of New York* (4th ed., 2 vols.; Syracuse, 1852) and on J. S. Jenkins, *History of Political Parties in the State of New York* (Auburn, 1846), as well as on the more recent monographic studies.

Witt Clinton.   In a closely fought election, Tompkins went down to defeat, although the Bucktails won both houses of the legislature.

The new alignment that had been formed by 1820 established the broad outlines of parties in New York for more than a generation.   The Bucktails, under the effective leadership of Martin Van Buren and his associates in the Albany Regency, maintained their unity and became, after 1827, the Jacksonian Democratic party.   Tightly disciplined, the party successfully avoided the factional wrangling that had previously plagued New York Republicans, and not even the vicissitudes of presidential politics occasioned any disruption of its ranks.   The opposition, on the contrary, lacked unity.   Indeed, a major theme of New York politics from 1820 to 1837 is the effort of the opposition to form an effective coalition under adequate leadership.   Operating successively as the Clintonians, the People's Party, the Antimasons and National Republicans, and ultimately as the Whig party, the anti-Regency forces rivalled the Regency in numbers of supporters but lacked the clear sense of identity that distinguished their adversaries.

The Clintonians, as of 1820, were basically a coalition of Clinton's personal following from the old Republican party, the bulk of the former Federalists, and—very significantly—a large segment of Republicans from western New York, whose attachment to Clinton is explained in part, at least, by his zealous promotion of the Erie Canal.   The Bucktail-Regency party included most of the old Republicans, minus the western losses, the body of "high minded" Federalists who cast their lot against Clinton in 1820, and small but significant numbers of Federalists in certain Hudson River counties.

Subsequently, and especially after 1828, there were to be shifts in party dominance in local areas—such former Federalist-Clintonian counties at Greene, Columbia, and St. Lawrence moved into the Democratic fold and former Bucktail areas, in central and southern New York moved toward the Whigs.   But the fact of central importance is that the Bucktail-Regency-

Democratic party—in leadership, organization, and sense of identity—experienced a continuous history from 1820 through the Jackson era. In contrast, then, to the situation in New England, party formation in New York dates not from the divisions over the presidential question around 1828 but from the emergence of the Bucktail-Clintonian cleavage in 1819-1820.[5]

The new constitution of 1821, produced by a convention in which the Bucktails held an overwhelming majority, wrought important changes in the environment of politics. The franchise was made uniform and extended to adult male citizens who paid state or local taxes, served in the militia, or labored on the highways. Whereas in 1820 only about one-third of the adult males had been qualified to vote for governor and for state senators and another third had the privilege of voting for assemblymen and members of Congress, more than four-fifths of adult males were now eligible to vote for all officials. In 1824, the vote cast for governor was more than twice as large as that recorded in 1820. Despite the vast increase in the size of the electorate, it does not seem that the new voters upset the existing balance between the parties. Clinton, for example, received 50.9 per cent of the vote in 1820 and 54.3 per cent in 1824.

More significant in terms of practical political effects was the abolition of the Council of Appointment. "If the ingenuity of man," declaimed Governor Clinton with reference to the council, "had been exercised to organize the appointing power in such a way as to produce continued intrigue and commotion in the state, none could have been devised with more effect than the present arrangement."[6] The vast appoin-

5. The emergence of the Bucktail-Clintonian alignment is carefully traced by Hammond, *Political Parties*, I, 406-534. The persistence of the new alignment is corroborated by a study of county voting patterns after 1819. In my opinion Lee Benson, *The Concept of Jacksonian Democracy: New York as a Test Case* (Princeton, 1960), fails to appreciate the decisive importance of the polarization of attitudes and loyalties that occurred between 1817 and 1820.

6. Dixon Ryan Fox, "The Decline of Aristocracy in the Politics of New York," *Columbia University Studies in History, Economics and Public Law*, LXXXVI (New York, 1919), 231 n.

tive powers formerly vested in the council were now divided. Sheriffs, county clerks, and mayors of cities (except New York City) were made elective. All but the highest militia officers were made elective by their units. Principal state officials, such as the comptroller, treasurer, and secretary of state, were to be chosen by the legislature. The remainder of the appointive offices, including judges, were to be filled by the governor with the advice and consent of the senate. There was considerable sentiment in favor of making justices of the peace elective, but the Bucktail politicians, who regarded that office as extremely important to their organization, were not yet prepared to make such a sacrifice. The old Council of Revision, which had given such political power to the justices of the Supreme Court was also swept away, and the judicial structure was so revised as to end Federalist influence in that branch of government. Other changes made the governor elective for a two-year term, increased to eight the number of senatorial districts, moved the time for holding elections from April to November, and empowered the legislature to provide for the registration of voters.

The constitutional changes broadened the popular base of politics, increased the importance of the county as a political unit, reduced the role of personal influence, and introduced new methods for dispensing patronage. Voter participation which had rarely exceeded 50 per cent of adult white males even in congressional elections, soon rose to over 70 per cent. The introduction of elective offices at the county level gave added zest to politics and party organization. The abolition of the Council of Appointment—as well as the Council of Revision—ended a type of personalism that had long distinguished New York politics. The new appointive power vested in the legislature or in the governor and senate was, in the hands of the Regency, employed by a disciplined caucus to build and maintain a unified party.

The internal workings of the Bucktail-Regency party have yet to be explored and described, but some general description can be attempted. The Albany Regency, with Van Buren as the recognized leader, associated with such able men as William L. Marcy, Azariah Flagg, Benjamin Knower, Silas Wright, Benjamin F. Butler, Edwin Crosswell, and others, determined broad party strategy, occupied important offices, used their influence to guide the actions of caucuses and conventions, managed the equitable distribution of patronage, enforced reasonably high standards of governmental efficiency, and—above all—made a fetish of party unity. Very great reliance was placed on the caucus to unite party votes for those officials elected by the legislature, and all who participated in the party caucus were expected to abide unswervingly by its decisions. Where local appointments were involved, it was the custom of the caucus to respect nominations made by local party organizations, which, of course, had the effect of integrating the entire party structure. Party policy was set forth in the official organ, the *Albany Argus* and was faithfully reproduced in the other party papers throughout the state. Here, indeed, was "a body of men united" for the purpose of securing party dominance.

The durability of the party machine, and its leadership, was sorely tested, especially between 1822 and 1828, but despite severe shocks and even serious blunders in strategy it survived and acquired added strength. In 1822, Clinton having been advised by his friends not to seek re-election, the Bucktail candidate, Joseph Yates, was elected governor over negligible opposition. With Clinton in eclipse and the opposition temporarily dispersed and leaderless, the Regency turned its attentions to the presidential election and committed its support to William H. Crawford. When this strategy became clear, anti-Crawford elements, and anti-Regency politicians, sought to take the choice of electors out of the hands of the legislature and give the vote to the people. The Regency opposed the change, and in 1823 a "People's" party, in favor of the popular choice of electors, was formed. By 1824 this movement had assumed large dimensions, and in April plans were made for a state convention to put forward a gubernatorial candidate to oppose Colonel Samuel Young, who had been nominated by the Bucktail caucus. At this juncture Clinton re-entered the scene. The over-zealous Bucktails had removed him from his post on the Canal Board, and this "martyrdom" encouraged his friends to launch a drive to restore him to the governorship.

When the People's party convention met at Utica on September 21, with delegates from each county equal in number to the legislative delegation, it signalized, among other things, the replacement of the caucus by the state convention.[7] Never thereafter was the caucus used to make nominations for elective office. There had been occasional previous use of the state convention, or mixed convention, notably by the Federalists in 1816 and by the Clintonians in 1817, but the People's party convention established a pattern that was to endure. Unhappily for the leaders of the new party, Clinton's followers secured the ascendancy in the convention and nominated their hero on the second ballot. Many disillusioned adherents of the People's party withdrew in protest and refused to support Clinton in the campaign, with the result that the alignment was essentially the old one of Clintonians against Bucktails. And, as in the past, Clinton emerged the victor. The Bucktails suffered a second blow when, after devious intrigues in which Thurlow Weed played a prominent role, the legislature chose only four Crawford electors to twenty-five for Adams and seven for Clay. The ultimate defeat came when the New York delegation in Congress cast the decisive vote to make Adams president.

After this disastrous year, the Regency adopted the strategy of avoiding any premature commitment on a presidential candidate to be supported in 1828 and concentrated on keeping the party united. The efforts were successful. "Never was a political party in a better state of discipline," commented Hammond admiringly, "than was the Van Buren or demo-

7. Niles' *Register*, XXVI, 117; XXVII, 68.

cratic party in New York during the years 1826, '27, and '28."
Although Clinton was again elected governor in 1826, the
Bucktails continued to control the legislature, retained a large
share of the state patronage, and re-elected Van Buren to the
Senate in 1827. In the elections of 1825 and 1826, the Regency
had kept the question of the presidency out of state politics.
The opposition, which was strongly partial to Adams, was also
obliged to keep the presidential question in the background because of Clinton's well advertised preference for Jackson.

Van Buren, meanwhile, had decided late in 1826 to work
behind the scenes with other Crawfordites, and with Calhoun,
to bring into effect a national coalition against Adams. Not
until September, 1827, however, was the time deemed to be
proper to commit the Bucktails to Jackson. On September
26 Tammany came out for the General, the *Albany Argus*
quickly unfurled the Jackson banner, and in the November
state election the well ordered rank and file of the party went
to the polls to vote for candidates who bore the Regency-
Jacksonian stamp. Soon after the new legislature convened,
the triumphant Bucktails met in caucus on January 31, 1828,
and completed the formalities of aligning the party behind
Jackson by nominating him for the presidency. Although there
were minor desertions from the ranks when the party declared
its presidential preference, the delicate task of shifting from
Crawford to Jackson had been accomplished with such finesse
that the party scarcely experienced a tremor.

The fact that Clinton was well disposed toward Jackson
had complicated Van Buren's problem, but it had also involved
Clinton's pro-Adams supporters in disabling perplexities. The
death on February 11, 1828, of Clinton, who had been a party
in himself for a generation, facilitated the transformation of
the Clintonians into the Adams party. But the Adams or-
ganizers had to contend with the epidemic of Antimasonry,
which was now raging with special virulence among former
Clintonians in the "infected district" of western New York.

The pro-Adams members of the legislature began prepara-

tions for the 1828 campaign by meeting after the adjournment
of the legislature on April 21 and adopting resolutions hostile
to Jackson. Two months later, on June 10, an Adams state
convention met at Albany, adopted resolutions and addresses
in praise of their candidate, but deferred making any nomination for governor in the hope of working out some kind of an
understanding with the Antimasons. A second convention
was held on July 22 at Utica, when Smith Thompson was
nominated for governor and Francis Granger for lieutenant-
governor. The objective then was to induce the Antimasons
also to name Granger as their candidate for lieutanant-gover-
nor, thus effecting an alliance. But the plan failed, and the
Adams and Antimasonic parties ran separate tickets against
the united Bucktails.

The Bucktails, aware of the crucial importance of the
impending contest, met in state convention at Herkimer on
September 24 and nominated their strongest man—Martin Van
Buren—for governor, with Enos Throop as his running mate.
No nominations of presidential electors were made because
they were to be elected by districts, and it remained for conventions in each congressional district to select the candidates.
Because the voters of the state, for the first time, would have
the opportunity to vote simultaneously for both governor
and president, the campaign was a peculiarly lively one. Early
in August a "Young Men's" convention friendly to Adams and
Thompson assembled at Utica to manifest enthusiasm for the
ticket and adopt the usual address. Not to be outdone the
Jacksonian "Young Men" held a similar rally at Herkimer in
October to promote the general's cause.[8]

During the three-day election in November there was an
unprecedented outpouring of voters; 70 per cent of adult white
males went to the polls in comparison with the previous high
of 56 per cent in the 1824 state election. Van Buren secured

8. Niles' *Register*, XXXIV, 411; *New-York Enquirer*, Aug. 5, 1828. "Young
Men's" conventions were also held in Maine in 1828. I am not aware of such
conventions before that year.

a plurality of votes, although his total fell three thousand below that of the Adams and Antimasonic candidates. In the presidential race, Jackson electors polled slightly less than 51 per cent of the total vote cast. Jackson electors were chosen in eighteen of the thirty-four districts and, in accordance with the existing law, the whole body of electors chose two electors-at-large, both, of course, pledged to Jackson. So close was the election that it is appropriate to raise the question whether Jackson's candidacy helped or handicapped the Bucktail party. In view of the disparity in organization between the Bucktails and the Adams party, the narrowness of Jackson's victory— and that of Van Buren—suggests that the Bucktails won because their opponents were divided and in spite of a lack of popular enthusiasm for Jackson.

In a sense, the party situation in New York after 1828 remained much as it had been since 1820. That is to say, there was one well organized, durable party—the Bucktails, or Republicans as they continued to call themselves—and there was a disorganized opposition. The Republicans, under Regency leadership and with the time-tested machinery of caucus and convention operating efficiently, retained control of the state government and its considerable patronage until 1837. There were desertions from the party ranks, occasioned by differences over policy, patronage, or local issues, but these were balanced by accretions of strength. The party leaders shrewdly modified their policies on banking, canals, and tariff, and similar questions to suit the changing temper of the times, and, down to the disastrous panic of 1837, they provided their opponents with no "burning issue" that could be used to accomplish their defeat.

The opposition, meanwhile, remained divided. The problem, essentially, was to unite the Republican-Clintonian-Antimasons of western New York and the Federalist-Clintonian-Adams contingents in the rest of the state. After the election of 1828, the Adams organization collapsed, and the Antimasons

assumed briefly the role of the major opposition party.[9] By
1830 the movement had come under the control of professional
politicians who were less concerned with extirpating Masonry
than they were with overthrowing the Regency. At their state
convention in August, 1830, the Antimasons nominated Granger for governor and, with the Adams party not in the field,
appealed to all anti-Regency voters. Granger's vote, nearly
48 per cent of the total and almost four times that polled by
Southwick in 1828, was impressive, and it seemed to indicate
that an anti-Regency coalition had indeed been effected. At
this juncture the exigencies of presidential politics again complicated the picture.

Looking forward to 1832, a large meeting of Clay supporters in New York City on December 31, 1830, resolved that the
time had arrived "when a party in opposition to the general
administration" should be formed, and took steps to that end.[10]
A state convention in Albany early in June, 1831, appointed
delegates to the National Republican Convention and set up a
detailed plan of party organization. The New York leaders
of both the Clay and the Antimasonic parties were hopeful
that they would be able to endorse the same presidential and
state candidates in 1832, but the nomination of William Wirt
by the national Antimasonic convention threatened to impede
this plan. Nevertheless, the difficulties were overcome and
both parties united behind Granger for governor and an
ambiguous electoral slate made up of both Clay and Wirt men.
The Regency was again hard pressed, but it directed its attack
against the incongruous character of the coalition, gained some
support from anti-Regency Masons who were outraged by the
Antimasons, and eked out a narrow victory for William L.
Marcy and for Jackson.

9. For my discussion of the role of Antimasons in New York politics I have
drawn mainly upon Charles McCarthy, "The Anti-Masonic Party, A Study of
Political Antimasonry in the United States, 1827-1840," *Annual Report of the
American Historical Association*, 1901, I; G. G. Van Deusen, *Thurlow Weed*
(Boston, 1947), and Hammond, *Political Parties*, II.

10. Niles' *Register*, XXXIX, 303. For the report of this Clay convention
see *ibid.*, XL, 278-9.

Despite the strong showing of the opposition in 1832, a genuine merger under a united leadership had not yet been effected, and in 1833 the Regency scored a one-sided victory in the legislative election. Early in 1834 the Antimasonic party, having outlived its usefulness, was formally disbanded. Soon a new coalition—bearing the name Whig—was taking form. The ostensible basis for the new rally was opposition to Governor Marcy's plan to lend funds to state banks to tide them over the crisis occasioned by the deflationary policies of the doomed Bank of the United States. Local protest meetings, anti-Regency in tone, culminated in the proposal by the central committee of the New York City Whigs that a state convention should be held in September. This call was later endorsed by the Whigs in the legislature. When the 122 delegates assembled at Utica to nominate the youthful William H. Seward for governor, the foundations were laid for the coalition of opposition elements that would soon overthrow the Regency.

Seward was defeated in 1834, after the most rousing campaign New York had ever witnessed, and for the next three years the Whigs exhibited little zeal. In 1836, with Van Buren and Marcy heading the ticket, the Republicans registered their most lopsided triumph since 1822, even though the total vote cast was far below that of 1834. But 1837 brought disaster. The Whigs, profiting by the discontent engendered by the Panic, were swept into control of the legislature. A year later, Seward was elected governor. Even the Regency could not withstand the forces engendered by economic adversity.

By 1838 the Whig party was united, efficiently organized, and brilliantly led. A host of able men—Thurlow Weed, William H. Seward, Francis Granger, Millard Fillmore, and Luther Bradish—most of them younger men who had first risen to political prominence with the Antimasons, furnished the party leadership. A strong central committee, generally obedient to Weed's guiding hand, directed the party. Fortified after 1837 with state patronage and inspired by the colorful appeals of

Horace Greeley, editor of the party organ, the Whig organization matched that of the aging Regency in potency and professional efficiency. At last, after two decades of fighting a phantom-like opposition, the Democrats were confronted with a substantial and worthy foe.

There are obvious differences between the circumstances associated with party formation in New York and in New England. In New England, and indeed throughout most of the states, party formation was closely related to presidential politics. In New York, however, the contest for the presidency did not occasion a reorganization of parties. The Bucktail-Republican party, having acquired leadership, organization, and discipline by 1820 survived virtually intact through the turbulent Jackson era. The fact that New England moved overwhelmingly to the support of its native son in 1824 and 1828 affords a partial explanation of the difference in behavior. The extraordinary ability of the Regency in maintaining party unity is another factor. Most significant, however, is the fact that in New York a unique kind of transition had taken place from a two-party situation that pitted Republicans against Federalists to a new two-party situation that saw Bucktails arrayed against Clintonians.

Eleswhere, either the Federalists had survived as a distinct party—conspicuously in Massachusetts and Delaware—or they had retired from politics—as in New Hampshire and Connecticut—or they had formed a loose alliance with a dissident Republican faction, as in Pennsylvania. In no other state, however, had new parties comparable to the Bucktails and Clintonians emerged before 1824 to succeed the earlier Federalist-Republican cleavage. In New York, these pre-existing parties became identified in 1824 and afterwards with opposing presidential candidates. Again, this is not to say that the alignment that assumed form by 1820 endured without any alteration. There were changes in allegiance by individual voters and by blocs of voters, as well as by political leaders of some prominence. But when New York is compared with other states in the period, the most striking aspect of its politics is the durability of the alignments that existed before 1824 and the moderateness of the shifts that occurred after that date.

New York politics was also distinguished by the close balance of the parties, by the coincidence of alignments in both state and national elections, by extremely high voter participation, and by a pronounced tendency toward higher voting in presidential than in off-year elections.   Only on very rare occasions after 1817 did the victorious candidate in a gubernatorial or presidential election receive as much as 52 per cent of the total vote cast.   Oddly enough, the Bucktail-Republicans registered their most lopsided victory in 1836, one year before their downfall, when they polled 54 per cent of the vote. The alignment of parties was virtually identical in both state and national elections.   That is, the anti-Regency party was also the anti-Jackson party.   This need not necessarily have been the case, and in several states—Rhode Island, Pennsylvania, Georgia, and Indiana are relevant examples—there were different alignments in state and national elections.

The intense competition between parties doubtless contributed to the high rate of voter participation.   Using the data of the New York censuses, which purport to enumerate those actually qualified to vote, it would appear that in the presidential elections participation fell below 80 per cent only in 1836 (71 per cent) and reached highs of nearly 94 per cent in 1840 and 1844.   In presidential years the vote for governor closely approximated that cast for president.   In those years when only a gubernatorial election was held, the vote was markedly smaller than in presidential years.   It usually ranged between 71 per cent and 74 per cent, except in 1834 (88 per cent), 1838 (82 per cent), and 1842 (81 per cent). Although this pattern of peak participation in presidential years was not uncommon, it was not universal.   It would, of course, seem to indicate a higher degree of interest in national than in state politics.

The structure of party organization in New York, which

has yet to receive the intensive study it merits, probably underwent little change after 1822, despite the introduction of the
device of the state convention in 1824. The legislative caucus
continued after 1824 to be a major instrument for enforcing
party discipline. The spoils system, which meant political jobs
for those who staffed the party machinery, continued to be
a strong feature of New York politics. And the corporate
management of the Bucktail party continued to be vested in
the Regency. It is possible that the management of politics
was more highly professionalized in New York than in most
states and that therefore the party as an institution with its own
vested interests was more developed in New York than elsewhere, but such judgments can not be confirmed on the basis
of available information. It does seem noteworthy, though,
that in a state marked by such regional and even local diversity,
so much authority was focused in the state party leadership,
rather than in city or county "bosses."

NEW JERSEY

New Jersey offered many contrasts to New York, not the
least of which was the relative simplicity and stability of its
politics. Small in area and population, this state was remarkably homogeneous with respect to the social and economic condition of its people. There were no jarring antagonisms
between classes or sections, or between metropolis and hinter-
land; no established aristocratic elite capable of monopolizing
political power and no self-conscious minority groups chafing
under a sense of oppression. The structure of government was
as elementary, as uncomplicated, as that of any state. Despite
the absence of sharp cleavages, parties were formed at an early
date, engaged in unremitting strife, and developed sophisti-
cated techniques of management. Vestiges of the first party

system survived as late as 1827, after which old loyalties were extensively reshuffled to produce a new party alignment.

The state's constitution of 1776, adopted hastily in a period of crisis, made as few alterations as possible in the familiar colonial structure of government but did concentrate virtually all authority in the legislature. Each county had one member in the upper house, or council; representation in the assembly was roughly apportioned among the counties on a population basis. Members of the legislature were elected annually in October, at which time the counties also chose sheriffs and coroners. The legislature in joint-meeting annually elected a governor, appointed all other state officials, including judges and militia officers, and even such county officials as justices of the peace and county clerks. This vast patronage was to be the great prize for which parties contended.

After 1797 the township was the polling unit, voting was by ballot, and state elections were held on the second Tuesday and Wednesday in October. Voting privileges were enjoyed by all inhabitants worth £50, a requirement that was redefined in 1807 to exclude females, Negroes, and aliens and to substitute a taxpaying qualification for the vague property limitation. After 1807, nearly all adult white males were eligible to vote. Congressmen were elected from the state at large—other than in 1798 and 1812—and were usually chosen in October, except in presidential years. Presidential electors were popularly elected beginning in 1804, except in 1812, and were also chosen from the state at large. It will be apparent that there were only two electoral units in New Jersey, the counties and the state, a circumstance that facilitated and simplified the task of party organization. At the state level party agencies were created to nominate congressmen and electors and to manage the distribution of patronage. Within the counties machinery was devised to nominate legislators and county officials and to conduct election campaigns.

New Jersey had manifested unanimous support for the Federal Constitution, and in 1789 it sent to Congress a delegation all of whose members were to give unstinting support to the administration and to become identified eventually with the Federalist party. Subsequently controversies developed within the state over Hamilton's policies, the Jay Treaty, and the measures taken to suppress the Whisky Rebellion, but it was not until 1797 that this dissension was organized on a party basis. In that year the foundations of the Republican party were laid when a "Farmer's Ticket," deriving its greatest support from Morris, Essex, and Sussex counties, entered the field against a Federalist slate. During the ensuing three years strong Republican county organizations, using the delegate-convention system, secured dominance in Sussex, Morris, and Essex and strenuous organizing efforts were launched in other counties as well. By 1800 party lines were drawn throughout the state for a major contest.

The Republicans were unsuccessful at the state election in October, but two months later they won the state-wide congressional election. In the following year they captured the legislature, and with it control of the governorship and the state patronage. Thereafter, except when the parties were tied in the legislature in 1802, and in 1812, when the Federalists capitalized on anti-war sentiment to recapture a majority in the legislature, the Republicans were clearly the dominant party. After their defeat in 1800 the Federalists did not even enter another state-wide contest until 1808, and they made two final bids in 1812 and 1814. They held a competitive position from 1812 through 1815, but thereafter their strength was confined to a few counties—Bergen, Somerset, Middlesex, Burlington, and Cape May—that continued to send Federalist candidates to the legislature even as late as 1827. Although old party distinctions survived, party organizations in many counties disintegrated after 1816, and there were numerous successes achieved by "union" tickets or by independent candidates.

The Republicans owed much of their early success to the vigor of their leaders and the superiority of the organization.

Aaron Kitchell of Morris County had initiated the task of party building in 1797, and through the co-operation of such other political figures around the state as William S. Pennington of Essex, Joseph Bloomfield of Burlington, and Ebenezer Elmer of Cumberland, the party was mobilized for victory. By 1800, following a plan suggested by Kitchell, several counties had created a convention-type organization, with delegates from each township meeting to nominate candidates for the legislature. In preparation for the state election in 1800, representatives from most of the counties met in Princeton on September 30 to adopt an address and stimulate campaign enthusiasm. More important, a second convention was held on December 2, 1800, in Trenton in order to nominate five candidates for Congress. These were the origins of the Republican state convention, which was to meet biennially until 1826.[11] The New Jersey Republican party was the first in the nation to establish the state convention on a regular basis, although there had been earlier conventions in Pennsylvania in 1788 and 1792. In addition to the state convention, the Republicans also made effective use of the legislative caucus, which managed the distribution of state patronage and even served as a clearing house for recommending appointments to federal positions.

The Federalists were less methodical than their opponents in their party organization. A Federalist "convention," made up of leaders from various parts of the state, assembled in Trenton on November 13, 1800, to name a congressional slate, but except on rare occasions thereafter—notably in 1812 and 1814—the Federalists had no formal state organization. At the county level, the Federalists relied mainly on county mass meetings to endorse nominations, but in certain counties, Middlesex and Burlington conspicuously, they had elaborate organizations.

11. (Newark) *Centinel of Freedom*, Oct. 7, Nov. 18, Dec. 2, 9, 1800; Joseph Bloomfield, *To the People of New Jersey*, Sept. 30, 1800, Broadsides Collection, Rutgers University Library.

Because the Federalists so rarely challenged the Republicans in state-wide elections, voter participation varied greatly. In 1808, when both parties put forth intensive efforts in the presidential and congressional elections, nearly 72 per cent of the adult white males voted, and this level was approximated in 1800 and 1814. Normally, however, only one-third of the eligible electorate went to the polls. In elections of members of the legislature, especially in those counties where the parties were closely balanced, participation was at a high level, frequently exceeding 75 per cent. Campaigns were conducted largely through the medium of the party presses and by local canvassing committees. Candidates were not expected to engage in speech making or other direct appeals for votes, and they usually adhered to this traditional code.

The routine pattern into which New Jersey politics had settled was temporarily disrupted by the presidential election in 1824. Late in 1823 political leaders began to utter cautious expressions of support for particular candidates, but it soon became apparent that the Republicans would not reach agreement on one man. Samuel Southard, secretary of the Navy and former senator, favored Calhoun but discreetly posed as a neutral, while Mahlon Dickerson, New Jersey's senior senator, was an ardent Crawford man. Half of the state's congressional delegation declared for Adams, and Clay had a small but ardent following in the early maneuvering. There was initially little evidence of Jackson sentiment, until the Pennsylvania endorsement in March.

The Jackson boom was really launched at a public meeting in Salem on June 9-10, 1824, out of which came a call for the friends of the general throughout the state to send delegates to a convention to be held on September 1 in Trenton. The Trenton meeting, which attracted delegates from only seven of the thirteen counties, named an eight-man electoral ticket, three members of which were well-known Federalists. The chairman of the convention, and leading promoter of the Jackson cause in the state, was the notorious Colonel Samuel

Swartwout of New York City. Aaron Ogden Dayton, Federalist nephew of Jonathan Dayton—who had been implicated with Swartwout in the Burr conspiracy—served as secretary of both the Salem and Trenton meetings.[12]

When the regular Republican state convention assembled on October 19, it was disclosed that the now-formidable Jackson forces had entered into a coalition with the Crawford adherents. In control of the convention, they forced the adoption of an electoral slate made up of three Crawford men and five Jacksonians. The irate supporters of Adams, surprised by this development, withdrew from the tumultuous convention and then named their own electoral slate. Not content with a partial ticket, the Jacksonians held yet another "convention" on October 25 and formed an all-out Jackson slate, which they commended to the electorate in a stirring address as the "People's Ticket."[13]

The election began eight days later, and the New Jersey voters experienced the unfamiliar excitement of participating in a genuine contest for the presidency. Only once before—in 1808—had they been given the opportunity to vote for opposing slates of electors, and on that occasion 33,000 votes had been cast. Now—in 1824—only 18,400 men went to the polls, or approximately one-third of the eligibles. Jackson scored a surprising one-thousand vote triumph over Adams, carrying nine of the thirteen counties. No small share of the credit for Jackson's victory could be attributed to the zealous leadership provided by former Federalists, who eagerly climbed aboard the Jackson bandwagon, which had been driven by Colonel Swartwout.

After the election, excitement quickly subsided and voters returned to their traditional party loyalties. But in 1826, when the regular biennial Republican state convention met, discord immediately developed over the presidential question.

12. *Bridgeton Observer,* June 26, 1824; (New Brunswick) *Times,* Sept. 22, 1824; (New Brunswick) *Fredonian,* Sept. 8, 1824

13. (New Brunswick) *Times,* Sept. 22, Oct. 24, 1824; (New Brunswick) *Fredonian,* Oct. 27, 1824; *Bridgeton Observer,* Oct. 30, 1824.

The convention broke up in disorder—never to meet again—and the Jackson and Adams factions met separately, each to nominate a congressional ticket.[14] In the ensuing election the Adams party scored an easy victory, but the test was not a decisive one, for the Jacksonians had decided to wait until 1828 to wage a determined campaign.

In 1828 the Jacksonians led off with a state convention held on the anniversary of the Battle of New Orleans. They named their electoral ticket and appointed a central committee headed by a former Federalist, Garret D. Wall. The Adams convention, meeting on Washington's birthday, also included numerous former Federalists, two of whom—Theodore Frelinghuysen and Aaron Leaming—were among the electors nominated. Quite obviously, the era of proscription had ended, and the new parties eagerly embraced both Republicans and Federalists. Subsequently, in October, both parties again held conventions to name congressional candidates. Months were devoted to vigorous campaign activities. In the October state election, the Adams party secured a decisive margin in the legislature, and a month later they repeated their victory in the presidential election, carrying all but four counties. The intensity of the campaign effort brought 45,000 voters to the polls, approximately 72 per cent of the adult white males.

The new party alignment that had been formed by 1828 proved to be durable, although the composition and leadership of both parties—and especially the anti-Jacksonians—remained unstable down to 1834. The Adams party, dispirited in 1829 because of the loss of their personal figurehead, offered little resistance to the Jacksonians, who won control of the legislature and elected Peter D. Vroom, a former Federalist, to the governorship. Mobilized behind Clay in 1830, the National Republicans made a strong comeback and triumphed in the congressional contest. The party balance remained exceedingly close through the presidential election of 1832, which the

14. (Trenton) *Emporium*, Sept. 30, Oct. 21, 1826; (Bridgeton) *West Jersey Observer*, Oct. 7, 1826; (New Brunswick) *Fredonian*, Oct. 17, 25, Dec. 13, 1826.

Jacksonians won by the narrowest of margins. Meanwhile, party politics became involved in the rivalry between two major transportation interests in the state. The Jacksonians became identified with the Camden and Amboy Railroad "monopoly" and the National Republican–Whigs were affiliated with the rival New Jersey Railroad. For the ensuing few years party politics was in many ways a projection of transportation politics.

National-Republican strength fell off sharply in 1833—as it had in 1829—because once more the party had lost its national leader. But it soon found a new basis for unity and for arousing excitement in the agitation that followed Jackson's removal of the deposits. The exploitation of the bank issue came to a head in April, 1834, when delegates from all parts of the state convened in Trenton, ostensibly to memorialize Congress on the subject of the deposits and to applaud the actions of Senators Theodore Frelinghuysen and Samuel Southard, who, in opposition to the instructions of the Jacksonian legislature, had taken a pro-Bank stand. But the real purpose of the meeting was to launch the Whig Party. It was the state committee appointed by this bank convention that issued the call for a Whig State Convention to be held in August to prepare for the impending congressional elections.[15] The Democrats, despite numerous defections over the bank issue, remained substantially the same party in leadership and organization that they had been since 1828. With both parties again militantly mobilized, the state was convulsed by months of campaigning that resulted in an unprecedented turnout of voters and hard-won victory for the Democrats. For the next two decades Whigs and Democrats contended on nearly an equal basis, with the Whigs having a slight dominance from 1837 to 1848 and the Democrats asserting their superiority before and after those years.

The parties that emerged by 1828 were essentially new parties; they did not represent a continuation of the old parties

15. (Elizabeth) *New Jersey Journal,* Apr. 8, July 15, 1834.

under new names. The Republican party had foundered in 1826, split irrevocably over the presidential question. This split presented the former Federalists with an opportunity that they seized with avidity. Initially most conspicuous in the Jacksonian ranks, these long proscribed figures now found a welcome in the Adams party as well. The result was a drastic reshuffling of old connections and allegiances. Counties that had formerly been staunchly Federalist, like Cape May and Bergen, took different courses after 1824, as did former Republican strongholds, like Essex and Morris. There would seem to be no simple explanation for the new cleavage, any more than for the old. The division was not one of rural against urban areas, of old Federalist counties against old Republican counties, or of North Jersey against South Jersey. New identities were formed between 1824 and 1828, especially at the leadership level, and these identities were adhered to regardless of circumstances for the next two decades.

The new party system differed from the old in many ways, but most particularly in the close balance maintained between the parties and in the elaborateness of their organizations. Whereas the old Republicans had rarely faced a serious challenge between 1800 and 1824, the Democrats and Whigs competed on nearly an equal basis. Largely because of this intense competition, both parties erected elaborate structures, extending from the state conventions and state committees down to conventions and committees at the county level and a vigorous array of committees in each township. In 1832 the regular party structures were supplemented by organizations of "Young Men," operating as campaign auxiliaries at all levels of political activity. Conventions grew enormously in size, until it became customary for several hundred delegates to attend, as much for the purpose of stimulating enthusiasm as for providing a democratic basis for party decisions. Campaigns, too, became increasingly boisterous affairs, and extensive vote-buying, little practiced before, became a standard feature of every election.

The closeness of the party contests and the zealous efforts
of the expanded party apparatus stimulated voter participation. After 1828 it was a rare occasion when less than two-
thirds of the adult white males voted, and in 1840 and 1844
participation rose slightly above 80 per cent. After 1844, when
the governor was made elective by popular vote, participation
in the triennial gubernatorial elections tended to be somewhat
lower than in presidential elections. In general after 1828
national elections took precedence in popular interest over
state elections.

In striking contrast to New York and Pennsylvania, the
New Jersey parties were remarkably stable and had about the
same relative strength in both state and national elections. The
contrast is explainable in part because the Antimasons never
developed any considerable strength in New Jersey. The
Antimasons made their first appearance in Morris County in
1827 and subsequently acquired small followings in other
North Jersey counties.[16] They ran a congressional ticket in
1830, made up of one Jacksonian and five National Republicans and may have tipped the balance in that election to the
National Republicans. In 1832 they had a slate of Wirt electors in the field, which polled only 468 votes. However, had
these votes gone to the Clay ticket, Jackson would have lost
the state. Thereafter the party had little influence, and no
other third-party efforts were made until after 1852. The
tightness of party discipline may also be attributed to the
compact, homogeneous character of the state and to the pro-
fessionalism of the leadership in both parties. Within the
Jackson-Democratic party, for example, the state leadership
included an able, hard-working group of skilled politicians,
among them Stacy G. Potts, Garret D. Wall, and Peter D.
Vroom, who applied themselves assiduously to the tasks of
political management, and the Whigs were no less ably led.
Finally, a generally conservative attitude on the great issues
of the moment was to be characteristic of both parties, and

16. (Morristown) *Palladium of Liberty,* Nov. 1, 1827.

this circumstance, in some respects a consequence of the closeness of the party balance, also operated to keep the parties relatively indistinguishable in terms of doctrine.

PENNSYLVANIA

In no state, surely, did political parties present such indistinct outlines as in Pennsylvania. Although politics was conducted on a partisan basis from a very early date, the parties were loosely organized, rarely reflected sectional or ideological cleavages, and lacked effective state-wide leadership. The parties were usually badly balanced in voting strength, unstable in composition, and subject to chronic feuds between rival factions. Political alignments in state elections were often markedly different from those that prevailed in national elections. It would seem that the forces that shaped party loyalty in state contests were frequently in conflict with powerful counter forces that became operative in presidential elections, with disastrous consequences to party cohesion. The manifestations of instability persisted until 1840. Party formation in Pennsylvania, then, cannot be portrayed in terms of sharp and durable alignments, nor can transitions in political patterns be dated with precision.

The political history of Pennsylvania down to 1848 has been most ably dealt with in the series of monographs by Thayer, Brunhouse, Tinkcom, Higginbotham, Klein, and Snyder. Accordingly, the story is a familiar one and need not be rehearsed in detail here. It is necessary, however, to recapitulate the narrative of party development in order to relate the situation in Pennsylvania to the general structure of this study.

Pennsylvania has an unusually long tradition of partisan politics. Throughout most of its history as a colony there were two discernible parties, generally referred to as the Quaker and Proprietary parties, which in periods of crisis waged vigorous contests for control of the legislature. Possessed of rudimentary organization but endowed with able leaders, these Pennsylvania parties were probably as close to the modern concept of parties as those in any of the colonies. The internal controversies related to the issue of independence produced a reshuffling of old alignments, and it was the "radicals" who gained control and were responsible for the unorthodox and democratic constitution of 1776. This constitution itself provided a basis for partisan cleavage, and Constitutionalist and Anti-Constitution parties appeared. The establishment of the federal government, followed by the adoption of a new state constitution in 1790, eliminated many old causes of dissension and created both new issues and an altered political environment.

The constitution of 1790, although it was a more conventional document than that of 1776, gave Pennsylvania a framework of government that was still remarkable for its democratic features. Voting privileges were conferred on all adult male taxpayers, a provision that in effect approximated adult male suffrage. State elections were held annually on the second Tuesday in October and were conducted by ballot, with separate ballots and boxes for each office. The creation of voting districts within each county made the polls readily accessible to the electorate. Members of the assembly were elected annually from the counties, senators were chosen from districts for four-year terms, and the governor was popularly elected every three years. County officials were elective, as were municipal officials in Philadelphia and other cities. The governor was limited to serving three terms in any twelve-year period. He enjoyed vast appointive powers, but because of various circumstances his patronage was not effectively employed to build a disciplined party. Presidential electors were chosen at large by popular vote, except in 1800. Congressmen, except in 1788 and 1792, were elected from districts.

Like New York, Pennsylvania was a large and hetero-
geneous state, with a multiplicity of religious and national
groups and with definable geographic sections. Unlike New
York, however, its politics rarely reflected religious, national,
or sectional cleavages. Too, Pennsylvania had no heritage of
an aristocratic political leadership. The established Quaker
families and the Philadelphia merchants and bankers played
but a minor role in party politics, and there was no "landed
aristocracy" in the New York sense. In the absence of a
recognized "governing class" and with its egalitarian temper,
Pennsylvania exhibited a pronounced tendency to entrust political leadership to a motley assortment of adventurers, hack
journalists, spoilsmen, expatriates, hyphenates, and professional manipulators. Finally, Pennsylvania, always distinguished for its unswerving fidelity to the party of Jefferson,
rankled under the feeling that the claims of its sons to national
preferment received inadequate recognition from the managers
of the Virginia-New York alliance.

The emergence of parties in Pennsylvania during the first
decade of the federal period was in response to the stimulus
provided by national issues. In 1788, while the controversy
over the ratification of the constitution was still alive, rival
Federalist and Antifederalist groups held crude state conventions to nominate candidates for Congress. By 1790, however,
this basis of partisanship had disappeared, and Thomas Mifflin
was elected governor by an all but unanimous vote. Mifflin,
who was to serve for nine years, avoided any identification with
parties and did not use his patronage powers in a partisan
manner. Opposing congressional tickets were run in 1792,
but, again, they did not signify the formation of parties. It
was in the state elections of 1795, and even more in the presidential election of 1796, that party identities acquired meaning. In 1796, both the Federalists and the Republicans in the
legislature held mixed caucuses to nominate electoral slates
and establish rudimentary campaign committees. The Jeffersonian electors won by an exceedingly small margin in an

election that brought less than a quarter of the electorate to the polls. In the succeeding years, elections were contested increasingly on a party basis, and in 1799 the gubernatorial election that was to determine Mifflin's successor produced a major trial of strength. Although neither party as yet possessed much in the way of formal organization, informally constituted campaign committees engaged in strenuous propaganda efforts and stirred up sufficient excitement to more than double the vote registered in 1796. Thomas McKean, the Republican candidate, defeated his Federalist opponent, James Ross, in the closest two-party contest the state was to experience until 1829.

Within the next few years the triumphant Republicans consolidated their hold on the state, built local party organizations, and engaged in factional disputes over spoils. The Federalists were never able to challenge the Republicans in a statewide contest, but they also built strong organizations in several counties, some of which they dominated until 1824. Both parties were organized on the delegate-convention model, with the township primary as the basic unit. At the state level the legislative caucus was used to nominate candidates for governor and for presidential electors. Although the delegate-convention system ostensibly afforded party members an opportunity to participate in a democratic manner in party affairs, the system in fact was controlled by county politicians and officeholders, against whose dominance there were periodic outbursts of popular resentment.

Under Governor McKean the practice was begun of making political removals and appointments for partisan considerations. Because there was no formidable Federalist party to force the Republicans to unite against a common danger and because of the insatiable demands of local party chieftains for patronage, the governor's appointments were more a source of intraparty dissension than a weapon to enforce party discipline. For these reasons, too, and for others that might be detailed, the party caucus in Pennsylvania was a relatively weak instrument and party leadership was dispersed among a host of county politicians rather than concentrated in a state machine of the Regency type.

The first major fissure in the Republican party appeared in 1805 when a faction of "Radicals," headed by William Duane and Michael Leib secured control of the party caucus and nominated Simon Snyder for governor rather than the incumbent McKean. McKean's supporters, rallied by Alexander J. Dallas, took up the challenge, and, aided by Federalist votes, defeated the regular candidate. In 1808, fearful of a revival of Federalist strength and inspired by a common allegiance to Madison, the warring factions composed their differences and united in electing Snyder to the governorship. Once in office, Snyder broke with his early sponsors, Duane and Leib, who became the leaders of a dissident faction known as the "Old School Republicans." Leadership of the Snyder faction of "New School Republicans" was gradually assumed by John Binns of later "coffin handbill" fame.

As Snyder's nine years in office drew to a close, another major party rupture occurred. When the party caucus nominated William Findlay, the Duane-Leib faction appealed to popular sentiment against "caucus rule," sponsored a state convention at Carlisle on March 4, 1817, nominated William Heister as the Independent Republican candidate, and solicited Federalist support. Findlay won, but he was unable to solidify his position or heal the party breach, and in 1820 he was defeated by Heister. By this date factional divisions within the Republican party had become so complex that even contemporaries were at a loss to delineate them. The discord continued through Heister's administration. In 1823 the old Snyder faction, which was itself made up of many smaller power groups, rallied behind John A. Schulze.[17] The former

17. Schulze was nominated by a state convention that met at Harrisburg on March 4, 1823. Hezekiah Niles explained that the legislative caucus in Pennsylvania broke down when divisions occurred in the Republican ranks and party distinctions became blurred. "What they once believed to be good, and perhaps *was* so, had become liable to many important objections, and the

Duane-Leib faction, now under new leadership and known as the Amalgamation party because of its Federalist contingent, backed Andrew Gregg. Schulze was an easy victor, but once in office he did little to clarify the muddled condition of the party. Thus, on the eve of the presidential election of 1824 the old Republican party had long since succumbed to internal factionalism, a factionalism that seemingly bore no relation to issues, national or state, but was instead an outgrowth of power struggles among rival individuals and groups. The Federalists, still holding on to their partisan identity in county contests in certain areas, were eager but little rewarded appendages of the minority Republican faction.

Ambitious politicians looked to the presidential election in hope of backing a winner and assuming command of the splintered Pennsylvania Republicans. There was little sentiment for Crawford or Adams in the state, and Clay's prospects were calculated to be too slim to warrant support. Calhoun was favored by the so-called "Family" faction of the Schulze wing of the Republicans, which was led by S. D. Ingham, George M. Dallas, and John Sergeant. Enthusiasm for Jackson was first discernible among local politicians and newspaper editors, but by 1823 many prominent figures in the Amalgamation faction, conspicuously Henry Baldwin, James Buchanan, and M. C. Rogers, began to see the possibility of reconstructing their faction behind the popular general. Governor Schulze maintained an attitude of strict impartiality.

Arrangements had been made for a state convention of the Republican party to meet on March 4, 1824, for the purpose of agreeing on a presidential candidate and naming a slate of electors. As the date approached, the leaders of the Family faction, conscious of the rising sentiment in the state for Jackson, decided to join the stampede. Accordingly, on February 18, G. M. Dallas came out publicly for Jackson, and when the state convention met in Harrisburg, only one dissenting vote

convention system was substituted for the _legislative_ caucus." Niles' _Register_, XXIV, 241.

was cast against the nomination of Jackson.[18] Momentarily
united, the party-of-all-factions put forward Calhoun for the
vice-presidency, named an electoral slate, drafted an address,
and appointed a general committee of correspondence to manage the campaign. Backed by this coalition, which included
Federalist-Amalgamators along with every other recognizable
faction, Jackson won an easy three-to-one victory over slates
pledged variously to Adams, Crawford, and Clay. The vote
cast was less than a third as large as that polled in the 1823
gubernatorial election, when two-thirds of the eligible voters
had participated. Indeed, a smaller proportion of voters
turned out in 1824 than in the presidential election of 1816.

It would be improper to assert that there was a Jackson
party in Pennsylvania in 1824, except in a very loose sense.
Rather, all rival factions were united in the belief, which did
not diminish after 1824, that Jackson would ultimately gain
the presidency, and not until 1827 did leaders come forth to
attempt to rally support for Adams. In 1826 the neutral Governor Schulze was unanimously renominated by the state convention and was re-elected over negligible opposition. Preparations for the presidential campaign began in April, 1827,
when a Republican caucus coupled a strong endorsement of
Jackson with a call for a state convention to meet at Harrisburg on January 8, 1828. With harmony still reigning, the
convention nominated Jackson and Calhoun, arranged for an
electoral slate, and appointed a central committee as well as
corresponding committees in each county.

Meanwhile the supporters of Adams, with little assistance
from the national administration, had also met in convention
at Harrisburg on January 4 to nominate electors and improvise
an organization by appointing "vigilance committees" for each
county. Prominent among the Adams leadership were distinguished social, civic, and business figures, respected citizens
whose practical political experience was limited but who rallied
a following on the basis of their personal prestige. John Binns,

18. See *ibid.*, XXVI, 19-20, 39-42 for a full report of this convention.

the former "New School" leader, lent his questionable aid to the cause, as did most of the former Federalist newspapers and a considerable segment of the old Federalists.

Jackson again triumphed, this time by a two-to-one margin. Voter participation rose to nearly 57 per cent, a figure that had never before been equalled in a presidential election, although it had frequently been surpassed in gubernatorial elections. Momentarily it seemed that a new two-party alignment had emerged based on divisions over national politics. But several circumstances immediately arose to throw the party situation into confusion.

The defeat of Adams, of course, dealt a serious blow to his party, which virtually ceased to exist. New state issues, associated with the building of a network of canals and railroads, created intense rivalry among sections desirous of benefiting from the internal improvements and complicated party alignments. The rapid rise of political Antimasonry after 1828 and its persistence until after 1840 did not simplify matters. The partiality shown by the Jackson administration to the Family-Calhoun faction outraged the other factions in the Pennsylvania Jacksonian party and brought forth a renewal of intraparty strife. Finally, the stand eventually taken by the Jackson administration on the tariff and the bank, both of which were widely favored in Pennsylvania, confronted the state party with an awkward dilemma.

Throughout the period of Jackson's presidency Pennsylvania had what was virtually a dual system of politics. In national elections the state was strongly pro-Jackson, but in state elections the loosely knit Democratic party was closely pressed by the Antimasons and their allies. Not until after 1835 did alignments in state and national elections approach identity, and even then the inability of the Antimasons and Whigs to effect a complete merger and the recurrence of factional strife within the Democratic ranks made for instability and confusion.

Down until 1840, state politics took precedence over national politics; voting in state elections was significantly higher than in national elections. The crucial issues that absorbed popular interest were the state program of internal improvements, antimasonry, public education, banking policy, and constitutional reform. While these issues were influencing the course of state politics, the state parties had also to make some accommodation to national party positions on national issues. After 1842, by which time the major issues that had agitated state politics had been resolved, parties came to be defined largely in terms of national identifications, and a clear-cut two-party situation assumed form.

The major party in opposition to the dominant Democrats was the Antimasons. Originating in 1828 as a political phenomena in predominantly German areas in the southeast and in Scotch-Irish counties in the southwest, the movement combined an attack on Masonry and opposition to the state administration's canal policy with general antagonism to the Democratic party. Unlike its New York counterpart, it was not highly concentrated sectionally, produced few able leaders, and was slow to merge with the Whigs. At its first state convention on June 25, 1829, with delegates present from only thirteen counties, it nominated Joseph Ritner for governor. In the ensuing contest with George Wolf, the Democratic nominee, Ritner polled nearly 45 per cent of the total vote. The party maintained its strength in succeeding state elections and in 1832 prepared to contest both the gubernatorial and presidential elections.

Meanwhile, efforts had been launched by adherents of Henry Clay to form a party in his behalf, beginning with a public meeting in Philadelphia in April, 1831, and culminating in a state convention on May 29, 1832. The convention decided to make no nomination for governor but did name an electoral ticket. Later, on October 15, the Clay ticket was withdrawn and the electoral slate that had been prepared by the Antimasons was substituted. Thus the weak National Republicans prudently left the Antimasons to carry the brunt of the offensive against the Jacksonians. Ritner lost the governorship by only three thousand votes, but in the presidential election Jackson's margin exceeded twenty-five thousand. Ritner had carried twenty-one counties; Jackson lost only eight. In the German areas especially, Jackson showed greater strength than Wolf. The disparity in the voting patterns in the two elections was indicative of the lack of alignment between state and national parties.

The excitement produced by the withdrawal of the deposits stimulated efforts to mobilize the erstwhile National Republicans and pro-Bank sympathizers in a new Whig party. This movement led to the holding of a state convention on May 27, 1834, where an attempt was made to unite all opposition elements. But the Antimasons remained aloof and the Whigs again relapsed into the role of a minor third party. In the legislature they usually worked in concert with the Antimasons, but they had no permanent state organization, persisted in calling themselves "Democratic-Republicans," and did not even hold a state convention in 1835. In that year, favored by a split in the Democratic party which produced two rival Democratic candidates, the Antimasons elected Ritner to the governorship with plurality of the total vote. This "accidental" victory doubtless served to extend the life of the Antimasonic party in the state.

Once in power, and with a presidential election in the offing, the Antimasons began to divide into "exclusivists" and "moderates," with the former, led by Thaddeus Stevens, expressing support for Daniel Webster, and the latter, led by Ritner, favoring William Henry Harrison. The moderates controlled the state convention that met in December, 1835, and nominated Harrison for the presidency, whereupon the Stevens faction bolted. The Whigs, meeting at the same time, also endorsed Harrison, but, again, played a distinctly secondary role to the Antimasons. The Democrats healed the schism that had caused their defeat in 1835 and united behind Van Buren, who carried the state by a slender majority.

Gradually, ever since 1824, the once overwhelming strength of the Democratic party in national elections had declined, until by 1836 the balance was close.

Fortified by the patronage they had enjoyed during Ritner's three years in office the Antimasons continued to be the dominant partner in their alliance with the ineffectual Whigs. In 1838 Ritner sought a second term in office, but in a scandal-ridden election the Democrats regained the governorship with David B. Porter. Shorn of power in the state, and, in effect, isolated from national politics, the Antimasons—who were in actuality the "opposition" party in Pennsylvania—now had little excuse for maintaining their separate identity. But the party exhibited extraordinary tenacity; even the presidential election of 1840 did not bring about a complete merger of Whigs and Antimasons.

Preparations for the 1840 campaign began in May, 1839, when the Antimasonic state convention named an electoral ticket pledged to Harrison and Webster. In the following month a poorly attended Whig convention adopted resolutions favorable to Clay, whereupon a faction led by C. B. Penrose withdrew and issued a call for a convention of all elements in the state opposed to Van Buren. This call was echoed by the "democratic anti-Van Buren" members of the legislature on June 22, and arrangements were made to hold the convention in Harrisburg on September 4.

When the delegates convened, the president, John Parker, observed that he was "surrounded by whigs, anti-masons and conservatives," who were inspired by "a spirit of determination to merge all minor differences of opinion in the one grand and patriotic object of redeeming our beloved country from the grasp of the spoilers." A committee was appointed to choose delegates to the national "anti-Van Buren" convention, with instructions to exercise a delicate regard to any actions that had already been taken by "any portion of the anti-Van Buren party, so that the feelings of all may be respected and harmony restored." Resolutions were adopted paying high tributes to the talents of Henry Clay, "who should one day have the highest evidence of the nation's affection," but whose nomination would be fatal to the party. Harrison was then endorsed as the only man who could unite the "anti-Van Buren" party. Subsequently this self-styled "Democratic Anti-Van Buren Convention of Pennsylvania" issued an address in which it set forth in a remarkably candid manner the practical considerations that had dictated the choice of Harrison over Clay.[19]

Even this mobilization of the anti-Van Burenites did not mark the consolidation of a new opposition party. In the ensuing presidential campaign both the Whigs and the Anti-masons maintained their separate party organizations, although, of course, they supported the same electoral ticket and joined enthusiastically in the cabin raisings, mass rallies, and spectacular festivals that made the election such a memorable one.

The Democrats campaigned as energetically as their opponents, and the result was an unprecedented outpouring of the electorate and a 350-vote margin of victory for Harrison. No previous presidential election in Pennsylvania had brought more than 57 per cent of the adult white males to the polls; in 1840 participation rose to over 77 per cent, a figure not to be exceeded before the Civil War.

After 1840 the Whigs became the principal opponents of the dominant Democratic party. The Antimasons played only a minor role in the 1841 gubernatorial election, which resulted in the re-election of Governor Porter, and declined rapidly after 1842 when Thaddeus Stevens, their colorful and zealous champion, retired briefly from politics before himself assuming—albeit briefly—the Whig label. Efforts to reactivate the party in 1843 in behalf of the presidential candidacy of General Winfield Scott came to naught when Clay secured the Whig nomination. Pennsylvania political alignments were finally

19. See *ibid.*, LVII, 46-7, 190-91, for the proceedings of the convention and the address.

becoming simplified, at least in the sense that party identities had the same meaning in both state and national elections. Such had never really been the case in Pennsylvania before 1840.

Party formation in Pennsylvania, then, would seem to have been more strongly conditioned by state than by national influences. It was not the presidential elections of 1824, 1828, and 1832 that stimulated the formation of parties but rather the local circumstances that produced the Antimasonic party, and it was the Antimasons, whose connection with national politics was remote, who provided the major opposition to the Democrats for twelve years and, in time, contributed most of their following to the post-1840 Whig party. This is not to say, of course, that Pennsylvania politics was unaffected by national politics. But the contrast between the circumstances of party formation in Pennsylvania and New England, where the emergence of new parties can be related very closely to the contest for the presidency, is great. In this connection it would also seem to be significant that before 1840 voter participation tended to be much higher in state than in presidential elections. After 1840, when the parties were strongly oriented toward national politics, voter participation was higher in presidential than in gubernatorial elections. Parties were were reasonably distinct and well balanced in state politics by 1829, but they remained ambiguous in national politics until 1836, or even 1840.

Why Pennsylvania failed to develop the well organized, durable, and disciplined parties characteristic of New England and certain other middle states defies simple explanation, but the fact is apparent. Although general use was made of the delegate-convention system after 1800, and the legislative caucus came into use at the state level after 1796, organization remained loose and state leadership weak. The state convention, which had made a premature appearance in 1788, began to supplant the caucus in 1817 and became the customary instrument for making statewide nominations by 1824. But its adoption does not seem to have reduced internal factionalism nor enhanced the authority of state party leaders. Similarly, the abundance of state patronage did not, in Pennsylvania, serve as a cement for party organization. One receives the impression that from an early date the "better element" in the state exerted little political influence, with the result that politics became the business of men who were interested in the tangible rewards of jobs and money. There was considerable corruption, fraud, and even violence in the conduct of elections, and political management was oligarchic rather than democratic. Campaigns were more commonly focused on scandals, personalities, or local concerns than on broad issues of public policy. Candidates did not engage in personal canvasses until 1844, when the Whig contender for the governorship toured the state, and not until 1847, when the Democratic gubernatorial candidate broke all tradition, did a candidate make stump speeches.

DELAWARE

Delaware was distinguished above all other states for the stability of its politics. Parties were formed early, developed efficient organizations, competed vigorously on a remarkably equal basis, and exhibited amazing durability. For more than half a century political alignments established in the 1790's underwent little change; even in the Jackson era the transition from old to new party alignments was accomplished smoothly. One might well say that Delaware politics represented the ideal, uncomplicated model of American politics, a model that was but crudely approximated in every other state.

The state constitution of 1792, which replaced the frame of government that had been adopted in 1776, was entirely conventional and obviously patterned on that of Pennsylvania.

The governor was popularly elected for a three-year term and could not succeed himself. The legislature consisted of seven assemblymen and three senators from each of the three counties, the former chosen annually and the latter for staggered three-year terms. Sheriffs and coroners, were elected for each county, as were the assessors and inspectors of elections in each hundred. There was no unit of government corresponding to the township. Elections were held annually by written ballot on the first Tuesday in October with the county as the polling unit until 1811, when each hundred became the election district. The franchise was conferred on all free, white, adult males who paid any state or county tax and was therefore quite broad.[20] The state was a unit for congressional elections, even during the decade 1813-1823 when Delaware had two congressmen. Presidential electors were chosen by the legislature until 1832. Problems of party organization were minimized, then, because there were but three obvious political units—the state, the county, and the hundred—in which parties had to function.

Party alignments in Delaware were durable, among other reasons, because they reflected stable geographic, cultural, and economic cleavages within the small state. New Castle county in the north was industrial, relatively urban, and had a numerous and politically vigorous Presbyterian and Scotch-Irish contingent. Kent and Sussex counties were rural, agricultural, predominantly English in national origin, and strongly Methodist or Episcopalian. From an early date, New Castle was the Democratic-Republican stronghold and the two lower counties were Federalist. Because of the rural dominance, and because political leadership was customarily exercised by elaborately interrelated gentry families, who took seriously their political prerogatives, the state was always conservative in its political sentiments.

During the Revolutionary and post-Revolutionary eras,

20. A new state constitution in 1831 provided for biennial elections, extended the terms of the governor and senators to four years, and retained taxpayer suffrage.

politics at the county level brought forth contests between rival factions that could loosely be described as "conservatives" and "radicals." By 1795 old factional labels were being replaced by the new party names, Federalist and Democratic-Republican. Initially the Federalists held the preponderance of strength, but the Democratic-Republicans, with their superiority in New Castle, were soon making an effective challenge. In 1795 the Federalists were sufficiently concerned to hold a convention at Dover, the delegates to which were informally appointed rather than elected, for the purpose of agreeing on a candidate for governor. In that year, and again in 1798, the gubernatorial election was contested on a party basis and the Federalist majority was small.

By 1800 the Democratic-Republicans had drawn abreast of their rivals, and a year later they repeated their triumph by winning the congressional election by fifteen votes. But the Federalists soon reasserted their superiority, and thereafter the only Republican successes came in congressional elections in 1810, 1816, 1818, and 1820, and in the gubernatorial elections of 1810, 1820, and 1822. In 1821 and 1822 they secured control of the legislature. But, again, the Federalists regained dominance and carried every state election through 1826. The party balance was almost invariably extremely close; at no time could either party risk the hazard of confidence. Too, except in 1816, when there was dissension in the Federalist ranks, party solidarity was proof against any manifestations of intraparty factionalism. Regardless of the course of national politics, Delaware parties remained as they had been from decade to decade.

Both parties in Delaware evolved organizational structures that ultimately came to resemble one another closely. The starting point was the county mass meeting. "Soon after the election of President Adams, in 1797," reminisced Hezekiah Niles, "the *first* regular democratic meeting, or 'caucus,' that I have heard of as being held in Delaware, was convened at Wilmington. It consisted of 50 or 60 persons, of whom I was

the junior. . . ."[21]   Niles related how a small group of six or
seven men, of which he was a member, directed party strategy.
They met informally, agreed on courses of action, and then
"spread the word" of what was to be done. This informal
system continued for some years until the managers made the
mistake of letting their "personal preferences to stand opposed
to the wish of the people." "From that time," Niles observed,
"the delegate system superceded caucussing, *which had been
slain at the polls.*"[22]   Although the record is not entirely clear,
it would seem that the county mass meeting, controlled by
Niles and his associates, made county nominations and appointed what were, in effect, campaign committees in the
hundreds. In 1802 these hundred committees became elective.
Later, but earlier than 1810, the hundred committees met in
county convention, thus replacing the mass meeting as the
nominating agency. The change to the delegate-convention
system, referred to by Niles, may possibly have occurred after
1804, when the Democratic-Republicans suffered an unex-
pectedly severe defeat.

While the county machinery was developing, formal procedures were also being perfected for making nominations for
state-wide offices. In preparation for the gubernatorial election in 1801 there were proposals for a state convention to
select the Democratic-Republican candidate, but the matter
was arranged instead by correspondence among committees
appointed by the county mass meetings. But in 1802, with a
congressman to be elected, committees appointed by the three
county mass meetings met in convention at Dover on June 5
and nominated Caesar Rodney. Thereafter it would appear
that the state convention was regularly established and that the
Federalists soon copied the device from their opponents. Federalist county organization was similar to that of the Democratic-Republicans, although the Federalists did not complete

21. Niles' *Register*, XXXIX, 252.
22. *Ibid.*, XXVII, 38-39.

the transition to the county delegate-convention system until after 1820.

That Delaware, unlike most states, never used the legislative caucus method of nominations is explainable, I believe, on the basis of the peculiar sectional-political division in the legislature. The Democratic-Republicans, for example, invariably had the seven assemblymen and three senators from New Castle, but, except in 1821 and 1822, they rarely had members of their party from Sussex or Kent. A "caucus" of the Democratic-Republican members of the legislature, therefore, could hardly pretend to represent more than the party sentiment in one county. The Federalists faced a similar problem. The solution to the problem was the state convention.

If the Delaware political scene was stable, it was not unexciting. The closely balanced parties, with their extensive campaign machinery in each hundred, contested every election with great zest. Voters were exhorted, canvassed, and entertained with steer-roasts, fish-fries, and turtle feasts. The result was that Delaware had, on the average, the highest voter participation of any state over the period before 1824. In the gubernatorial election of 1804, which restored Federalist supremacy, 82 per cent of the adult white males voted. Rarely did this figure fall below 60 per cent in any state election, although it never again rose above 74 per cent before 1828. The explanation for the consistently high voting rate is to be found essentially in the close balance of the parties.

Delaware was the only state in which in 1824 the old parties still retained their original identity and undiminished vigor. The presidential election of that year had no discernible effect on the election of members of the legislature. Neither party was united in support of a presidential candidate, and the legislature, after some intricate maneuvering, chose two Crawford electors and one pledged to Adams. In Congress, Delaware's lone representative, Louis McLane, voted for Crawford.

After 1824 politics resumed its traditional course, with the Federalists holding a narrow edge over their rivals.

Not until 1827 were there clear signs that old party identities were about to be replaced by new ones. In January of that year Louis McLane, still a Federalist, was elected to the Senate. Although he was uncommitted on the presidential question, he had privately decided to oppose the Adams administration, as well as the "Dover Junto" of Federalist state leaders. His antagonism may have originated in 1824, when the Junto frustrated his hopes of going to the Senate at that time.

An open rupture developed later in 1827 when McLane sought to dictate the choice of his successor in Congress. The Federalist state convention, meeting on August 27, nominated Kensey Johns, Jr., an Adams supporter, rather than McLane's favorite, James Bayard. Next, on August 28, Republican delegations from New Castle and Kent nominated Arnold Naudain, an Adams man, for the vacant seat. On the same day, Sussex Federalists partial to Jackson put forward Bayard as their choice. To add to the confusion, a Jackson state convention on September 4 placed Colonel Henry Whitely in the field. A subsequent meeting of the same convention replaced Whitely with Bayard, and an Adams state convention on September 18 induced Naudain to withdraw in favor of Johns. Thus after all the frenzied activity, the ultimate contest was to be between Johns and Bayard, identified respectively with Adams and Jackson. "The old names 'Democrat' and 'Federalist' are for the present, at least, entirely lost sight of in Delaware," reported the Wilmington *American Watchman* on September 21, 1827, "where they have been adhered to with such remarkable tenacity. You hear of no party names here but Adams-men and Jackson-men. An amalgamation of old parties has taken place."[23]

In this crucial election, Johns won Sussex and Kent and the

23. Quoted in John A. Munroe, "Louis McLane," Ch. IX. Professor Munroe generously made available to me the manuscript of his projected full-length biography of McLane, on which I have relied for much of my account of party formation in Delaware.

election; Bayard carried New Castle. McLane, the acknowledged leader of the Jackson party, worked valiantly to prepare for the elections in 1828, which would determine Delaware's electoral vote and its representative in Congress. But he met a brilliant adversary in John M. Clayton, who emerged as the leader of the Adams party. As the election drew near, McLane went on the stump to rouse the cohorts. Clayton, meanwhile, employed the powerful Federalist state organization, most of whose workers remained loyal to Adams, to good effect. Bayard was again defeated by Johns and the legislature had a large Adams majority because of the successes scored again in Sussex and Kent. The victory by the Adams party inaugurated a long period of Adams-National Republican-Whig supremacy in the state, which ended only with the collapse of Clayton's Whig machine in 1850.

The political alignment that came into existence in 1827-1828 strongly resembled that which had prevailed since the 1790's. It is not possible to determine the extent to which the Federalists entered the Adams party and their Republican adversaries the Jackson camp, but there is reason to believe that the political associations that had been formed over a period of more than thirty years were not easily dissolved. Some former Federalists of stature, like McLane and Bayard, broke with their old associates, as did some former Republican leaders, like Arnold Naudain. But it seems doubtful that there was extensive reshuffling of loyalties. Sussex and Kent produced Whig majorities, while New Castle was heavily Democratic. In any event, the pattern that appeared in 1828 was durable; the readjustment to the new party designations was accomplished within a year and became immediately operative in both state and national elections. Party machinery, already highly developed, was not affected significantly by the inauguration of a new era, nor was there any departure from the tradition of stability and conservatism.

Although the balance between the parties continued to be remarkably even, the Democrats were rarely able to achieve supremacy. They won the governorship in 1832 and 1846 and elected a congressman in 1838, but scored no other state-wide victories before 1850. How the party managed to sustain itself, especially in Sussex and Kent, in the face of almost constant defeats, is difficult to understand. Yet they customarily polled around 48 per cent of the total vote in state-wide contests. This intense interparty competition, coupled, perhaps, with the introduction of the popular election of presidential electors in 1832, produced an even higher level of voter participation than had prevailed previously. In 1840, in both the gubernatorial and presidential elections, 83 per cent of the adult white males voted; in 1844 a record high of 85 per cent was reached. Never, after 1832, did voter participation fall below 70 per cent.

No student of the history of American politics can observe the well ordered, uncomplicated pattern of Delaware politics without suppressing the vain wish that all states might have been as stable and regular in their political behavior. It is not indulging in fantasy, however, to remark that there seems to have existed in all states a tendency toward the "model" conditions that prevailed in Delaware. This would seem to be so apparent that one might justifiably regard every other state as a deviation from the Delaware norm and then confine one's attention to attempting to account for the deviations.

MARYLAND

On the basis of its form of government Maryland could properly be classified as "southern," but in its political behavior it was closely akin to the Middle States. It was, in fact, the southernmost state to develop a vigorous and durable two-party politics during the period of the first American party system. For over two decades these parties were well organized, closely balanced, and exerted sufficient appeal to induce high voter participation. This vitality of the parties is especially remarkable in view of the fact that there were, between 1792 and 1836, no state-wide elections in Maryland. With the reorganization of parties after 1824, Maryland was among the first states to readjust its politics to the new national alignments that formed behind Jackson and Adams.

The Maryland constitution of 1777, which was not substantially altered until 1837, could hardly be described as democratic. A House of Delegates was elected annually and was made up of four delegates from each county and two each from the cities of Baltimore and Annapolis. The Senate was chosen by an electoral college, elected every five years. Nine senators represented the "Western Shore" of the state and six the "Eastern Shore." The legislature by joint ballot chose a governor and five councillors annually. County government was largely managed by appointed boards, although the governor selected the sheriff from among two men who were popularly elected in each county. There was no township government.

The quinquennial elections of senatorial electors were held in September, the regular state and congressional elections on the first Monday in October, and the presidential elections on the second Monday in November. Suffrage was originally confined to those who owned fifty acres or possessed £30 personal estate, but in 1802 the privilege was extended to white, adult, male citizens who had resided twelve months in the county or city. In 1799 the counties were divided into election districts for polling purposes, and in 1801 the change was made from *viva voce* voting to the ballot. Except in 1789 and 1792, presidential electors were chosen by districts until 1836, and congressmen, except in 1789 and 1790, were always elected from districts. The political units in Maryland, therefore, were the county—for the election of delegates, senatorial electors, and sheriffs—the congressional district, and the presidential district.

Also significant as a unit of party organization after 1800 was the election district.

Maryland's avoidance of state-wide elections resulted from the determination of the rural counties to prevent domination of the state by metropolitan Baltimore. The weight of Baltimore in the political scale was less than its population merited because of the system of representation in the legislature as well. With district elections for Congress and presidential electors, the influence of Baltimore could, in effect, be limited to its own immediate area, and by allotting the city only two delegates, whereas the least populous county had four, the constitution guaranteed rural supremacy. Not until dissatisfaction approached revolution was this inequitable arrangement altered in 1837, and even then the concessions were confined chiefly to modifying representation in the lower house. There were actually three district sections in the state—the Eastern Shore, Baltimore, and the remainder of the Western Shore. When the governor was made popularly elective in 1837, it was with the proviso that he must be chosen from each of the three sections in rotation. Political groupings in the state, especially in the early 1800's reflected these sectional differences.

Political parties assumed form in Maryland shortly before 1800, although there had been organized political activity much earlier. In 1788 the legislature enacted a complicated law dividing the state into districts for the first congressional election but required that every voter should vote for a candidate from each district. This act stimulated the Federalists in the legislature to hold a mixed caucus to agree upon a general ticket, which was later endorsed by a meeting in Baltimore. The anti-Federalists also ran a ticket that was evidently the product of an informal conference. In 1790, when congressmen again were elected on a general ticket, the state was seriously agitated about the recent decision to locate the federal capital on the Potomac. A meeting in Baltimore nominated what was termed the "Chesapeak ticket" and a group of legislators from the Western Shore put forward a "Potomac ticket." The tentative use of the legislative caucus as a nominating device in Maryland soon disappeared, for state-wide elections were abandoned after 1792. Too, the early distinctions between Federalists and anti-Federalists, as well as between Chesapeake and Potomac, yielded to new distinctions arising out of national politics.

Before 1800 party designations were extremely loose, candidates were usually self-announced, and formal party organization was lacking. In the presidential election of 1800, however, candidates for elector identified themselves with Adams or Jefferson and engaged in a most active campaign that extended from March to November.[24] In the October state elections, legislative candidates ran on a party basis. The elections gave the Republicans a majority in the House of Delegates for the first time and resulted in an even division of the state's ten electoral votes.

Within the next few years, an elaborate delegate-convention type of organization—with the election district as the primary unit—was instituted by both parties. In 1803, for example, the Federalists in Frederick County held a convention of delegates chosen from each election district, which agreed to support four candidates for the House of Delegates. The convention also appointed a committee to meet with a similarly chosen committee from Montgomery County to agree on a Federalist candidate for Congress. In presidential years similar arrangements were made for nominating presidential electors.[25] By 1804 the Republicans in Prince George's County were also using the delegate-convention, and in time its use was extended generally. Previously there had been some use of the mass meeting as a nominating device in the counties.

Along with their organizational apparatus, the Maryland politicians developed a popular style of campaigning, seemingly much in advance of other states. In 1800, the several

24. (Annapolis) *Maryland Gazette*, Mar. 20, June 26, Sept. 11, 1800.
25. *Frederick-Town Herald*, July 9, 30, Sept. 10, 24, 1803.

candidates for presidential elector went around their districts delivering addresses to the voters. General Samuel Smith, a Jeffersonian elector, was accused of attending every public meeting in his own county and several in neighboring counties. It was also a pleasant custom for the parties to advertise barbecues, at which there would be speeches by the candidates. In September, 1803, the voters of Anne Arundel County were advised that a beef would be roasted at Orndorf's tavern "at which time it is expected a discussion of politics will take place by the candidates that offer to represent said county in the next general assembly."[26] When the Republicans won a hard fought victory in Frederick County in 1802, they celebrated by parading through Fredericktown in the evening carrying ornamented lanterns inscribed with mottoes. What with the barbecues, stump speeches, parades, newspaper propaganda, and conventions galore, the Maryland electorate was both stimulated and entertained and responded to election appeals in sizable proportions. Over 44 per cent of the adult white males voted in the 1800 presidential election, a proportion which was matched only in New Hampshire, and nearly 57 per cent participated in 1812. Many counties on occasion turned out over 80 per cent of their eligible voters, and on at least one occasion Baltimore City came suspiciously close to 100 per cent.

Republican supremacy in Maryland, established in 1800, continued down to the eve of the War of 1812, when the Federalists, using the label "Friends of Peace," made a strong comeback. Although the Republicans won a majority in the electoral college in 1811, thus assuring a wholly Republican Senate for the next five years, the Federalists gained such overwhelming superiority in the House of Delegates that they were able to elect four successive Federalist governors during the war period. The Republican strongholds were Baltimore City, Baltimore County, and the counties on both sides of the upper Chesapeake. The Federalists were dominant in the lower counties of the Eastern Shore and in the western coun-

26. *Ibid.*, Sept. 1, 1803.

ties. Federalism in Maryland—as in Delaware and even in New York—was strongest in the rural areas. Most counties tended to be heavily unbalanced in favor of one party. Baltimore County, for example, had greater than a two-to-one Republican majority in 1812, and in Baltimore City the ratio exceeded three-to-one. Some of the Federalist counties, like St. Mary's, Somerset, and Worcester, gave their candidates 80 and even 90 per cent of the total vote. But despite the imbalance from county to county, party strength on a state-wide basis remained fairly even.

Federalist strength reached its apogee in 1816, when the party gained control of the Senate for the first and only time and also secured a large majority in the House of Delegates. But by 1818 the Republicans had regained the House of Delegates, and it became apparent that Federalism was crumbling. One Federalist editor attributed the defeat to "schisms, broils, personal altercations, and neglect in attending the polls."[27] For many years the party had been divided into a moderate wing, of which Roger B. Taney was the leader, and an exclusivist faction led by Alexander Contee Hanson. The disheartened party attempted a final bid for power in 1821, in the quinquennial senatorial election, but was badly beaten. In the succeeding few years, traditional party distinctions became blurred, party discipline—both among Federalists and Republicans—became lax, and in many counties "anti-caucus," or independent candidates upset regular nominees.

With the old parties disintegrating, the presidential election of 1824 initiated a tendency toward a new alignment of parties. Sentiment in the state was almost evenly divided between Jackson and Adams, with minor support for Crawford and negligible backing for Clay. In the October state elections, some candidates declared their positions on the presidential question, but in most counties the contests were divorced from national politics. Because the presidential electors were to be chosen by districts, no state-wide nominating

27. (Annapolis) *Maryland Gazette,* Oct. 15, 1818.

device was employed, and the electors were apparently either self-nominated or put forward by informal meetings. There is no evidence, at least, of extensive new party machinery.

The election resulted in the choice of seven electors for Jackson, three for Adams, and one for Crawford. Of the popular vote, however, Adams had 14,698 votes; Jackson, 14,523; Crawford, 3,333; and Clay 695. Maryland led the nation in voter participation; nearly 54 per cent of its adult white males voted. But this was not an extraordinary turnout for Maryland and fell below the mark set in the 1812 presidential election.

The new party alignment forecast in the presidential election did not immediately become operative in state elections. In 1825, elections for the legislature went off much as usual, with considerable confusion of party identities. But in 1826, with a quinquennial senatorial election, as well as members of the House of Delegates and Congressmen to be elected, there were signs that a new order was emerging. In every county, candidates were under pressure to declare their preference for Jackson or Adams, and old party distinctions faded. A major sensation of the campaign was provided by Virgil Maxcy, a former Federalist who was assuming prominence as a Jackson leader. Maxcy, who had favored Calhoun in 1824, with Adams as his second choice, had consented to run for Congress on the understanding that the issue of his presidential preference would not be raised. But when his supporters demanded that he pledge himself to Adams, Maxcy issued a lengthy statement announcing his withdrawal from the race and his support for Jackson. In the election of the electoral college, there were reportedly two factions, "one in favor of a Liberal or mixed Senate, the other for making the selection entirely from the old democratic party."[28] Although party identifications were still vague, it was believed that the new Senate, chosen by the "Liberal" electors, had a majority of Jacksonians.

28. *Ibid.*, Sept. 21, 1826.

It was in 1827 that new parties, aligned behind Jackson or Adams, assumed clear form.   The organization of a Jackson party got under way at a meeting held in Skinner's long room in Baltimore on March 7, "for the purpose of adopting some measures preparatory to the next Presidential election."[29]   In addition to adopting an address that lauded Jackson, it proposed the holding of a state convention in Baltimore on May 24.   The Jacksonians in each electoral district were urged to hold meetings and appoint delegates.   The chairman of the meeting, Alexander M'Kim, was authorized to appoint the delegates from Baltimore City.   During March and April, there was much activity among the Jacksonians as meetings were convened to name the convention delegates.   In some counties resolutions and addresses were adopted and committees of correspondence were appointed.   On the designated day, eighty-four delegates from the several electoral districts met at the Athenaeum in Baltimore, drafted and ordered to be printed the customary address, appointed a central committee—of which Taney was the chairman—to direct the campaign, and left it to the party agencies in each district to nominate electors.[30]

Similar preparations were being made by the friends of Adams.   A meeting at the Exchange in Baltimore on May 5 recommended that the Adams adherents in each county should assemble and appoint delegates to a convention to be held in Baltimore on July 23 "for the consideration and adoption of such measures as shall appear needful to bring out a full and fair expression of the will of the People of Maryland and sustain the Administration of the United States. . . ."[31]   At the same time a central committee for Baltimore was named and was instructed to set up an elaborate organization within each ward of the city.   The state convention, attended by 154

29. *Ibid.*, Mar. 8, 1827.

30. *Address of the Jackson State Convention to the People of Maryland . . .* (Baltimore, 1827); (Annapolis) *Maryland Gazette*, May 31, 1827.

31. (Washington) *National Intelligencer*, May 8, July 25, 27, 31, 1827; Niles' *Register*, XXXII, 354.

delegates representing every county except Allegany, met on July 23, and, after organizing and appointing various committees, adjourned till the following day. Then a lengthy address was adopted and ordered to be printed and a central committee of seven men from Baltimore was appointed to communicate with committees of correspondence in each county.

The purpose of both of these state conventions—the first ever held in Maryland—was not to make nominations but rather to carry forward the organization of the parties. Former Federalists played prominent roles in both conventions, although they may have been somewhat more influential in the Jackson than in the Adams party. Stimulated by these state conventions, local party organization quickly became established on the pattern that had been created in the early 1800's. Primary meetings were held in the election districts to choose delegates to county conventions, which in turn appointed delegates to congressional district and electoral district conferences. In many counties the new party apparatus was functioning in the state election in 1827, which gave the Adams party a majority in the House of Delegates. With this election, the old party designations had been replaced by the new.

There was virtually no cessation of political activity as the parties continued their preparations for 1828. In some districts presidential electors had been nominated as early as September, 1827; in others action was deferred until after the state election. In June, 1828, county conventions met to nominate candidates for the House of Delegates and to name committees of vigilance to superintend the campaign. Everywhere candidates were making appeals for votes. The state election in October increased the size of the Adams majority in the lower house, but it brought no relaxation of party excitement about the presidential contest. In November the voters thronged the polls in every election district in unprecedented numbers. Only in New Hampshire was there an equal display of interest as slightly more than three-fourths of the eligible voters cast their ballots.

The outcome of the election was a standoff. Adams won six electoral votes and Jackson five, and the margin between them in popular votes was less than a thousand in a total vote of over fifty thousand. The Jackson electors were chosen from the districts encompassing Baltimore and its environs; the other districts were all for Adams. Because the districts were created of counties and parts of counties by a partisan legislature, they obviously represented a gerrymander and for that reason several of them were fairly closely balanced in party strength. Within individual counties, however, there was wide disparity in strength, and a sectional pattern that pitted the Baltimore area against the rest of the state was evident.

The new party alignment did not disintegrate after the defeat of Adams; rather it persisted with occasional readjustments until the 1850's. The Jacksonians won control of the legislature in 1829 and were able to elect Thomas K. Carroll, a former Federalist, to the governorship, but a year later they were routed by the "Antis," as their opponents were called. Late in 1830 the Antis began to make plans to mobilize behind Clay, and on February 17, 1831, a meeting of anti-Jacksonians from both branches of the legislature assumed leadership of the movement. It was declared to be "expedient that a national convention be held, to which the people of all the states shall be invited to send delegates, in which their will can be authentically ascertained, and that concert of action produced, which is essential to the success of our cause."[32] Accordingly, delegates from all the states were invited to meet in Baltimore on the second Monday in December. The caucus further proposed that the anti-Jacksonians in each congressional district in the state should appoint a delegate to the national convention; two delegates-at-large—representing the Eastern and Western shores—were named by the caucus itself. In the year that followed Baltimore was to play host to three national political

32. Niles' *Register*, XL, 28-29.

conventions, the first ever held in the United States. The Antimasons met September 26-28, 1831; the National Republicans, on December 12-16; and the Democrats, on May 21-23, 1832.

In contrast to the high degree of excitement that had prevailed in 1828, the 1832 elections were relatively quiet. Because both parties were already well-organized and electors were again to be chosen by districts, neither party found it necessary to hold a state convention. Instead, electors were placed in nomination as they had been in 1828. The October state election gave the National Republicans a two-to-one majority in the House of Delegates, and in the presidential elections—because the districts had been shrewdly redrawn by the anti-Jackson legislature—Clay secured seven of the states ten electoral votes. This division was hardly a fair representation of the relative strength of the parties, for Clay's majority in a total vote of 38,256 was only 52 votes. The area of preponderant Democratic strength was confined to Baltimore, the counties of the upper Chesapeake, and the two westernmost counties. For reasons that are not apparent, voter participation fell far below the level that had been reached four years earlier; only 56 per cent of the adult white males voted.

The transformation of the National Republicans into Whigs was accomplished smoothly in 1834. Shortly before the state elections in that year the "Whig Committee of the City of Baltimore sometimes partially acting as a Central Committee for the State of Maryland" issued a call to all who were opposed to the Jackson administration to vote in the forthcoming elections.[33] In March, 1835, Whig legislators and other officials met in caucus at Annapolis and recommended that Whigs refrain from making presidential nominations until a state convention could be held.[34] Such a convention met in December, and Harrison and Tyler were nominated. In 1836, for the first time since 1792, the electors were chosen from the state at

33. (Washington) *National Intelligencer*, Oct. 1, 1834.
34. *Ibid.*, Mar. 26, July 11, 1835; Niles' *Register*, XLVIII, 63.

large. The Whigs used conventions in each district to name electors, with two-electors-at-large being appointed by the Whig legislative caucus.[35] The Democrats held a state convention in Baltimore on May 18, 1836, to approve the nomination of Van Buren and Johnson and name their electoral ticket. The election resulted in a victory for the Whigs by a safe margin; nearly 68 per cent of the adult white males voted.

In the years after 1836 Whigs and Democrats continued to vie for control of the state until the American party supplanted the Whigs in 1855. The party balance remained close. After 1838, when the governorship became elective by popular vote every three years, the Democrats won the office consistently except in 1844. In presidential contests, however, the Whigs did not meet defeat until 1852. Voter participation remained high, reaching peaks of 85 per cent in the presidential election of 1840 and 81 per cent in the gubernatorial election of 1844. Voting in presidential elections tended to be slightly higher than in state elections. The long-established convention system, based on the election districts and the counties, continued to function effectively and the state convention acquired additional functions and importance when the state became a unit for the election of a governor and presidential electors.

Far too little is known about Maryland politics; consequently any generalizations about party formation in that state have to be limited to the meager evidence available.[36] It is

35. (Washington) *National Intelligencer,* Dec. 29, 1835.
36. After this section had been written, M. H. Haller's excellent article, "The Rise of the Jackson Party in Maryland, 1820-1829," appeared in the *Journal of Southern History,* XXVIII (Aug., 1962), 307-26. His findings, happily, corroborated my own investigations, and I concur with his interpretations. The Jackson party in Maryland, Haller found, "grew primarily out of practical political needs, out of the search for alliances and for office by displaced politicians, and out of the external pressures created by the formation of national parties dedicated to Andrew Jackson and John Quincy Adams. The Maryland Jackson party developed primarily as a coalition of dissident politicians, composed of former Federalist leaders, personal followers of John C. Calhoun, Republican followers of William H. Crawford, and ambitious younger politicians. Jackson leaders in Maryland, as they were painfully aware, had no distinctive economic issues or legislative program to rally their supporters; instead, they argued that Jackson and his followers possessed superior personal

quite clear, however, that the state had a long tradition of two-party politics before 1824 and that new party alignments, related to the contest between Jackson and Adams for the presidency, had been formed by 1827. The easy transition from the old party system to the new seems to have been facilitated by the readiness with which former Federalists and former Republicans laid aside ancient animosities and amalgamated in the new parties. Too, there was no Antimasonic enthusiasm to create a diversion. One of the most conspicuous and interesting features of politics in the state was the popular, and even entertaining, style of campaigning that enlivened elections. One receives the impression that if politics was regarded as sinful in New England and sordid in Pennsylvania, it was looked upon as a highly sociable activity in Maryland.

CONCLUSIONS

All of the Middle States entered the era of the second party system with a long background of experience in conducting politics on a two-party basis. There was, of course, wide variation in the durability of the original party alignments. The Federalists retained their dominance in Delaware until 1827 and were capable of challenging the Republicans in Maryland until 1818 and in New Jersey until 1815. They made their last bid for power in New York in 1816, and in Pennsylvania, although they never came close to obtaining a majority after 1800, they maintained some sense of identity until 1824.

Unlike their brethren in New England, the Federalists in the Middle States showed less disposition to "retire" from participation in politics once their party had been beaten. Instead they held doggedly on to control in certain counties,

---

qualifications for office. They were, in short, united chiefly in a desire to secure the victory of Old Hickory and of his loyal followers in Maryland."

as in New Jersey and Pennsylvania, or entered into alliances with dissident Republican factions, as in New York and Pennsylvania, or were sustained by the fading of old party identities, as in Maryland. In very general terms, the old Republican parties in New England retained their exclusiveness and their monopoly of political power until 1824, whereas in the Middle States, the Republicans had met various fates, ranging from near disintegration in Maryland through factionalism in Pennsylvania and new party formations in New York, to relative solidarity in Delaware and New Jersey.

The party situation in each of the Middle States in 1824, then, differed considerably, a circumstance that was to affect party formation in the Jackson era. Only in Delaware did the old parties continue to contest vigorously on a nearly equal basis. In New Jersey party distinctions survived, but the Federalists were a hopeless minority. Factionalism and amalgamation had all but destroyed parties in Pennsylvania, while in Maryland political identities had become ambiguous. New York presented the unique instance of new parties supplanting the old. One important consequence of the relative breakdown of the old party system in the Middle States was that new parties were not to form primarily from schisms in the Republican ranks, as in New England. In turn, the situation enabled former Federalists to play from the first a prominent role in the leadership of the new parties and especially—outside of New York—in the new Jackson party.

Parties had acquired extensive organization after 1800 in all the Middle States, but nowhere was the organization as highly centralized at the state level as in New England nor was the legislative caucus so powerful. These differences could largely be attributed to the fact that the state was generally less important as a political unit in the Middle States. Forms of party organization varied, but in every state the delegate-convention system was operative for nominations below the state level, with the township as the primary unit in New York, New Jersey, and Pennsylvania, the hundred in Delaware, and the election district in Maryland. The state convention was established in New Jersey in 1800 and in Delaware two years later. The legislative caucus gave way to the state convention in Pennsylvania between 1817 and 1824 and in New York in 1824. Maryland, with no state-wide elections after 1792, lacked either the state convention or caucus. The differences in the structures of party organization from state to state is explainable largely in terms of differences in the structures of government. Except in Delaware and Maryland, the Federalists seem to have been less attentive to organization than their opponents, although whether this neglect was attributable to their supposed aristocratic scruples or to other factors—such as their lack of federal or state patronage and their minority position—it is difficult to judge. The relative importance of patronage in the Middle States, as compared with New England, can scarcely be evaluated on the basis of the available evidence, but it would appear that especially in New Jersey and Pennsylvania, and conspicuously in New York, avidity for the spoils of office exerted a powerful influence in politics.

In the Middle States, as in New England, interparty contests in elections had produced high levels of voter participation, although—unlike New England—these levels were to be surpassed in the post-1824 era. In all of the states except New York, where the suffrage was restricted until 1822, there were elections in which 70 per cent, or more of the adult white males voted. Delaware produced consistently large turnouts of voters, followed in order by Maryland, Pennsylvania, New Jersey, and New York. In general, there was a direct relationship between the closeness of party competition and the size of the vote. Voting in presidential elections, for obvious reasons, tended to be lower than in state or county elections, especially after 1812. There was not in the Middle States the abrupt shrinkage of the vote that occurred in New England with the collapse of Federalist opposition because, as has been explained, the Federalists in the Middle States did not "collapse" or retire.

The revival of the contest for the presidency in 1824 had a very different political impact in the Middle States than it did in the New England. In New England the old Republican party had survived and was dominant, and it gave overwhelming support to its sectional favorite, John Quincy Adams. In the Middle States the party situation was much more complicated and varied and there was no sectional favorite.   In New York and Delaware, where electors were chosen by the legislature, Crawford was the major opponent of Adams but there was no immediate realignment of parties on the issue. In Pennsylvania involved political circumstances produced overwhelming support for Jackson against weak and divided opposition, but the resultant Jackson party had one dimension in presidential elections and quite another in state elections. There was in Maryland a marked polarization of the electorate behind either Adams or Jackson, but the election did not create new party identities.   Even in New Jersey, where the election produced as clear and as even division as in any state, old party designations survived.   Although Jackson was decidedly the popular favorite only in Pennsylvania, there was no strong manifestation of enthusiasm for any of the other candidates. The apathy, and doubtless the indecision, of the electorate was reflected in the low voter turnout (Pennsylvania, 20 per cent; New Jersey, 31 per cent; Maryland, 54 per cent).

By 1828 the party situation had changed dramatically. Adams and Jackson parties contended on nearly an equal basis —except in Pennsylvania—and voter participation was extremely high. The new party formations dated from 1826 in New Jersey and from 1827 in Delaware and Maryland. In each of those three states the parties were from the first closely balanced in strength and were similarly aligned in both state and national elections. A Jackson party coalesced in Pennsylvania in 1824, but there was no real opposition party until 1829, when the Antimasons assumed that role. For the next decade the National-Republican-Whigs remained a minor party, and the Antimasons included in their ranks most of those who were opposed to both the state and national Democratic administrations. Pennsylvania remained heavily Democratic—or Jacksonian—in national elections until 1836, but in state elections there was less disparity between the strength of the parties. In New York, new party formations had come into being by 1820, with Bucktails pitted against Clintonians. The Bucktails became Jacksonians late in 1827; the Clintonians, though less well united, continued in opposition as Adams men, National Republicans, and Antimasons. Not until the demise of the Antimasons in 1834 did the opposition elements assume a common identity under the Whig label. But the opposition, whatever its description, was able to offer severe competition to the Bucktail-Democratic party in both state and presidential elections throughout.

There exists a strong presumption that the new party identities assumed in 1828, before the emerging national parties had begun to acquire distinctive philosophies and policies, tended to persist for more than two decades. This conclusion is suggested in part by the obvious stability of the balance between the parties after 1828 and in part by a study of election statistics and contemporary observations. There were many notable shifts in the allegiance of political leaders, especially between 1834 and 1837, and there were minor party realignments in some localities, but there was no major readjustment of party loyalties, except perhaps in Pennsylvania, where parties did not become stabilized until around 1836.

In no other section of the nation were party lines drawn more closely than in the Middle States. The average margin between the percentages of the votes obtained by the presidential candidates of the major parties in the elections of 1828 through 1844 was 10, 5, 5, 5, and 2 as compared with the nationwide figures of 36, 33, 11, 11, and 9. To put it differently, the winning candidate received more than 53 per cent of the popular vote once in New York, never in New Jersey, twice in Pennsylvania, once in Delaware, and twice in Maryland. Except for Pennsylvania before 1836, all were "doubtful" states, although Maryland, Delaware, and New Jersey tended to be Whig and Pennsylvania and New York tended to be Democratic.

Just as was the case with New England, so also in the Middle States there was a marked tendency for the section to swing as a unit in the same direction in presidential elections. The Democrats were weaker in every state—except New York—in 1836 than they had been in 1832, and the general decline continued in 1840. Democratic gains were registered in every state in 1844, but the trend was reversed in 1848. The Whigs carried every state in 1848 but lost every state in 1852. The shifts in party balance, as has already been noted, were not considerable—usually not more than a few percentage points— but they are clearly discernible and they exerted an important effect on the outcome of national elections. Because of the evenly matched strength of the parties, the Middle States were truly the political balance wheel of the nation. Why were parties so conspicuously well balanced in this section? Many answers might be offered, but for the present it might suffice to suggest that this was the section to which national parties "accommodated," rather than to New England, the South, or the West.

The intensity of interparty competition, as might be expected, produced a very high rate of voter participation. Roughly speaking, 70 per cent of the adult white males voted in 1828, and although there was a slight falling off in the two succeeding presidential contests, the average soared to over 80 per cent in 1840 and remained close to that level in 1844. For the section as a whole, of course, the pre-1840 figures were not exceptional when compared with participation during the years before 1824. It was in 1840 that the dimensions of the electorate suddenly expanded to unprecedented proportions. In general, interest in state elections approximated that in national elections, although Pennsylvania tended to produce higher turnouts for state elections until 1840 and New Jersey manifested greater activity in presidential years.

Forms of party organization underwent relatively little change after 1828. The state-convention system had been well established in New Jersey and Delaware long before that date and was an accepted feature of the Pennsylvania scene by 1824. New York abandoned the legislative caucus in favor of the convention in 1824 and Maryland held its first state convention in 1827. Although Pennsylvania was notorious for the laxity of its party discipline, strong leadership groups—like the Regency in New York, the Clayton machine in Delaware, or the "little Regency" in New Jersey—dominated party affairs.

One receives the general impression that the parties were managed very largely by office-holders, who assumed a highly businesslike attitude toward their tasks and who had a strong vested interest in party politics. The extent to which party conventions, for example, were made up of office-holders could only be ascertained through prodigious research, but it must have been very considerable, judging from contemporary comments. The reputation that politicians in the Middle States had acquired much earlier for being avid seekers after patronage, as well as for venality, was enhanced in the Jackson era.

Campaign techniques became increasingly theatrical. Political speeches by candidates, which had become a common practice in Maryland before 1800, spread slowly to other states, although the Democratic candidate for governor in Pennsylvania was regarded as having broken a precedent when he went on the stump in 1847. New York experienced what may be regarded as the first of the new-style spectacular campaigns in 1834, when the Whigs stirred up extraordinary excitement in behalf of Seward. Everywhere, by 1840, old restraints had been abandoned and mass enthusiasm was stimulated by every imaginable device, including parades, rallies, barbecues, tireless orators, cabin raisings, and hard cider, or its equivalent.

To what extent did the party identities that had become established by 1828 represent a continuance of loyalties acquired during the period of the first party system? The available evidence indicates that in New York and Delaware old alignments persisted, with the New York "Bucktails" and the Delaware Republicans becoming Jacksonians. Elsewhere the situation is less simple, partly because the old party identities had become blurred before 1824. In New Jersey, where the dominant Republican party split in 1826 into Adams and Jackson wings and where numerous Federalists assumed positions of prominence in the Jackson cause, there was obviously much shuffling of allegiances. In Maryland and Pennsylvania, too, although by a somewhat different process, it would appear that former political adversaries found themselves allied in behalf of either Jackson or Adams. In contrast to New England, where former Federalists generally were denied opportunities for political leadership—especially within the Jackson party—the Middle States adhered to no such practice of proscription. In New Jersey, Pennsylvania, Delaware, and Maryland, such former Federalists as Vroom, Buchanan, McLane, and Taney were representative of large numbers of their brethren who found in the Jackson cause a long-awaited chance to move to the center of the political stage.

CHAPTER V

PARTY FORMATION
IN THE
OLD SOUTH

Turning from a consideration of England and the Middle States to what can be styled the Old South —Virginia, North Carolina, Kentucky, Tennessee, and Georgia —one immediately becomes aware of certain characteristics that, at least for the purposes of political analysis, defined the region. Overwhelmingly rural, predominantly agricultural, more or less dependent on slave labor, and largely immune to the economic and demographic changes that influenced the northern states, the Old South had a style of politics that reflected both inherited tradition and contemporary social realities. It had, as well, a particular set of concerns about its place within the nation that were to exert profound effects upon the formation of its parties. Again, however, it is necessary to observe that despite general similarities, each state could be regarded as a special case, with attributes that marked it off decidedly from the others.

Except in Virginia and North Carolina, the first party system had never become well-established in the region, and even in those two states it had all but disintegrated by 1824. Having had little or no experience with two-party politics, or with the operation of elaborate party machinery, the Old South entered the era of the second party system with a very different background from the states to the north. Southern politics retained a strong flavor of localism and personalism. Because

177

the state was much less important as a unit of political action than was the county and because partisan identities were of slight importance in most election contests, candidates for office relied on their personal appeal and on their connections with men of influence in their constituencies. Politics could therefore be managed with a minimum of formal machinery.

The revival of the contest for the presidency, which soon stimulated the formation of parties in the Middle States and New England, did not have a comparable effect on the Old South—except for Kentucky—until after 1832. Not until after Jackson had been re-elected and the question of who might succeed him had come to the fore did the monolithic character of southern politics suddenly crack. Cleavages appeared in state after state in 1834, and by 1836 there were two parties everywhere. These parties were defined most obviously by their attitudes toward Van Buren.

Even after the new alignments had formed and politics was conducted on the basis of contests between fairly well matched parties, southern practices remained distinctive. The parties were slow to adopt the extensive organization of their northern counterparts, and major political figures retained an unusual degree of freedom from party discipline. The new alignments, however, proved to be remarkably durable and evenly balanced for the two succeeding decades.

VIRGINIA

Virginia, the oldest and most stable political community in the United States, was remarkable for the simplicity of its governmental and political institutions. For reasons which are so well known that they need not be recapitulated here, the state had inherited from its colonial past an ordering of political relationships among socio-economic groups that persisted

at least through the first half of the nineteenth century. Political privileges were confined to the freeholders, and office
holding and the control of political affairs was largely the
prerogative of the landed gentry, who held distinctly aristocratic concepts about their role. In no state were conventional
democratic procedures and beliefs more firmly resisted, or
with greater success.

The Virginia Constitution of 1776 vested virtually complete governmental authority in a two-house legislature, elected on the basis of a severely restricted franchise. The House
of Delegates, made up of two delegates from each county and
one each from the cities of Norfolk and Williamsburg, was
elected annually. The Senate contained twenty-four members
elected from districts; one-fourth of the members were chosen
at each annual election. The legislature elected a governor
annually, together with a small advisory Council of State, and
appointed the higher judicial officers.

The suffrage was restricted to freeholders possessed—after
1785—of fifty acres of unimproved, or twenty-five acres of improved, land, although more liberal provisions were made for
voters in the two cities. Precise studies of the effects of these
suffrage restrictions are lacking, but it would appear that at
least half of the adult white males were disfranchised. Voting
was *viva voce*, except in presidential elections after 1800. The
county was the polling unit, a factor that operated to restrict
the exercise of the franchise because in numerous counties vast
distances made access to the single poll difficult. The same
circumstance also had the effect of giving undue weight to
those living in or near the county seat. Because residence was
not a requirement, it was possible for a man who had freeholds
in more than one county to cast more than one vote. Such
plural voting was facilitated by the fact that before 1830 the
April state elections were held on different court days in each
county. Congressmen were invariably elected from districts,
but presidential electors were chosen from the state-at-large
beginning in 1800.

There were no elective officials below the state level, except in the cities. The county courts, made up of the justices of the peace, were in practice self-perpetuating bodies, as were also the vestries, which exercised limited authority in local matters. Sheriffs and coroners, usually drawn from the personnel of the county courts, were appointed by the governor. The court, because of its wide powers and the great prestige of its members as well as because of the stability of its personnel, was the focal center of Virginia politics. Recruited from the leading men of the county, from its ranks were drawn the principal civil and military officials and most legislators as well. Because they did not owe their office to popular election, the members of the court enjoyed unusual independence and occupied a secure base from which to conduct their political operations.

The basic constitutional structure was not fundamentally altered until 1851. Two features, however, were subjects of controversy for many decades. The system of apportionment in both houses of the legislature discriminated against the increasingly populous western area of the state and produced insistent demands for reform. In 1816 a modest revision of the senatorial districts did little to allay western discontent, and the problem continued to create sectional antagonisms after the unsatisfactory adjustments made by the constitution of 1831. At that time, unable to agree on any one of several proposed formulas, the convention arbitrarily reapportioned both houses but did so in such a way as to continue eastern dominance. A second issue was suffrage reform. Increasingly after 1815 there were petitions from the large disfranchised segment of the population for an extension of the suffrage. The constitution of 1831 produced a redefinition of voting requirements that was so complex as to be unintelligible, but it did confer the franchise on certain non-freeholders, most particularly, leaseholders and householders. This change increased the electorate appreciably but probably left about one-third of the adult white males still voteless. Not until 1851 did Virginia finally adopt adult white male suffrage.

Many circumstances, therefore, combined to give Virginia a singularly simple, or at least not highly organized, style of politics. A limited franchise, a social structure dominated by recognizable gentry families, an oligarchic local governmental system, a paucity of elected officials—all these factors rendered complex party organization unnecessary, as did the simplicity of the electoral system. There was little need for local party organization both because the county court members and their connections were equipped to manage party affairs in an informal manner and because the only officials to be elected at the county level were the delegates. There was little incentive, either, for the development of an elaborate organization at the state level, for only in presidential years were there state-wide elections. Within senatorial and congressional districts, party matters could be arranged by consultations among prominent men.

There was relatively little, then, in the way of formal party machinery—of the type found in the northern states, for example—but this does not mean that parties did not exist. Rather, party management was carried out by informal arrangements within the small but active group that provided political leadership in each locality and throughout Virginia as a whole. Again, because of the essential simplicity of the electoral system and the well-ordered nature of Virginia society, such informal devices could be effective.

Although the elite group that dominated Virginia politics had much in common in the way of social background, economic standing, and aristocratic concepts, they were not in agreement on political issues, a fact that was abundantly illustrated in the early years of the new federal government. There had been strong differences of opinion over the merits of the constitution, and comparable differences over public policy after 1789 provided the basis for a loose, and constantly shifting, two-party alignment. Within the legislature, and in the contests for congressional seats, politicians took positions for, or in opposition to, the policies of the national administration. Obviously, the presence in Virginia of such figures as Jefferson and Madison on one side and Washington, Henry, and Marshall on the other gave special significance to the controversy. By 1795, when party designations had assumed some clarity of definition, the Federalists were in a minority position, with strong bases of support in both the Tidewater and the Shenandoah Valley. The party was able to win only one electoral vote for Adams in 1796, but in the succeeding three years it maintained and even increased its strength. It constituted sufficient menace to the dominant Republicans, at least, to occasion a change in the method of choosing electors from the district to the general-ticket system, a move designed to insure that Jefferson would receive all of the state's electoral votes in 1800. Jefferson, in fact, obtained nearly 80 per cent of the popular vote.

Federalism lingered on after 1800, and with the emergence of the "Quid" faction in the Republican party, there were prospects of a Federalist revival after 1807. Co-operating in opposing the election of Madison in 1808 and in state and congressional elections in subsequent years, the odd alliance kept party strife alive in the state. But the Quids were virtually eliminated from the scene in 1813, and by 1816 the remnant of Federalists, now chiefly confined to the Valley, gave up what had become a hopeless contest. After that date, party contests as such were non-existent. A new generation of political leaders, all nominally committed to the Republican party and espousing doctrines of "Old Republicanism" in opposition to the nationalist philosophy represented by Clay and Calhoun, held sway in national politics. In state politics issues associated with constitutional reform, internal improvements, and economic readjustments absorbed interest and frequently produced sectional alignments in the legislature. To all appearance, Virginia had become a one-party state.

The challenge presented by the Federalists had resulted,

however, in the creation of a device for state-wide party management that merits examination. The need for such a device became apparent when the legislature provided for the choice of presidential electors by general ticket in 1800. Some method had to be devised for producing agreement on a party slate of electors. Accordingly, on January 21, 1800, ninety-three Republican members of the Virginia legislature and other "respectable citizens" met at the capitol in Richmond and adopted an electoral ticket. In addition, they established a "General Standing Committee" of five members and appointed corresponding committees for each county. The central committee communicated with the county committees by means of circular letters, issuing detailed instructions about the preparation of written ballots that were to be used for the first time in the state.[1] The Federalists, meanwhile, adopted a similar plan of organization.

By 1808, when the regular Republican supporters of Madison were faced with opposition from both Republican and Federalist adherents of Monroe, the caucus machinery had become well developed. In preparation for the impending election a meeting of about 120 legislators favorable to Madison was held on the evening of January 21, 1808, at the Bell Tavern in Richmond with Robert Taylor, speaker of the Senate, as chairman and Thomas Ritchie, editor of the *Richmond Enquirer,* as secretary.[2] An electoral slate was prepared, with legislators from each congressional district proposing nominees. A permanent corresponding committee of five was then appointed. All five—William Foushee, Sr., Peyton Randolph, Samuel Pleasants, Jervas Storrs, and Ritchie—were residents of Richmond and vicinity. Subsequently Abraham B. Venable was added to the committee and John H. Foushee was named as treasurer. The caucus appointed a three-man cor-

1. The proceedings of this important caucus, one of the earliest of which we have detailed knowledge, may be found in *Calendar of Virginia State Papers,* ed. by W. P. Palmer, *et al.* (11 vols.; Richmond, 1875-1893), IX, 74-78.

2. The course of politics in 1808 may be traced in detail in the *Richmond Enquirer,* Jan. 23–Nov. 1, 1808.

responding committee for each county, again on the nomination of local legislators. These committees, which were later augmented to seven members, usually included at least one legislator. Additional meetings of the caucus to complete arrrangements for the campaign were held on January 28 and February 4.

In the months that followed, the central committee issued circular letters to the county committees urging that every effort be made to turn out a large vote for Madison and instructing them to prepare written electoral ballots equal to the total number of voters in each county. The Monroe partisans, in caucuses held on January 23 and 25, made similar preparations. The Federalists were divided. One wing, with leadership provided from Augusta County, valiantly put forth a ticket pledged to support Pinckney and King and sought to correspond with other Federalist committees in the state. The Richmond Federalists, on the other hand, decided to back Monroe and broadcast an address in his behalf. In the course of the campaign the Madisonian county committees were active in sponsoring mass meetings, at which appropriate resolutions were adopted in support of the candidate. Madison scored an extremely lopsided victory over Monroe; the vote for the Federalist ticket was negligible.

The Richmond Junto, with Ritchie's *Enquirer* as its organ, played a prominent role in Virginia politics.[3] Its personnel changed, but the loose organization under its direction was not altered substantially for forty years. Despite the vicissitudes of state politics and the constant shifting of intraparty

3. Considerable mystery still shrouds the operation of the Richmond Junto, but Harry Ammon has revealed something of its membership and mode of operation. The Junto, which was not called by that name until 1823, included from fifteen to twenty men, most of whom resided in the eastern counties and made Richmond their headquarters. Knit together by family and business relationships, this group exerted great influence on the Republican caucus and effectively dictated the choice of the central committee, through which it controlled the party apparatus. The leader of the Junto in the early years was William Cary Nicholas, and he was succeeded by Spencer Roane. Harry Ammon, "The Richmond Junto, 1800-1824," *The Virginia Magazine of History and Biography*, LXI (1953), 395-418.

factional alignments, the Junto was a factor of continuity in the Republican party, and under its guidance the party rallied together every four years to support its choice for the presidency. Ritchie's influence in party affairs has never been fully assessed, but it would appear to have been considerable. His talents were usually devoted to conciliation and to maintaining cordial relations with New York and Pennsylvania Republican leaders, a strategy to which he was to adhere—despite opposition from ultra elements in the Virginia party—after 1824. It was also Ritchie's policy to try to occupy a middle ground between the extremes of state rights and positive nationalism, and here again he encountered difficulties after 1824.

It would not be correct to liken the Richmond Junto to Van Buren's Regency, for the Virginia Republican party lacked the cohesion and discipline of the New York Bucktails. Virginia politicians, because of the very nature of the state's political and social structure, were far more individualistic and independent of organizational control than the New York breed. Moreover, the efforts of the Junto were directed largely toward national politics, whereas the Bucktails were more involved with state politics. Actually the Virginia scheme of party organization found its closest counterpart, of all places, in Massachusetts, whose centralized Federalist machine might well have served as a model for the Junto's apparatus.

The lack of serious competition between parties, the restrictive suffrage requirements, and the general inaccessibility of the polling places made for remarkably low voter participation, at least in presidential elections.[4] The contest between

4. During a debate in the House of Delegates in 1830 on a bill to establish a separate election district in Franklin County, one legislator detailed his objections to the proposal. It was, he contended, a general principle that candidates should be present at the polls in order that they might explain their views to the people. They could not meet this obligation if there were two polling places in their constituency. Moreover, if people could travel to the court house on business, they could get there to vote. A proponent of the measure explained that the residents of the proposed district were sixteen to eighteen miles from the court house. There were about 150 voters, of whom

Jefferson and Adams in 1800 brought only a quarter of the adult white males to the polls, and this was the highest participation registered until 1828. Fewer than 18 per cent of the adult white males voted in 1808 and 1812, and in the two succeeding elections the vote fell to 6 per cent and 4 per cent. In no other state were the effects of apathy and a restricted franchise quite so apparent.

State elections, and especially contests for seats in the House of Delegates, aroused far more interest than did presidential elections and frequently brought most of the eligible electors to the polls. Indeed, judging from the large number of cases of disputed elections, often involving the charge that unqualified persons were allowed to vote, heated campaigns might produce a turnout that exceeded the number of legal voters. Campaign methods remained essentially unaltered from those employed in the late eighteenth century, which were so admirably described by Charles Sydnor in his *Gentleman Freeholders* and in Robert Munford's delightful play, *The Candidates*. Candidates offered themselves for election and—with their connections—solicited votes according to a code of etiquette that proscribed political speeches but condoned the old practice of treating the voters who came to the polls. Mass meetings were used occasionally, not for the purpose of making nominations but to adopt resolutions on issues of the moment. Polling procedures reminiscent of practices in vogue at county elections in Elizabethan England made for colorful and lively scenes, with the candidates and their retinues in attendance and the body of freeholders following the state of the poll as each voter's choice was announced. What influences were exerted on the voter as a result of the fact that his vote was given orally can only be surmised, but the practice was appropriate to the Virginia style of politics.

With the approach of the presidential election of 1824, the

only 15 or 20 customarily voted; "the rest," he said, "were completely disfranchised by the inconveniences of their situation." The bill passed. *Richmond Enquirer*, Dec. 16, 1830.

long subdued interest in national politics began to revive. The Virginia Republican party held the allegiance of virtually all of the politically active men in the state, but, as has already been mentioned, the party had only a rudimentary organization and included within its broad ranks political figures of considerable independence and great disparity of views. The one feature that gave the Republicans some sense of unity and continuity was the quadrennial caucus to determine the party's stand on the presidency and reconstitute the central committee and its subordinate county committees of correspondence. In the early calculations regarding the most acceptable successor to Monroe, Crawford and Adams were the men most frequently mentioned. Clay, Jackson, and Calhoun had little backing, especially among leading politicians.

The campaign really got under way when in October, 1823, Ritchie's *Enquirer* declared its support for Crawford, hailing him as the candidate whose political philosophy was most in line with the "Old Republican" states-right creed espoused by the Virginia party. The Adams cause, whose chief local advocate was Senator James Barbour, initially commanded wide sympathy, especially in the western counties, but as the campaign proceeded, sentiment for Jackson began to develop in the same area. Clay's support was not extensive, and Calhoun, because of his nationalist sentiments, never acquired a following. The lack of unity within the old party was revealed in January, 1824, when the legislators met in caucus to decide, in effect, whether Virginia's congressmen should participate in the proposed congressional caucus, already under severe attack. More than a fourth of the legislators, most of them from the western counties, remained aloof from the meeting, which proceeded to endorse the congressional caucus and—by implication —the nomination of Crawford.

After the thinly attended caucus in Washington had placed Crawford in nomination, the Virginia caucus reconvened on February 25, adopted an electoral slate pledged to Crawford, appointed a ten-man central committee, and named corresponding committees for each county. Again, however, 73 out of 236 eligible legislators, most of whom were partial to Adams or Jackson, did not participate in the caucus. In the months that followed, the machinery directed by the Junto worked in the traditional manner to advance the interests of its candidate. The adherents of Adams, Jackson, and Clay, laboring under obvious disadvantages, attempted to weld together campaign organizations based on corresponding committees and popular mass meetings. In the final months before the election there were efforts to unite all of the anti-Crawford, or anti-Junto, forces behind a single electoral ticket, but the fusion movement was unsuccessful. The election itself attracted surprisingly little interest. Fewer than 12 per cent of the adult white males voted, which was the lowest voter participation of any state. Crawford won with 56 per cent of the popular vote; Adams was second, closely followed by Jackson; and Clay received only negligible support. Jackson's strength was greatest in the southwestern counties; Adams ran best in the western counties.

The election of 1824 ended the none too substantial solidarity of the Virginia Republican party, but it did not provide a lasting basis for new party alignments. For the next decade at least, and really until 1837, there was considerable fluidity in the party situation, with frequent shifts of allegiance by prominent political figures and blocs of the electorate. The one constantly stable factor throughout this period was the unswerving loyalty of Ritchie, the Junto, and the major portion of the Republican caucus to Jackson and subsequently to Van Buren. Otherwise, the composition, leadership, and philosophies of the parties in any particular year varied depending upon the identity of the presidential candidates, the dominant issues of the moment, and the relationships among rival political chieftains. This fluidity was especially characteristic of the years down to 1834, by which time the foundations had been laid for the Whig party. Virginia parties, it may be noted again, lacked the disciplined character of parties in most northern states.

With Adams installed in the presidency and Crawford eliminated as a possible future candidate, the Junto seemingly was confronted with a bleak prospect. It was soon apparent from the tone of Ritchie's *Enquirer* that there could be no thought of endorsing Adams. On the other hand, long behind-the-scenes negotiations with the erstwhile supporters of Jackson, Crawford, and Calhoun in other states continued for over two years before Ritchie and his associates were prepared to join openly in the coalition that was to put Jackson in the White House. The general did not commend himself strongly to the conservative Virginia political community, but he seemed to be the only alternative to Adams. It was presumably the assurances received from Van Buren during his visit to the state in the spring of 1827 that prompted the *Enquirer* to come out for Jackson in April, 1827.

The Adams forces, lacking the cohesion and traditional authority of the Junto, found it difficult to organize. They included in their ranks only a small minority—possibly one quarter—of the members of the legislature and could not, therefore, legitimately use a legislative caucus as the authentic voice of the party. They turned, instead to a state convention. The proposal for such a gathering apparently originated in King George's County, where a meeting of Adams adherents on September 18, 1827, proposed that all who were opposed to Jackson throughout the state should meet at their county court houses on the first day of the November court session and appoint delegates to convene in Richmond on the first Tuesday in January for the purpose of preparing an electoral ticket and making arrangements for the campaign.[5] Other counties took up the proposal and soon "Anti-Jackson" meetings were being held in numerous counties, especially in the Valley and the West. In October an Adams committee was

5. (Washington) *National Intelligencer,* Sept. 26, 1827.

chosen in Richmond, which undertook to make local arrangements for the convention.

On the appointed day some two hundred delegates, representing most of the counties, met in the capitol in Richmond for Virginia's first state political convention.[6] During the course of the five-day session, the convention agreed on an electoral slate, headed by Madison and Monroe, resolved to support Adams and Rush, and adopted a lengthy address, thirty thousand copies of which were ordered to be printed. A central corresponding committee was appointed and was authorized to name corresponding committees for those counties which had not, through public meetings, already created such bodies. In the campaign that ensued, the Adams central committee worked against heavy odds in behalf of its candidates and was highly critical of the governor for appointing as commissioners of elections in each county none but Jackson adherents. To counteract anticipated partiality at the polls, large "vigilance committees" were to be selected in each county.[7]

The Junto-Jackson party was induced to modify its customary procedures and hold a mixed caucus-convention. This move was dictated in part by mounting criticism of the caucus system and in part by the fact that several western counties whose legislators were hostile to Jackson, would not be represented in a pure caucus. Accordingly, such counties were invited to send delegates to sit with the party's legislators. With Thomas Ritchie in his habitual role of secretary, the "legislative convention" assembled on January 13 and completed its labors three days later. Jackson and Calhoun were formally endorsed as candidates, an electoral ticket was named, and the usual central committee and county committees were appointed. A motion that the central committee be requested

6. In 1812 a Federalist convention met in Staunton and nominated an electoral ticket, but only eighteen counties were represented. (Raleigh) *Star*, Oct. 9, 1812.

7. *The Virginia Address* [n.p., n.d.]; Niles' *Register*, XXXIII, 333.

to prepare an address to the people was, for unexplained reasons, defeated.[8]

The election gave Jackson, who secured 70 per cent of the vote, an easy victory. Adams had his greatest strength in western Virginia and along the Potomac, areas that were deeply interested in the internal improvements issue. The Tidewater and Piedmont, strongholds of conservative views, went heavily for Jackson. Despite its one-sidedness, the election had created sufficient interest to send voter participation up to nearly 28 per cent of the adult white males, exceeding the previous high set in 1800. If a contemporary estimate that there were about forty-five thousand legally qualified voters in the state is correct, then over 85 per cent of the eligibles went to the polls.

The Junto-Jacksonian party seemed to be in an impregnable position following the election, but as the new national administration pursued its troubled course in Washington, opposition mounted in Virginia. Attacks came from two very different sources. The mildly nationalist westerners, who had backed Adams in 1828, provided the base for a weak Clay party and found allies in the commercial centers of Richmond and Norfolk. More disquieting was the attitude of numerous influential political leaders of the state-rights school, who did not venture to focus their attack on Jackson but who took a strong stand in opposition to his northern heir apparent, Martin Van Buren. Ritchie was conscious of the need to hold a middle ground between the nationalists of the west and the eastern localists; he was also apprehensive of a possible alliance between the two extremes. Accordingly, he and his associated party leaders sought to avoid a sharp cleavage on the Van Buren issue. Three party caucuses that were held between December, 1831, and March, 1832, readily endorsed Jackson for renomination but could reach no agreement on the vice-presidency. At the Democratic National Convention in May,

8. *Ibid.*, XXXIII, 334, 357. This "legislative convention," as it was called, was attended by 170 members of the legislature and 23 special deputies. It was thus more of a caucus than a convention.

the large Virginia delegation cast its vote for a local son, P. P. Barbour.

Subsequently a small Jackson-Barbour Convention assembled at Charlottesville and accepted the electoral ticket that had been regularly named by the party caucus but proposed an elaborate plan whereby the electors would be pledged to vote for whichever vice-presidential candidate received the most votes in an informal referendum at the time of the election. When the electors, who were ostensibly not committed to a particular vice-presidential candidate, refused to agree to the scheme, the Barbour group appointed its own electoral slate. Their candidate, however, who was soon to be appointed to the Supreme Court, announced his withdrawal from the contest at the end of October, and the effort was frustrated. The Barbour movement was extremely significant, for in that it represented a potent state-rights, anti-Van Buren sentiment within the Jackson party, it forecast the explosion that was to take place in 1834. The movement was not confined to Virginia; it had considerable strength in North Carolina, South Carolina, and Alabama as well.

The Clay party possessed little in the way of party machinery nor was it fortified by any hope of success. Delegates to the Baltimore National Republican Convention were appointed by local assemblages in such centers of Clay enthusiasm as Winchester, Norfolk, and Richmond, and a state convention met at Staunton in July to adopt an electoral ticket. But Clay failed to equal the vote that Adams had received and Jackson substantially increased the size of his majority, winning nearly three-quarters of the popular vote and carrying all but seven counties. Despite the expansion of the suffrage that had been granted under the new state constitution, voter participation rose only slightly. The election did not provide an accurate reflection of political sentiment in the state, for—with the withdrawal of Barbour—there was no opportunity for the anti-Van Buren feeling to manifest itself. The Junto, by skillful maneuvering, had won another easy victory, but there were to be no more such lopsided triumphs in the years ahead.

The coalition of extremes that Ritchie had feared took place in 1833, and the Jackson party found itself confronted with an opposition that, although lacking in cohesion, could unite at least in attacking "executive usurpation" and the succession of Van Buren to the presidency. Jackson's reaction to South Carolina's nullification of the tariff of 1832 was an important factor in causing the latent antagonism of state-rights leaders to burst forth. The removal of the deposits invigorated the Clayite, pro-nationalist elements to renew their attack on the administration. Both groups could agree on the wickedness of the chief executive's action in the removal incident, and they joined together in the legislature to pass a resolution condemning the action. W. C. Rives, who upheld Jackson's policies, was forced to resign from the Senate and the coalition replaced him with Benjamin Watkins Leigh, the idol of the eastern, state-rights faction. In the 1834 state elections the Jacksonians lost control of the legislature to the Janus-like opposition, which now began to glory in the name of Whig. In 1835 the Democrats waged an all-out campaign, emphasizing the obvious incongruity of the Whig position, regained a majority in the legislature and soon forced Leigh and Tyler out of the Senate. The alignments that appeared in 1834 were to prove to be highly unstable, but from that year we can begin to date the recreation of a durable, competitive two-party situation.

As the presidential election of 1836 approached, the Democratic party, momentarily purged of its extreme state-rights wing, agreed, despite some misgivings, to back Van Buren. But when the eccentric Richard M. Johnson was nominated by the National Democratic Convention for the vice-presidency, the Virginia delegation rebelled and announced that it would under no circumstances support him. When the "legislative convention" of Jacksonian legislators and elected delegates met in Richmond on January 11, 1836, an electoral slate pledged to vote for Van Buren and William Smith of Alabama was adopted. At the same time, more than usual effort was devoted to perfecting the party's campaign machinery. By this time there were effective Democratic organizations in many counties, which had begun to assume the function of making local nominations; the county committees, however, were appointed as in the past by the legislative convention, which also reconstituted the state central committee.

The Whig opposition could agree on antagonism to Van Buren but on little else. A Whig legislative caucus, after serious disagreement between the two wings of the party, named an electoral ticket and endorsed Hugh L. White for the presidency but could reach no accord on his running mate. The western, nationalist wing of the party was unhappy with this decision, for they favored William Henry Harrison rather than White. They sponsored a convention at Staunton on July 4, attended by delegates from twenty counties, which endorsed the electoral slate that had been adopted at Richmond but labelled it "The Union Anti-Van Buren Harrison Ticket." As a concession to the eastern wing of the party, they announced support of John Tyler for the vice-presidency.

The Democratic party, with its superior organization and its claim to represent the continuation of the old Republican tradition, carried the state for Van Buren, but the discordant Whigs polled nearly 44 per cent of the popular vote. There was no sharp sectional pattern in the voting. About 35 per cent of the adult white males cast ballots.

The opposition to Van Buren, contrasted with the overwhelming support given to Jackson in 1832, was compounded of many factors. Perhaps the most important was that Van Buren was neither a southerner nor a hero. Virginia had never cast its electoral vote for a northern man, and the mere fact of Van Buren's candidacy afforded malcontents a basis for opposition. Also involved was antagonism to the dominant Junto clique, which was unable to please or appease all factions; concern about "executive Tyranny" and the abuse of power by the federal government; and discontent with specific policies of the Jackson administration. But it is difficult to avoid the conclusion that the Whig party emerged in Virginia when it did—and with such strength as it manifested—primarily because as a southern state, with southern fears and attitudes, the Old Dominion was reluctant to see a northern man in the presidency.

The disastrous business panic that hit the country early in Van Buren's administration and the president's insistence that Congress enact his independent treasury scheme created new grounds for controversy and provided the occasion for more shifts in party loyalties. A "conservative" faction, headed by W. C. Rives, emerged within the Democratic party and, after holding the balance of power for a time in state politics, moved into the Whig camp by 1840. At the same time such erstwhile state-rights Whigs as R. M. T. Hunter, L. W. Tazewell, and W. F. Gordon, perhaps in emulation of Calhoun, returned to the Democratic party. The party balance in state elections was extremely close; the Whigs secured a majority in the House of Delegates in 1838 and held it for four years, but neither party could rely on the firm support of its members. As the margin of strength between the parties narrowed, so, too, did the differences in their philosophies. Both Whigs and Democrats were now seeking support in all sections of the state and both embraced spokesmen of conflicting interests and viewpoints.

The Democratic party, threatened by the rising tide of Whiggery and by internal dissension, made extraordinary efforts to solidify its ranks for the state and congressional elections in 1839. Recognizing that a crisis existed, the Democratic caucus issued a call for a "convention of the friends of the present administration" to meet in Richmond in March, 1839. Each county, town, and borough was invited to send one or more delegates to join with members of the legislature. Ritchie's authoritative *Enquirer* stressed the urgency of the meeting. "We wish to animate and confirm our friends, and

convince them of the importance of the present crisis...,"
read the appeal, "to bring out strong men in all counties,
and secure concert of action—to reiterate and vindicate our
great principles—to counteract the designs of our political
opponents, who predicate their success on fomenting family
quarrels, and to agree upon measures which, if boldly and
vigorously pursued, will ensure us a decisive and glorious
triumph."[9]   The convention adopted a carefully worded address that was designed to woo the "Conservatives" and state-
rights men alike, but its effect was not apparent.   The Whigs
and "Conservatives" in the legislature also adopted addresses
to the voters.   In more areas of the state than ever before,
popular sanction was sought for party efforts by using delegate
conventions to nominate candidates for the legislature and for
Congress.   The old Virginia style of informal politics was giving way to new methods occasioned by the intensification of
interparty strife.

Preparations for the climactic presidential election of 1840
began early.   The Democrats, in accordance with what had
now become established custom, held a convention made up of
elected delegates and members of the legislature in February,
1840, with Ritchie still in his vital post of secretary.   An
electoral slate was named and the usual compaign apparatus
was created; but, in the interest of avoiding internal dissen-
sions over candidates, it was decided not to send a delegation
to the Democratic National Convention.   As the campaign
approached its final stage, the Democrats aped the flamboyant
Whigs by holding a state convention early in September at
Charlottesville, solely for the purpose of manifesting party
enthusiasm.   Over five hundred delegates attended, listened to
orators, and reported on prospects in their respective baliwicks.

The Whigs, though conscious of their own internal differences, approached the campaign with hope and ardor.   On
the recommendation of Whig Central Committee in Richmond, a state convention met at the Presbyterian Church in

9. *Ibid.,* LV, 375-76.

Staunton, September 25-26, 1839. This well-organized meeting resolved to send a delegation to the Whig National Convention and, while expressing a preference for Clay and N. P. Tallmadge of New York as the party's standard bearers, pledged its "hearty and zealous" support to whoever might be nominated. The spirit of the convention was exemplified when one delegate sought to have an address to the people adopted. He was quickly squelched, whereupon the president of the convention delivered a closing address in which he "invited the Whig party to 'sink or swim' with their principles, but never with men."[10] A second Whig state convention in February, 1840, adopted an electoral ticket, strengthened the party organization, and ordered printed fifty thousand copies of an address that praised Harrison and explained that the bank, the tariff, and internal improvements were no longer significant issues. Rather, excutive tyranny must be overthrown.

To manifest beyond doubt that a new era had arrived in Virginia politics, the Whigs held a "monster convention" in Richmond, October 5-6, which was reputedly attended by fifteen thousand people. The hero of the occasion was none other than Daniel Webster, who so charmed the multitudes with his dignity and oratorical powers that he was invited to deliver a special speech to the Whig ladies of Richmond at an evening meeting. On the second day of the festival W. C. Rives, a recently welcomed convert to the party, testified to his new faith in an address that lasted for four hours. All around the state old inhibitions vanished as campaign orators, log-cabin raisings, barbecues, conventions, and vigilance committees whipped up unprecedented popular excitement. Both parties were organized as they had never been before; the party committee was assuming the role so long filled by the gentry of the county court.

The election of 1840 signalized the maturing of the new political order that had been emerging since 1834. The in-

10. *Ibid.*, LVII, 125-27.

tensive efforts of the two sectionally balanced, well-organized parties were responsible for a 60 per cent increase in the size of the vote over that which had been cast in 1836. There could have been few eligible voters in the state who did not respond to the popularly expressed appeals of the Whigs or the Democrats. Nearly 55 per cent of the adult white males voted, as compared with 35 per cent in 1836. Van Buren eked out a victory by the margin of 1120 votes out of a total of over 86,000. But the election was significant mainly because it demonstrated that for the first time in its history, Virginia now possessed a competitive, well-balanced, two-party system. This condition of parties was to persist until the Civil War, although the Whigs after 1854 became first Americans and then Constitutional Unionists. The Democrats never lost a state-wide election, but they were compelled to take cognizance of the strength of their adversaries. The continued party competition, and the adoption of white male suffrage in 1851, ultimately brought voter participation to peaks of nearly 72 per cent in the 1855 gubernatorial election and 70 per cent in the presidential election of 1860.

Party formation in Virginia offers many contrasts to the process in the northern states. Whereas new party alignments had taken shape in the North generally by 1829, not until after the presidential election of 1832 did lasting alignments appear in Virginia, and it was not until 1839 that these alignments became reasonably stable. Opposition to the old Junto-Republican party in 1824, 1828, and 1832 had been weak, sectionalized, and lacking in continuity. The old party, itself, was a loose aggregate of factions and local leaders, drawn together quadrennially by the caucus and the Junto. Party discipline was not a conspicuous feature of the Virginia political tradition, with the result that independent politicians moved easily from one faction or party to another. But between 1834 and 1839, both parties elaborated their organizations, increased their discipline, altered their campaign techniques, and broadened the nature of their appeal. In few states did the changeover from the old to the new style of politics represent so great a transformation as in Virginia.

NORTH CAROLINA

North Carolina bore many broad resemblances to Virginia in its form of government, political attitudes, and course of party development. Its constitution, like that of Virginia, was based on restricted concepts of democracy and left local government in the hands of appointed county courts. Its dominant political creed emphasized localism and condemned extensions of federal authority. Its early political parties were loosely organized and ill matched. New parties did not emerge until late in the Jackson era. But North Carolina was, when compared with Virginia, a relatively primitive state economically, socially, and culturally, lacking an aristocracy comparable in size, wealth, and prestige to the Virginia gentry. Its political practices reflected these differences in many subtle ways.

Governmental powers in North Carolina were vested largely in a two-house legislature and in the county courts. The House of Commons, in which each county had two representatives and each borough one, and the Senate, composed of one member from each county, were elected annually. The legislature chose a governor annually, who was given little authority and who was checked by an executive council. Judges and other state officers were elected by the legislature; justices of the peace were recommended by the legislature and commissioned by the governor for good behavior. The justices formed the county courts, which operated in much the same way as in Virginia. Congressmen were elected from districts; presidential electors were chosen by the legislature in 1792 and 1812, by districts between those dates, and by general ticket beginning in 1816. The county and the congressional district were thus the important units of political activity and remained so until 1835.

North Carolina, like New York, had a dual suffrage system. All adult male taxpayers could vote for members of the House of Commons, but only those freeholders possessed of fifty acres of land could vote for state senators. In effect this meant that virtually all adult white males could exercise the lesser franchise but only half of them had full privileges. State elections were held annually in August; voting was by ballot; elections lasted three days (until 1823); and after 1800 it was common to hold the poll in three different places within the county. Sheriffs were made elective in 1830 and county clerks in 1833. It will be apparent that government in North Carolina rested on a much broader base than in Virginia in that there was an opportunity for nearly all men to participate in elections. The dual suffrage system was not seriously questioned until 1848. There was, however, continual dissatisfaction with the basis of apportionment in the legislature, which tended to give disproportionate representation to the eastern counties.

Republican and Federalist parties had emerged in North Carolina around 1795 and continued to wage an uneven contest in some areas down to 1816. The Republicans were always dominant in the legislature and held most of the congressional seats as well, but their opponents exhibited remarkable staying powers. In 1812 nearly one-third of the legislators were classed as Federalists; the proportion had not altered greatly by 1815. After 1815, doctrinal distinctions, which had long since become blurred, faded entirely, and partisanship ceased to be a factor in elections. Campaigns were fought on the basis of personalities, although the old Republican party continued to maintain some sense of identity and leadership with reference to national politics.

One of the vestiges of the earlier party strife that survived was the Republican legislative caucus. In addition to nominating presidential electors, when such action was appropriate, it was also employed to secure agreement on the party's gubernatorial choice and may have been used to regulate other appointments by the legislature. Unlike its Virginia counterpart, however, it did not create a central committee or county corresponding committees. Although it was severely attacked, especially in the Federalist press, it never entirely died out and attempted to assert its authority in 1824.[11] Aside from the caucus, there was little in the way of formal party machinery. Candidates were self-nominated or were put forward by cliques in each county or congressional district.

There was a rough-and-tumble quality to North Carolina politics, regardless of the condition of parties. Candidates were not only required to treat the voters to liberal rations of liquor, they were also expected to engage in a personal canvass, and it was not unusual for them to meet their opponents in political debate. By the 1820's, at least, stump speaking at church suppers, militia musters, and other social occasions had become commonplace. The candidates also availed themselves of letters to the press and printed circulars to extol their virtues and repel the slanderous attacks of their adversaries. The colorful campaign practices met a warm response from the electorate. Indeed elections frequently became so heated and fraught with violence that their duration was reduced from three days to one in 1823 in the interest of restraining intemperance and turmoil.

Even fraud was not unknown. One enterprising voter in Wayne County in the congressional election of 1808 was apprehended in the act of stuffing the ballot box. His ballot was found to contain ten small ballots, each one-sixth of an inch wide, on which were written the name of the congressional candidate. His ballot for state senator contained five similar small ballots.[12] The tumult and corruption at the polls was a frequent topic of comment in the press. "How contemptible

11. (Raleigh) *Minerva*, Dec. 1, 8, 1808; (Raleigh) *Register and North Carolina Gazette*, Oct. 20, 1820; (Salisbury) *Western Carolinian*, Jan. 6, 1824.

12. (Raleigh) *Minerva*, Sept. 1, 1808. This is the earliest reference I have found to this manner of "stuffing the ballot box."

and degrading it is," declaimed one editoralist, "to see gentlemen assembling at such places, treating, fawning and courting,
nay *soliciting* the suffrage of men to *honor* them with a seat in
the Legislative Councils of the State—Gracious God! If this
is independence, save us, we beseech thee, from participating
in the blessings it imparts."[13]

Perhaps because of the personalized and turbulent nature
of the campaigns, voters flocked to the polls in large numbers.
In the congressional election of 1800, for example, available
returns from fifteen counties indicated that 61 per cent of the
adult white males voted; in at least two counties the participation exceeded 80 per cent. Figures for twenty-seven of the
state's sixty-two counties for the congressional election of 1810
show that 74 per cent of the adult white males voted. Long
after genuine party contests had ended, and campaigns were
conducted largely on the basis of personalities, voter participation continued at a high level. In North Carolina, as in certain
other southern states, the extent of voter participation seemingly bore little relation either to the existence of competitive
parties or to elaborateness of party machinery. One can only
conclude that, for many reasons, elections were an enjoyable
experience to the voters, who reacted enthusiastically to other
than purely partisan appeals. Voting in state and congressional
elections, which were usually held at the same time in August,
brought forth greater participation than the November presidential elections.

The revival of the contest for the presidency in 1824 had
the effect of stirring new interest in presidential politics, but
not until after 1832 did durable parties, aligned to contest both
state and national offices, emerge. Following the lead of Virginia, Willie P. Mangum and other "Old Republican" chieftains in North Carolina became committed to Crawford as
the successor to Monroe, and ten members of the state's congressional delegation participated in the small caucus in Washington that nominated him for the presidency on February 14,

13. (Raleigh) *Register and North Carolina Gazette,* Aug. 4, 1820.

1824. Earlier, on December 24, 1823, members of the legislature friendly to Crawford had met in the Senate chamber at Raleigh, formed an electoral ticket, and appointed a central committee of correspondence of seven members to promote Crawford's election. Apparently only about 80 of the total of 196 legislators attended the caucus, which had previously been the object of attack by those hostile to Crawford. These opposition elements, initially disposed to support Calhoun, had already begun preparations to launch a "People's Ticket."[14]

Among the chief promoters of the "People's Ticket" were Charles Fisher, a Calhoun adherent, and William Polk, a former Federalist of great wealth, who was an ardent promoter of Jackson's cause. Behind the scenes negotiations among Fisher, Polk, and other politicians who were antagonistic to the Crawford faction, resulted in the preparation of an electoral ticket that was endorsed by well-managed public meetings in various parts of the state. When Calhoun was eliminated from the race, most interest focused on Jackson, but the "People's Ticket" sought the support of Adams and Clay men as well. The movement, in effect, represented a challenge to the old political leadership in the state and appealed strongly to former Federalists and disgruntled Republicans. Both factions, despite weak organization, endeavored to wage campaigns in behalf of their tickets, relying on mass meetings, circulars, newspapers, and informal communication among local politicians. Much was made by the sponsors of the "People's Ticket" of the fact that the Crawford faction had used a caucus to nominate their electoral slate. The election resulted in a surprising defeat for the old regime; Crawford polled only 43 per cent of the vote. About 42 per cent of the adult white males voted, which was high compared with other states but well below the participation in the August state election.

By 1827 the issue was no longer Crawford *versus* Jackson, but Jackson *versus* Adams, and the old Crawford faction moved easily into the general's camp. The lines that had been

14. (Salisbury) *Western Carolinian*, Jan. 6, 27, Feb. 10, 1824.

formed for the 1824 election had been swiftly obliterated, and
politics in the state again bore little relation to partisanship.
The presidential election of 1828 brought about a brief revival
of party strife, but the contest was an unequal one and did
not provide a new basis for parties.

On December 20, 1827, fifty-five delegates met in Raleigh
to hold an Adams State Convention, the first state convention
to be held in North Carolina.   The meeting named an electoral ticket, selected a central committee of correspondence,
and adopted an interesting address.   Parties in the past, it was
stated, had been founded on measures, not on men.   The
impending election was different.   "It is not a conflict between
opposing principles, but a conflict between opposing men, and
combinations of men.   It is founded on no recognized differences about measures; but on a competition for power and
place." Adams, it concluded, was the better man.[15]

The Jackson partisans, avoiding the much maligned caucus,
experimented with new nominating machinery.   A meeting of
pro-Jackson legislators on December 24, 1827, in response to
resolutions adopted earlier at a mass meeting at Fayetteville,
chose a state central committee headed by William Polk and
urged that Jacksonians in each county should appoint delegates to meet in district conventions and choose electors.   In
actuality, the electors were selected at an informal meeting of
party leaders and—with one exception—were accepted by the
district conventions.   In the ensuing election Jackson secured
almost a three-to-one margin over his opponent; the relatively
high voter participation—nearly 57 per cent—may be regarded
more as a testimony to the general's popularity than to the
urgency of the contest.

With Adams' defeat, his party, if such it could be called,
collapsed, and party distinctions were soon obliterated.   As
the presidential election of 1832 drew near, there was very
little pro-Clay sentiment evident; more significant was the

15. *Address of the Administration Convention Held in the Capitol at
Raleigh, December 20, 1827* [n.p., n.d.].

mobilization of opposition to Van Buren. The Jacksonians at the time possessed little sense of unity, lacked organization, and had no stable leadership. Instead, there were rival factions, all ostensibly loyal to Jackson, but competing with one another for power and place.

One faction, led by John Branch, who had served as Jackson's secretary of the navy until he resigned at the time of the upheaval in the Cabinet in 1831, rebelled against the nomination of Van Buren for the vice-presidency. Branch, a Calhoun admirer, was instrumental in arranging for an anti–Van Buren "convention" that met at the governor's residence in Raleigh on June 18, 1832. With delegates present from only eighteen counties, this conference declared that Van Buren was "odious" because of his tariff views and nominated a partial electoral slate pledged to Jackson and Barbour. The remainder of the electors were to be named by district conventions. A central committee, headed by William Polk, was set up to work for the Barbour ticket.[16] The bulk of the Jacksonian Republicans refused to follow Branch, and, under the leadership of Romulus Saunders, remained loyal to the nominees of the Baltimore Convention.

The Jackson–Van Buren slate received 21,006 votes; the Barbour and Clay tickets polled 4,255 and 4,533 votes respectively. Small though these opposition votes were, they were a forecast of the future union of Branch's following with the mildly nationalist Clay contingent. It is also significant that only 32 per cent of the adult white males voted in 1832, as compared with 57 per cent in 1828. The heavy decline is probably attributable in large part to North Carolina's lack of enthusiasm for Martin Van Buren, the northern heir-presumptive to the presidency.

Several circumstances combined in the next few years to produce in North Carolina durable and highly competitive parties. The opposition to the succession of Van Buren, together with such issues as the nullification controversy and the

16. Niles' *Register*, XLII, 304.

withdrawal of the deposits, were made the basis for the organization of the Whig party. The strength of the anti-Van Buren forces was greatly augmented in February, 1834, when the extremely influential Willie P. Mangum broke with the national administration, carrying many figures of lesser influence with him. In the congressional elections of 1834, for the first time in a generation, contests were bitterly fought on national issues, rather than personalities, and the split between Democrats and Whigs became pronounced. The polarization occurred so suddenly, as it did in many southern states, as to be dramatic. To what extent it represented the successful efforts of political leaders to capitalize on hostility to Van Buren and to what extent the division reflected other factors would be difficult to determine.

Party development was also influenced by the adoption of a new state constitution in 1835. Western discontent with the old system of representation was partially allayed by a new arrangement under which 120 members of the lower house were to be apportioned among the counties according to federal population and 50 senators were apportioned among districts on the basis of taxes paid. Borough representation was ended. State elections were to be biennial in August, in even-numbered years; congressmen were chosen in odd years. Most important, the governor was to be popularly elected for a two-year term. Although the old dual suffrage system was retained, taxpayers were eligible to vote in gubernatorial elections. These changes, and particularly the provision for an elective governor, made the state a more important unit of political activity than it had previously been and greatly encouraged state-wide party organization. Moreover, to the degree that sectional antagonisms over the apportionment issue were lessened, the new parties could appeal strongly to both eastern and western regions.

The Whigs had taken the initiative in promoting constitutional reform and continued to display more energy and imagination than their lethargic Democratic rivals in building a strong party organization. At the end of the legislative session in December, 1835, the Whig legislators, and other prominent figures in the party, met to plan for the 1836 elections, which would involve not only the election of a president but also the first popular election of a governor and a new legislature. A central committee of seven persons residing in or near Raleigh was set up, together with five-member committees of vigilance and correspondence for each county. The latter were authorized to expand their size, and one Whig county committee soon had 215 members. The county committees were instructed to appoint delegates to meet in district conventions to agree on the nomination of presidential electors, whose names were to be reported to the central committee by May 1. They were also urged to propose the names of suitable gubernatorial candidates. The conference named Hugh Lawson White as the party's presidential candidate. Within a few weeks sentiment had mobilized behind Edward B. Dudley for the governorship.

The Democrats lagged for behind the Whigs in their campaign preparations, relying on traditional informal methods of management until 1839. R. D. Spaight, the incumbent governor, was accepted as the party's candidate without resort to formal nominating procedures. District conventions, arranged by local leaders, nominated Van Buren electors. The campaign for the governorship, as well as for the presidency, was fought almost entirely on national issues. Dudley set the tone of the Whig appeal by denouncing Van Buren. "To say all in one sentence," Dudley declared, "He is not one of us. He is a Northern man in soul, in principle, and in action, with not one feeling of sympathy or interest for the South."[17] The aggressive Whig tactics brought 67 per cent of the adult white males to the polls in August and gave Dudley a substantial victory. When the presidential election was held in Novem-

17. J. G. De Roulhac Hamilton, "Party Politics in North Carolina, 1835-1860," *The James Sprunt Historical Publications*, XV, Nos. 1 and 2 (Chapel Hill, N.C., 1916), 36.

ber, only 53 per cent of the adult white males voted, and Van Buren secured the state's electoral vote by a comfortable margin.　The 1836 elections confirmed and climaxed the trend toward the polarization of parties that had been under way since 1834.　After that year, although there were minor shifts of allegiance, especially in 1837, the leadership cores of both parties remained stable and the voters generally adhered loyally to their new-found party identifications.

Preparations for the 1840 elections stimulated both parties, and especially the Whigs, to extend and elaborate their party machinery.　Both parties held state conventions—the Whigs on November 12, 1839, and the Democrats on January 8, 1840 —to nominate candidates for governor, choose delegates at large to the national party conventions, name central committees, and adopt party platforms.　District conventions chose electoral candidates and county vigilance committees directed campaigns at the local level.　The Whig apparatus extended down to the level of the precinct and made effective use, too, of "young men's" auxiliaries.　Both parties employed the caucus to maintain discipline in the legislature; the Whigs are credited with having introduced the spoils system in the distribution of patronage in 1840.　Within each party a "Raleigh Clique" directed party strategy, and the Democratic *Standard* and the Whig *Register* gave authentic voice to the views of the party managers.

Campaign methods became increasingly popular in style. By 1840 the opposing gubernatorial candidates were holding joint debates throughout the state, barbecues and mass rallies were in great vogue, and scarcely a person was not drawn into the excitement of the election drama.　The North Carolina Whigs, like their brethren elsewhere, heralded the new era with a monster, two-day festival at Raleigh on October 5, 1840, which according to report was attended by twelve thousand of the faithful.

The ably managed Whig machine scored sweeping victories in 1840 in both the gubernatorial and presidential contests.

Voter participation reached the unprecedented height of 83 per cent in both elections, levels that were never to be exceeded in the state. Both parties were genuinely state-wide in character and latitudinarian in their political principles; they were distinguished chiefly by the greater vigor that marked the Whig leadership. The ascendancy obtained by the Whigs in 1836 was retained until 1850, when the Democrats first won the governorship. Thereafter the Whigs never achieved a state-wide victory, although they remained in a challenging position until 1860. Voter participation averaged close to three-fourths of the adult white males and tended to be somewhat higher in gubernatorial than in presidential elections, except in 1840 and 1844.

New party alignments, then, were slow to form in North Carolina, but when they emerged between 1834 and 1836, they soon proved to be durable and closely balanced. Party organization, which had been negligible before 1836, had by 1840 become highly elaborate and well adapted to the new, popular style of politics. Parties became defined not on the basis of state issues but rather in relation to national politics. Adams in 1828 and Clay in 1832 had aroused little enthusiasm, but the prospect of Van Buren as president in succession to Jackson created a strong division of sentiment. The loose coalition that had supported Jackson suffered heavy losses, and these dissidents combined with such diverse elements as the Branch-Barbour, state-rights faction and the western, pro-Clay group to form the Whig party.

KENTUCKY

Kentucky stands forth as a conspicuous exception to the generalization that the South remained politically monolithic until after 1832. In that state new and durable party alignments had been formed by 1828. The parties quickly adopted elaborate organizations, based on the convention system, and contested both state and national elections. Why Kentucky, which had so much in common politically with Virginia, North Carolina, and Tennessee afer 1836 should have deviated so sharply from those states in the preceding decade is not difficult to explain. Kentucky had Henry Clay, and in Kentucky—alone among the southern states—Clay commanded sufficient popular support to provide a secure base for opposition to Jackson. Elsewhere in the South it was the prospect of Van Buren as a successor to the presidency that stimulated the formation of parties. But in Kentucky it was the choice between Jackson and Clay, first presented in 1824, that shaped party loyalties.

Kentucky had much in common in its political institutions with its parent state of Virginia, but its constitution also reflected strong democratic influences. Like Virginia, it adhered to a county court system that permitted no popular participation in local government and to *viva voce* voting. Government at the state level, however, was more democratic in form than that of most of the older states. Under the constitution of 1799, the second adopted by the state, voting privileges were enjoyed by all adult white male citizens who had resided two years in the state or one year in a county. At the annual state elections, held on the first Monday in August and the two days following, a legislature apportioned on the basis of eligible voters was chosen. Representatives were elected from the counties for one-year terms and senators were elected from districts for staggered four-year terms. The governor was chosen by popular vote in the presidential years—together with a lieutenant-governor—and was not eligible to succeed himself. Congressmen were elected by districts at the state elections in odd years. Presidential electors were elected from districts until 1828, when the general-ticket plan was introduced. The county was the polling unit, but the constitution sanctioned the creation of election precincts and they were established in some counties from an early date.

The county courts, self-perpetuating as in Virginia and vested with authority to name other county officials, were important centers of political influence, but they did not play so dominant a role as in the mother state. In the 1830's around one-fourth of the members of the state legislature were also members of the county courts in Kentucky, but the proportions in Virginia and North Carolina were twice as large. The captain's company, the basic unit of militia organization, seems to have been a significant center of political activity in a community where military prowess was highly valued.

The county was not the exclusive center of political management that it was in Virginia because of the use of districts in electing senators, congressmen, and electors and because of the interest that attached to the popular, state-wide election of the governor. Moreover, the Kentucky county courts, as the products of a new society, did not have behind them the generations of prestige and the established traditions of their Virginia counterparts. And they had to contend with an electorate that was broad, rather than restricted, tumultuous, rather than respectful.

Kentucky elections were anything but sedate. The assembling of several hundred voters from a county at election time, and the average county in 1824 had a thousand voters, could lead to many abuses ranging from mere riots and tumults to vote buying and fraudulent multiple voting. On occasion a determined faction would seize control of the polling place and forcibly prevent its opponents from voting, sometimes with the connivance of a partial sheriff. It was not uncommon, either, for a county to produce more votes than the number of its adult white males. Voters were imported from neighboring Tennessee, and in some counties where election precincts had been created it was possible for an elector to vote both in his own precinct and at the county seat. Because the election lasted for three days, voters could easily attend the polls in

several counties. Campaign techniques were suited to the
exuberant nature of the electorate, and voter participation was
high. The gubernatorial election of 1800 attracted 61 per
cent of the adult white males to the polls, despite a lack of
party organization and a multiplicity of candidates, and, except
in 1804, when there was only one candidate, subsequent elections produced almost precisely the same turnout down to 1820.

There was little semblance of party politics in Kentucky
before 1820. Federalism never became an effective force, and
by 1800 the state was all but unanimously Jeffersonian. In
the absence of opposition, the Republicans were under no
pressure to organize their forces, and contests for office were
conducted largely on the basis of personalities. Indicative of
the lack of party machinery was the candidacy of sixteen men,
all self-nominated, for the four posts of presidential electors in
the northern district in 1804. In 1812, however, when some
organized sentiment favorable to De Witt Clinton appeared,
the Madisonians adopted measures to meet the threat. On
October 9 a meeting was held at Georgetown, in the third electoral district, at which a committee of seven was appointed to
correspond with similar committees in other counties and arrange a district meeting at Paris on October 26. The Paris
convention, attended by thirty-four delegates from seven counties, agreed on four men to be supported as Madison electors
and adopted an address to the voters. In the ensuing election
the Madison ticket polled over 5,000 votes to 289 for the
Clintonians.[18] In 1816 an attempt was made to organize opposition to Clay in the congressional election. The Lexington
Western Monitor proposed that two delegates should be appointed from each militia company in the district to assemble
and agree on a candidate. Only sixteen delegates appeared at
the appointed time, but they proceeded to nominate John
Pope, an alleged Federalist, and adopted an address. Clay was
easily re-elected. Such organizational activities seem to have
been exceptional prior to 1820, but they do suggest familiarity

18. (Lexington) *Reporter,* Oct. 10, 24, 31, Nov. 25, 1812.

with the use of delegate conventions.   I have found no evidence
that the legislative caucus was employed in Kentucky, and
there is every indication that it was not used for the nomination of candidates for governor, congressmen, or electors.

The economic distress occasioned by the Panic of 1819 was
responsible for the injection into Kentucky politics of an issue
of such urgency and magnitude that it became the basis of
party alignments.   By January, 1819, all the banks in the state
had been forced to suspend specie payments, debtors were
under severe pressure, business was at a standstill.   Among the
remedies proposed, the most popular called for stay laws, to
save debtors from bankruptcy, and a new bank endowed with
power to issue fiat money.   Proponents of these measures became known as the "Relief" party and their opponents were
"Anti-Relief."   In 1821 the controversial legislation was enacted.   Two years later the bank was declared unconstitutional
by the Kentucky Supreme Court.   Unable to remove the
members of the court, the Relief-controlled legislature in 1824
created a new court.   The party battle continued, now between the "Old Court" and "New Court" men.   By 1826 the
Old Court party had secured the ascendancy, the economic
crisis had passed, the New Court act was repealed, and the
issue ceased to be agitated.   But between 1819 and 1826 the
two parties waged a series of bitter contests in the course of
which the old personalized, informal style of politics gradually
gave way to organized efforts to mobilize the electorate on the
basis of "measures, not men."

In 1820, with sentiment running strongly in favor of "relief," three candidates pledged to the popular cause entered
the race for governor in opposition to a lone Anti-Relief champion, and John Adair, a Relief man, won with a plurality of
the vote.   The excitement engendered by the contest, and the
issue around which it focused sent voter participation to a new
level as three-quarters of the adult white males voted.   In 1824
the Relief party concentrated its support behind General James
Desha, who was easily elected and carried with him a Relief

majority in both houses of the legislature. The contest continued in the state elections of 1825 and 1826. Both parties by now had organizations in the counties, towns, and captain's companies, rallying the voters to support either the Old Court or the New Court. The Old Court party triumphed in both years and in December, 1826, repealed the New Court act. By that year, with the court issue presumably settled, party allegiance was being determined increasingly by the presidential question and the Old Court-New Court distinctions faded.

As the struggle between the Old Court and New Court parties approached its climax in 1824, popular interest was temporarily diverted by the presidential election. In November, 1822, after the adjournment of the legislature, members of both houses had met to recommend unanimously support of Henry Clay for the presidency and to issue an address extolling the virtues of Kentucky's favorite son. Because of the general popularity of Clay and the preoccupation with state issues, the presidential race attracted little attention until after the August state election in 1824. By that time, however, Jackson's candidacy had acquired some local support, and the adherents of both men began, somewhat belatedly, to make serious campaign preparations. The state had been divided into three districts, two of which were to choose five electors each while the third district was allotted four electors. Some machinery was obviously required within each district to arrange slates of electoral candidates.

Clay's cause was sponsored by a five-man central committee, presumably named by the pro-Clay legislators and headed by William T. Barry, a New Court man who four years later was to be the Jacksonian candidate for governor. Among other activities this committee stimulated the holding of district conventions. For example, on July 26, 1824, the Clay adherents in Franklin County met at the courthouse and appointed Francis P. Blair, soon to become a distinguished Jacksonian, to meet with delegates from other counties in the district at Paris on August 9 and nominate five electors. Delegates from fifteen counties convened on the appointed day and, after deciding that each county delegation should have the same vote as in the legislature, proceeded to arrange an electoral ticket and adopt an address. Similar conventions were held in the other two districts, both of which had appointed Clay electors by mid-October.[19]

The Jacksonians were lacking in effective leadership and could construct only a rudimentary organization. At a meeting in Georgetown, Scott County, on August 28, 1824, the general's friends appointed a five-man committee to correspond with other similar committees that might be appointed throughout the state. The committee was also authorized to endeavor to arrange a district convention, appoint the necessary delegates, and publish an address. Several weeks later, on October 2, the Frankfort Jacksonians met at the Capitol, created a correspondence committee, and appointed a delegate to a district convention that was to be held at Cynthiana.[20] In contrast to the excitement that had marked the state election in August, the presidential campaign was remarkably quiet. Nearly sixty-five thousand votes had been cast in the gubernatorial election; little more than one-third that number of voters went to the polls in November. Clay was an easy victor, winning more than 70 per cent of the popular vote and all of the electors.

The temporary alignment that occurred in connection with the presidential contest bore no direct relationship to the existing state parties, and the elections of 1825 and 1826 were fought on the court issue rather than on the presidential question. But by 1827 the political situation was undergoing a major transition. The state-centered parties disintegrated, and new parties were formed in preparation for the presidential election of 1828. Old Court and New Court men laid

19. (Frankfort) *Argus of Western America* (hereinafter, *Argus*), Aug. 4, 18, 25, Sept. 22, Oct. 20, Nov. 3, 1824.
20. *Ibid.*, Sept. 8, Oct. 6, 1824.

aside their antagonisms and joined together in support of—or in opposition to—General Jackson. With Clay no longer a candidate, but with his considerable influence enlisted in behalf of Adams, the race promised to be less one-sided than it had been in 1824.

The first test for the new parties came in the 1827 elections, which produced a legislature that was almost evenly divided between Jacksonians and Adams men and a congressional delegation in which the Jacksonians held a seven-to-five edge. The Jackson party organization, as described by Major Allan Campbell in a letter to the general, operated in secrecy. Under the leadership of a central committee in Louisville, committees were set up in each county, with sub-committees in town wards and captain's companies to canvass the voters. The charge was later made that the Adams forces employed similar tactics.[21] After the state elections both parties abandoned any pretext of secrecy and, pleading that the underhanded combinations of their opponents had forced them to it, began to construct elaborate party machinery.

The Jackson campaign was launched by a meeting of his friends at the Mansion House in Frankfort on August 20, a day when the sheriffs from all the counties came to the capital to present the election returns from their counties. After adopting resolutions expressive of their joy at the successes already attained, those present proposed that a dinner should be held at Cedar Cove Spring, near Frankfort, on September 10. A committee of twenty was instructed to make the necessary arrangements and invite "such distinguished citizens and soldiers as they may think proper."[22] The dinner was a festive occasion, with over five-hundred Jacksonians in attendance. The day began with a military parade, after which two Revolutionary soldiers were appointed presidents for the occasion. Then came the barbecue, followed by numerous toasts and

21. John S. Bassett, ed., *Correspondence of Andrew Jackson* (7 vols.; Washington, D.C., 1926-35), III, 333-34; (Frankfort) *Argus*, Sept. 26, 1827.
22. (Frankfort) *Argus*, Sept. 5, 1827.

band music. "All was harmony and good feeling." The assemblage found an opportunity to adopt lengthy resolutions extolling Jackson and denouncing Adams and also sanctioned "associations of honest citizens devoted to truth and correct principles." Other arrangements of a more practical nature, soon to be revealed, were also made.[23]

Among those who had played a prominent role in planning the Cedar Cove Spring conclave was Amos Kendall, the remarkably able editor of the Frankfort *Argus of Western America*. Two weeks later Kandall charged that the opposition was secretly organized and declared that the Jacksonians must take prompt action to counteract the devices of the coalition. Accordingly he proposed that the friends of Jackson in every county should hold meetings to appoint delegates to a state convention to be held in Frankfort on January 8. For the first time, Kentucky would choose its electors on a single state-wide ticket, rather than by districts as in the past, and it was essential that the Jacksonians agree on a set of candidates for electors. A week later Kendall broadened his original proposal with the suggestion that it might also be desirable to unite the party behind a single candidate for governor. There can be little doubt that arrangements for the convention had been thoroughly discussed at Cedar Cove Spring and that politicians in every county were prepared to act on Kendall's cue. During the ensuing weeks, meetings were held in counties throughout the state at which delegates were chosen and committees of correspondence and vigilance were appointed to manage local party affairs.[24]

The sudden flurry of activity in the Jackson camp roused the Adams men to undertake comparable preparations. The editor of the Louisville *Focus,* a leading Adams journal, noting that the Jacksonians had "come to the determination to organize their party in the most efficient manner for carrying on

23. *Ibid.,* Sept. 12, 19, 1827; (Frankfort) *Commentator,* Sept. 15, Oct. 6, 1827.
24. (Frankfort) *Argus,* Sept. 26, Oct. 10, 1827; (Frankfort) *Commentator,* Sept. 29, Oct. 6, 1827.

the electioneering campaign," recommended that "arrangements of a similar nature should be adopted to meet and counteract them." The editorial went on to urge that county meetings be held to appoint delegates to a state convention, together with county committees.[25] The proposal, which was obviously made with some authority, was favorably received, and during the following weeks the county politicians were busy with preparations for the state convention. The proceedings in Boone County were typical. The Adams supporters met on December 3 and organized by appointing a chairman and secretary. Resolutions were then adopted praising the "American System," Adams, and Clay. Five delegates were named to attend the state convention, together with a correspondence committee of eight and a vigilance committee of seventy-five members. It was the assignment of the latter committee to distribute information, canvass the electorate, and guard the polls.[26]

The Adams State Convention, the first such party meeting ever held in Kentucky, met in Frankfort on December 17 and continued in session for three days. The legislature was meeting at the same time, and many legislators played prominent roles in the convention. Sixty-two counties sent delegations, varying in size from one to eight members. The business was conducted in a most methodical manner with several committees to discharge particular functions. After naming an Adams electoral slate, the convention considered the propriety of nominating candidates for governor and lieutenant-governor. It was agreed that while "in ordinary times this subject should not necessarily connect itself with the Presidential Election," the existing circumstances made it desirable to act. After two men had declined the honor, Thomas Metcalfe, a member of Congress, received the gubernatorial nomination, with J. R. Underwood as his running mate. The convention adopted the usual address and appointed a state central committee of

25. *Ibid.,* Sept. 29, 1827.
26. *Ibid.,* Oct. 13–Dec. 27, 1827.

thirteen members, seven of them residents of Frankfort, to correspond with similar committees in other states and with the county committees.[27]

The Jackson Convention, which also took three days to complete its deliberations, was attended by some two hundred delegates from sixty-two counties. Organized in the same thorough manner as the Adams Convention, the Jackson meeting experienced no difficulties in adopting an electoral slate pledged to Jackson and Calhoun but had to resolve internal differences over the nomination of state candidates. After considerable behind-the-scenes negotiations, William T. Barry, erstwhile Clayite and New Court champion, received the gubernatorial nomination and John Breathitt—an Old Court man —was a last-minute choice for the lieutenant-governorship. Later, after harmony had been achieved, it was reported that there had been "some unfortunate jealousies between new and old court men belonging to the great Jackson party, in relation to the candidates for Governor and Lieutenant Governor." The convention named twenty-two men to a state committee of correspondence and vigilance and displayed remarkable inventiveness by requesting each county committee to raise funds and transmit them to the party treasurer, who would expend them in support of the cause. Equally remarkable, Barry and Breathitt both appeared at the final session and addressed the convention.[28] The Jackson Convention was, in almost every respect, a model affair, conducted with professional skill of the highest order. If, as the available evidence suggests, Amos Kendall and Francis Preston Blair were the leading architects of the smooth-functioning party machinery, they must be accorded high rank among American political technicians.

There was only a brief respite between the adjournment of the conventions and the beginning of several hectic months of electioneering. Barry took to the stump early in the spring

27. *Ibid.*, Dec. 27, 1827.
28. (Frankfort) *Argus*, Jan. 16, 1828.

and set out to canvass the entire state. Metcalfe's congressional duties kept him in Washington until May, when he returned to Kentucky and launched into an extensive speaking tour. The presidential question, state issues, and personal abuse all were thoroughly exploited by the champions of the two parties. Clay worked valiantly in behalf of the Adams party, which was really the Clay party. The state elections in August must have been the most exciting ever held in Kentucky, for 77 per cent of the adult white males voted. The results showed the two parties to be almost equal in strength. Barry lost the governorship by less than a thousand votes, but the Jacksonians won the lieutenant-governorship and majorities in both houses of the legislature. Barry's defeat was attributed to the refusal of some Old Court Jacksonians to vote for the man who had been chief justice of the New Court.

After the state election, the presidential campaign held the center of the political stage. Party committees, many of them enlarged to include vast numbers, worked unceasingly to arouse the electorate for the second great battle in the interparty war. But Adams lacked the appeal of Clay. He fell more than seven thousand votes short of the total that Metcalfe had received in August while Jackson ran slightly ahead of Barry's total. Voter participation declined to 71 per cent. As subsequent elections were to demonstrate, the poor performance of Adams did not accurately reflect the strength of the party that supported him; rather it showed the handicap that confronted a northern candidate running in opposition to Jackson. Indeed, the relatively large vote given to Adams in Kentucky was more a tribute to Clay—and to the effectiveness of the new party organization—than an expression of genuine regard for Adams.

The parties that had been formed in 1827 proved to be durable. The anti-Jackson party, momentarily weakened after 1828, because its prospects on the national scene were clouded, revived late in 1830 when it glimpsed the hope that Clay would be the candidate to oppose Jackson. On September 17, 1830, a public meeting in Winchester called on "the friends of the union of the states and the American system" to make plans for a state convention, to be held in Frankfort on December 9. In due course this convention nominated Clay for the presidency, overhauled the party machinery, appointed delegates to the Baltimore National Republican Convention, and arranged for another state convention to be held in 1831 for the purpose of naming electors. The Jackson party, meanwhile, was engaged in similar preparations.[29]

Soon the state was engrossed in another year full of campaign activities leading to the state election in August, 1832, and the presidential contest in November. Both parties were well-organized in all parts of the commonwealth and sought to exceed the efforts they had put forth in 1828. The Democrats, with John Breathitt as their gubernatorial candidate, were victorious by the narrowest of margins in the August election, which brought nearly three-fourths of the adult white males to the polls. But, again, the party lines that had maintained for the state election could not be held against the force of Clay's candidacy. No man, not even Jackson, could beat Clay in Kentucky. In a total vote that was only a few hundred less than that cast in the state elections, Clay outdistanced Jackson by over four thousand votes.

The Clay party, which adopted the Whig label in 1834, gained in strength after 1832 and remained dominant in the state for twenty years, usually by a substantial majority. Not until Buchanan's victory in 1856 were the Democrats able to win a presidential election, although they captured the governorship in 1851 with a plurality of the total vote—occasioned by the irregular candidacy of Cassius M. Clay—and in 1859, when the old parties were breaking under sectional strains. Voter participation, which sagged to 60 per cent in the 1836 elections, revived in 1840 and reached an all-time high in 1844, when over 81 per cent of the electorate voted in the state

29. (Lexington) *Kentucky Reporter*, Sept. 15–Dec. 15, 1830; Niles' *Register*, XXXIX, 90, 234.

election and 80 per cent in the presidential election that brought a final defeat to Clay's hopes. Except in 1836, voter participation continued to be slightly higher in state elections than in presidential elections, perhaps because of the added interest of races for seats in the legislature. The convention system, introduced so effectively in 1827, continued to be employed, especially for managing state-wide nominations.

What was peculiar about party formation in Kentucky was, of course, the fact that it took place so early and that the new parties proved to be so durable. This situation contrasts sharply with the experience of Virginia, North Carolina, and Tennessee. The explanation, as has already been suggested, is to be found in the influence exerted by Clay on the Kentucky scene, an influence he did not have in the neighboring states. It was Clay's popularity that sustained the Adams party in 1828, and it was Clay who led his party to victory over Jackson in 1832. The rough balance of forces in the 1828 elections in Kentucky had no counterpart elsewhere in the South. By 1834, when clear two-party situations emerged in other southern states, Kentucky had already experienced several years of politics conducted by well-organized parties that contested both state and presidential elections. The party loyalties acquired between 1827 and 1834 were, with the usual exceptions, retained into the 1850's.

TENNESSEE

Tennessee affords an excellent, although by no means unique, illustration of the fact that government and politics in an American state could be conducted over a long period of time without political parties. For nearly forty years Tennessee voters participated numerously and enthusiastically in elections that were contested by rival factions and local personalities, rather than by parties, and the candidates elected to office acknowledged no partisan loyalties. Not until 1834, when a combination of personal rivalries and antagonism to Van Buren served as a basis for partisan divisions, did leaders and voters begin to align behind opposing standards. This is not to say that politics was devoid of management before that date. Although the conventional party machinery was completely absent from the Tennessee scene, the state possessed politicians of great vigor and authority who, despite the lack of formal apparatus, were able to manipulate and control political affairs. Not until 1840 did the old, informal style of politics yield to the new era of the institutionalized parties, with their elaborate facade of conventions, committees, and other mechanisms.

Tennessee's style of politics was fashioned by many circumstances, but of primary importance was the dominant role played by William Blount and his associates from an early period. A land speculator of insatiable appetite, Blount was also an extraordinarily astute judge of men and a master of political maneuver. After acquiring enormous tracts of land in what was to become the State of Tennessee he served as the first governor of the Southwest Territory and subsequently as the first senator from the new state. It was Blount's strategy to attach to himself men of enterprise and talent who shared his interests in land speculation and politics. Thus he welded together a faction so powerful and able as to constitute an impregnable ruling elite. Such heroic pioneer figures as James Robertson and John Sevier, as well as promising young men like Andrew Jackson, were drawn into the Blount faction, where they were held together by Blount's impressive leadership and by the tangible rewards that accrued to members of the privileged circle.

Incorporating as it did the men who were outstanding in the state for their military prestige, economic position, and personal abilities, the faction could command wide popular support and monopolize the principal elective and appointive offices. The tradition of political management established by Blount and his cohorts was carried on after his death in 1800 by his half-brother, Willie Blount, who was succeeded in turn as the center of authority by John Overton. This type of management, it might be observed, was a characteristic feature of the newer, frontier states.

The oligarchic character of Tennessee politics could not be attributed to the state constitution which, with conspicuous exceptions, was democratic in form. All freemen who owned land or who had resided six months in a county were entitled to vote. All elections were by paper ballot, with the county as the voting unit until 1834, when general provisions were made for the creation of small election districts. Elections for members of the legislature, congressmen, and the governor were held biennially in the odd years. The legislature, both houses of which were equitably proportioned on the basis of taxable inhabitants, was the strongest branch of the government and possessed extensive powers of appointment. The governor, who was limited to three successive terms, was endowed with little authority, and his influence depended on his personal effectiveness.

If the state government was democratic in form, the same could not be said of the counties. The justices of the peace, who composed the county courts, held office for life and owed their initial appointments to the legislature. Although they were not self-perpetuating, as in Virginia and Kentucky, they enjoyed virtually the same degree of independence from popular control as their colleagues in those states. This situation was altered in 1834, however, when a new constitution made all county officials elective. In the federal sphere, congressmen were chosen from districts, and presidential electors were not elected on a state-wide basis until 1832.

Tennessee was from its inception as a state nominally Republican in its political allegiance; there was never any vestige of a Federalist party. National politics, then, played no part in molding alignments in the state. Neither was there any tendency for state-oriented parties to form on the basis of local issues, national antagonisms, or rival leadership cliques.

The lack of any broad and enduring cleavages was evidenced, for example, by the absence of contests over the governorship. John Sevier was elected to three successive terms over negligible opposition and was then succeeded by a Blount stalwart, Archibald Roane. The popular "Nollichucky Jack," who had become estranged from the Blount faction, defeated Roane in 1803 in one of the rare instances of a genuine contest and was easily re-elected for two more terms. When he was again forced to vacate the office because of the constitutional limitation, Willie Blount succeeded him for three terms, again virtually without opposition. Blount in turn was followed by Joseph McMinn, who won the office in a five-man race in 1815 and then easily held it for his allotted three terms. General William Carroll, second only to Jackson in military stature in Tennessee, overwhelmingly defeated his lone competitor in succeeding McMinn in 1821 and, with one interruption held the office until 1835.

In contrast to the tameness of the gubernatorial election, seats in the legislature and in Congress were the objects of intense competition. Self-nominated candidates, relying on their personal connections and their popular appeal, conducted extraordinarily intensive campaigns for these offices. When the young James K. Polk ran for the legislature in 1823, he spent several months canvassing Maury County, as did his opponent, in accordance with the general practice. Beginning with the militia musters in April and extending through until August, the candidates made up for the lack of any formal party campaign machinery by expending enormous energy in direct personal appeals to the electorate. By engaging in joint debates, speaking at barbecues and dinners, and enlisting, where possible, the support of the local weekly newspaper, aspirants for public office stimulated high interest in elections. It was not uncommon for over 70 per cent of the adult white males to vote for governor, despite the lack of competition for that office.

But they were, in reality, drawn to the polls by the excitement attending the contests for the legislative and congressional seats. In 1821, for example, the vote for governor indicated participation by over 82 per cent of the electorate, but an inspection of county returns shows that an even greater number of votes was cast for congressional and legislative candidates.[30]

During most of the period down to 1821 the Blount faction, under successive leaders and with changes in membership, continued to exercise a powerful influence in the higher levels of politics. Through the force of its prestige and its connections around the state, it was usually able to determine who should hold such major offices as the governorship, the United States senatorships, and seats in Congress, and its operations included also elections to the legislature. By 1821, however, a rival faction, led by Andrew Erwin, Newton Cannon, and Senator John Williams had coalesced and the old Blount faction, whose most prominent figures now were John Overton, Hugh L. White, John H. Eaton, and William B. Lewis, was seriously challenged. In that year, the Erwin forces backed General Carroll for the governorship and he defeated overwhelmingly the Overton candidate, Colonel Edward Ward.

It was at this point, as Charles G. Sellers, Jr., had so ably described the episode, that the Overton men conceived the idea of putting Jackson into the presidential race in a calculated effort to enhance their declining local political fortunes. Jackson, who was loosely identified with the Overton faction, had not for many years been prominent in politics

30. On the tangled question of the size of the vote in the 1821 elections, see *Nashville Clarion*, Aug. 22, 29, 1821; *Nashville Whig*, Aug. 15, 22, 1821; [Tennessee] *House Journal*, 14th Assembly, 1st Session, p. 91; MSS returns of 1821 Congressional election (incomplete), Tennessee State Library; Robert H. White, ed., *Messages of the Governors of Tennessee* (6 vols.; Nashville, 1952-63), II, 15 n. It would appear from the evidence that at least 53,440 votes were cast in the gubernatorial election, although the official canvass by the legislature recorded a total of only 38,584 votes. I cite this instance because it was common for the official returns to be far below the returns reported in the newspapers. Usually the reason for the discrepancy was the failure of county officials to make their returns in proper form and within the specified time, with the result that the votes of many counties were not included in the official canvass. This is but one type of hazard involved in the use of early election statistics.

and had held no civil office since 1804. The real objective of the Overton faction was to replace Senator Williams with one of their own men, and in 1823, when it became apparent that no other candidate could unseat Williams, they turned in desperation to Jackson, and he was elected to the Senate. Somewhat to the surprise of his original sponsors, Jackson's candidacy for the presidency elicited a favorable response in other areas of the nation, and by 1824 he was, of course, a serious contender for that office.

In the presidential contest only 216 votes were cast against Jackson in Tennessee in a dull election that brought but 27 per cent of the voters to the polls. This apparent unanimity did not, however, signify the cessation of political hostilities in Tennessee. In contests for seats in the legislature and in Congress, old rivalries persisted and many powerful political figures remained hostile to the Overton-Eaton-Lewis coterie, now closely associated with Jackson. Too, Jackson was notorious for the number of enemies he had made in the state, and these men, although they did not venture to take the hopeless step of supporting an opposing candidate, were less than ardent in their commitment to Old Hickory. If anything, politics in Tennessee became less coherent after 1824 than had been the case earlier, for now there was no dominant faction exercising an overlordship over affairs and there was a noticeable tendency for individuals without strong ties to either of the old factions—like John Bell or James K. Polk—to rise to prominence.

The vague no-party politics persisted through the presidential elections of 1828 and 1832, when on both occasions Jackson was the all but unanimous choice of the Tennessee electorate. Again, it is notable that in 1828 only 50 per cent of the voters went to the polls and in 1832 participation dropped below 30 per cent. Although he met with no opposition at the polls, Jackson had little or no control over politics in Tennessee, where nominal Jacksonians continued their intricate factional and personal contests. After 1832, with the

prospect of Jackson's political retirement in view, the opportunity was provided for politicians to array themselves in two
opposing camps, ostensibly on the basis of national issues and
the question of the succession to the presidency.

Some forecast of the new alignment could be seen in 1833,
when an effort was made to unseat Felix Grundy, who was
exceeded only by Polk in his fidelity to Jackson. Legislative
contests were fought on the issue of Grundy's re-election, and
although the opposition had a majority, it was unable to unite
behind a single candidate, with the result that Grundy was
finally chosen after fifty-five ballots. Most of those who led the
anti-Grundy faction, including Ephraim Foster and John Bell,
were soon to head the revolt against Van Buren. A second
crucial episode was the contest for the speakership of the House
of Representatives in June, 1834, between Polk and Bell. Despite the fact that Polk had Jackson's backing, Bell, supported
by anti-Van Buren, pro-Bank, and southern nullifier elements,
won on the tenth ballot. As a result of this conflict, Polk and
Bell became the central figures around whom the emerging
parties rallied in 1834.

More was at stake than mere personal rivalries. Bell and
many of his associates differed sharply with Polk on the Bank
issue. Even more to the point in terms of popular political
currents, they differed on the presidential question. Polk as
early as October, 1833, had committed himself to Van Buren,
who enjoyed little support among politicians or voters in
Tennessee. Bell, while continuing to insist on his loyalty to
Jackson, had declared against Van Buren but had some difficulty in deciding whom to back in opposition to Jackson's
designated heir.

This problem was solved when Senator Hugh Lawson
White, an early Jackson adherent who, among other considerations, felt that his loyalty had not been returned by the general,
consented to enter the presidential contest. White had been
a prominent and respected figure in Tennessee politics since
the territorial period, when he had served as secretary to Gov-

ernor Blount. Bell and his associates proposed to use White much as the old Overton faction had sought to use Jackson in 1824. The White movement was formally launched in December, 1834, when Bell called a meeting of the Tennessee congressional delegation—which Grundy and Polk refused to attend—for the purpose of adopting a letter requesting White to become a candidate. White readily assented, but the correspondence was kept secret for two months, until he had been put in nomination by the Alabama legislature.

White's candidacy, for obvious reasons, was extremely popular in Tennessee, and the small remnant of political leaders —notably Polk, Grundy, Carroll, and Cave Johnson—who were willing to follow Jackson even to the extremity of accepting Van Buren, faced a dismal prospect. In the state election in August, 1835, the venerable Governor Carroll, hitherto unbeatable, was overthrown by Newton Cannon, in part because he had declared for Van Buren. In the congressional contests, the Van Buren faction was able to run candidates in only four of the state's thirteen congressional districts. The new legislature nominated White for the presidency in October by a vote of sixty to twelve but then proceeded by a vote of sixty-nine to three to resolve that they approved generally of "the principles and policy, both foreign and domestic, of the administration of the federal government" under Jackson.[31]

It is clear that by 1836 politics in Tennessee was entering a new era. Formerly elections had turned largely on considerations of personalities and factional affiliations, with the result that there could be no real polarization of political alignments. Now, with the issue of the succession to the presidency to the fore, political leaders and voters throughout the state could identify with the opposing candidates. As has already been suggested, more was involved than the presidential question, but this matter served to dramatize the cleavage throughout the state. As yet neither party, if such a term can be used, possessed any formal organization nor

31. Niles' *Register*, XLIX, 178-79.

were there acknowledged differences on public policy to differentiate them.   Both protested their fidelity to Jackson and purported to differ only over the question of his choice of a successor.

After the 1835 state election, Polk and Grundy worked valiantly against heavy odds to advance the cause of Van Buren. Polk's victory over Bell for the House speakership in December, 1835, bolstered his position in Tennessee.   Many early White supporters began to have misgivings about his candidacy when they saw that, contrary to their hopes, he could expect no votes outside the South.   From July to November Polk, Bell, and other stalwarts on both sides stumped the state addressing huge throngs at dinners, barbecues, and mass rallies. For the first time, in effect, every voter in every part of the state was presented with the same choice—White or Van Buren. That the choice was a difficult one is evidenced, perhaps, by the fact that only 55 per cent of the electorate cast their ballots, in contrast to nearly 73 per cent in the 1835 gubernatorial contest.   White was an easy victor, polling nearly 60 per cent of the total vote, but considering the obstacles against which they had to contend, the Van Buren forces had every reason to be heartened by their showing.   This election of 1836 was extremely influential in establishing lasting party loyalties in Tennessee.   But the parties had yet to acquire distinctive platforms and regular machinery for making nominations and conducting campaigns.

The lack of party machinery was apparent in the state election of 1837, when the incumbent, Governor Cannon, was opposed by General Robert Armstrong, who had been urged to run by Jackson but who also had the backing of John Bell and Ephraim Foster, the most prominent figures in the anti-Van Buren party.   Both sides had tacitly agreed not to conduct the election on party lines and neither candidate campaigned actively.   Cannon, a popular figure, won without difficulty. It was after this curious contest that Polk assumed the undisputed leadership of the Van Buren party and set about almost single-handedly to create a party organization. At a public meeting that he arranged in Nashville on December 31, 1837, a central committee of sorts was constituted and elaborate plans were announced for the organization of committees in each county. But for reasons that are not easy to explain, his efforts produced little results. Meanwhile, the opposition was consolidating under the banner of Henry Clay, who was confidently expected to be their presidential candidate in 1840, and was beginning to use the Whig label.

In an effort to strengthen what might now properly be called the Democratic cause, and to advance his own ambitions for the vice-presidency, Polk announced his candidacy for the governorship at a party gathering in Murfreesboro in August, 1838. Then, through correspondence and consultations, he sought to get strong Democratic candidates to run in every district.

When Congress adjourned in March, 1839, he returned to Tennessee and spent the several months until the election touring every corner of the state, often engaging in joint debates with his opponent, Governor Cannon, and with his old adversary, John Bell. Polk directed much of his fire against Clay, who was not overly popular in Tennessee, and made much of his undeviating loyalty to Jackson and old Jeffersonian principles. Although he had no elaborate hierarchy of campaign committees to marshall the party faithful, he more than supplied the lack by his own incredible personal efforts. Never had Tennessee been so thoroughly canvassed, and by election day the excitement was intense. Nearly 90 per cent of the voters went to the polls, and they elected Polk by a small margin, together with a Democratic legislature. Once installed in office, Polk continued to function as a party leader and succeeded in giving to his party a sense of unity that it had not hitherto possessed.

Preparations for the presidential election of 1840 brought the process of party formation in Tennessee close to completion. Despite the fact that he was disappointed in his ambitions for the vice-presidential nomination, Polk was determined to attempt to carry the state for Van Buren. The Whigs, whose ablest leader now was Ephraim Foster, overcame their initial distaste for William Henry Harrison and, recognizing that extraordinary measures were called for, decided to introduce the convention system of party organization. At a meeting of Whig members of the legislature and other party notables on January 4, in the State House, which featured four hours of oratory by Foster, resolutions were adopted urging the Whigs of Middle and West Tennessee to hold county meetings to elect two or more delegates to attend a convention in Nashville on February 3. Meanwhile plans had been formulated for a convention of East Tennessee Whigs at Knoxville on February 11.

The Nashville convention, the first of its kind ever held in Tennessee, met as scheduled under the presidency of Newton Cannon. Electors for the nine districts west of the mountains were named, resolutions lauding Harrison and Tyler were adopted, and a committee was appointed to draft an address to the people. On the following day a committee of three was authorized to correspond with the Whigs of East Tennessee about naming two electors-at-large. The Knoxville convention in due course named four electors, agreed on the choice of White and Foster as electors-at-large, and published an address. Both conventions were efficiently managed and testified to the ability of Foster as a political organizer in the new manner.

The Democrats were stimulated by the activity of their rivals into adopting similar techniques. At a party gathering in Nashville on January 8, attended by Democratic legislators and other politicians from around the state, they viewed with some concern measures that had been taken by the Whigs. Charging that their adversaries had set up secret committees of vigilance in many counties, they rejected such clandestine operations and proposed that public meetings should be held "for the purpose of insuring harmony and concerted action." Noting that the Whigs at their meeting on January 4 had called for the election of county delegates to convene at Nashville, "thus setting the example of a resort to a State Convention as a means of organizing and uniting the Whig party," the Democrats announced plans for a comparable gathering. Each county was to hold primary meetings and appoint any number of delegates to attend a state convention at Nashville on February 11. Presumably to insure that adequate leadership would be provided at the county level, the meeting appointed three men in each county as members of a state committee and authorized them to correspond with county committees that would be elected at public meetings.

"Never did a more animating spirit pervade an assembly," exulted J. George Harris, editor of *The Nashville Union,* the party organ. "There was no adjournment for dinner, and the recess for supper was a very short one. The ball of democracy for the fall campaign was fairly put in motion."[32] Harris later felt called upon to justify such an innovation as a convention by pointing out that the Whigs had set the example, that such was "the accustomed mode of organization of both parties in all the other States around us, and indeed throughout the Union," and finally, that the party leaders "deemed it necessary *in self defense,* and with a view to secure harmony and concert in the Republican Party in the approaching contest."[33] Tennessee politics, for so long completely undisciplined, was now to be tamed by a party apparatus.

The hasty efforts of the Democracy to combat the tactics of their foes were not entirely successful. Despite a rash of articles in *The Nashville Union* explaining the virtues and necessities of the convention system, it proved to be difficult to create the requisite machinery in every county. Consequently, when the convention assembled in the State House, fewer than half of the counties were represented, some with scores of delegates but others with only one.

Despite this disappointing showing, the convention was

32. *Nashville Union,* Jan. 10, 1840.
33. *Ibid.,* Jan. 13, 1840.

well managed. Major Andrew Jackson Donelson of the state committee introduced a set of carefully prepared resolutions providing both for the choice of electoral candidates and the appointment of delegates to the Democratic National Convention, which were adopted without dissent. In like manner, J. George Harris, also a member of the central committee, proposed a set of resolutions lauding Jackson and Van Buren, attacking the Whigs, and extolling Polk's qualifications for the Vice Presidency. A committee of twelve, called the Central Democratic Corresponding Committee was constituted to communicate with county committees. The second day of the convention was largely given over to speeches by leading lights of the party and was climaxed by a visit to the hall by the venerable Jackson, who spent an hour listening to the oratory and nodding to old acquaintances.[34]

The campaign thus initiated was fought with the intensity that had become traditional in Tennessee, but with the added features of the networks of committees and the extravagant spectacles produced by the Whigs. Governor Polk, the electoral candidates, and host of other party orators stumped the state for months, addressing mass meetings of unprecedented size and enthusiasm. The Whigs excelled both in the strength of their organization and in their ability to popularize their cause. Their greatest achievement was the Southwest Whig Festival, held at Nashville in August and attended by some thirty thousand partisans from all the states in the region.

The Democrats tried as best they could to combat the theatrical appeal of log cabins, hard cider, and "Old Tip," but they were inadequate to the challenge. Van Buren again went down to defeat, although he polled a slightly higher proportion of the total vote (44 per cent) than he had received in 1836. The most striking feature of the vote, however, was its magnitude. Never before had more than 55 per cent of the electorate participated in a presidential election, but in 1840 just under 90 per cent of the adult white males voted. This unprece-

34. *Ibid.*, Feb. 12-14, 1840.

dented turnout signified that Tennessee politics, so long conducted with little or no reference to national politics, had at
last been placed on a new basis, characterized by competition
between two parties that defined themselves essentially in
terms of their positions on national issues.

The party alignments that had developed in Tennessee
after 1834 had assumed stability by 1840, both at the leadership
level and among the masses of the voters, and had become well
balanced. Indeed, few counties altered their political allegiance down to the Civil War. Although the Whigs won every
presidential election through 1852, the Democrats captured the
governorship in 1839, 1845, and 1849. After 1852 the Democrats won all state-wide elections, but never by an overwhelming margin.

The state continued to be resistant to the establishment of
elaborate party machinery. The Whigs held a state convention, March 4-5, 1841, in Murfreesboro for the purpose of
uniting the party behind a new gubernatorial candidate, James
C. Jones, who went on to defeat Polk, but in 1843 no conventions were called; Jones and Polk were both tacitly recognized as the obvious party candidates. The Democrats, in
particular, found it difficult to create a durable party apparatus, and they seem to have had many fewer able leaders than
the Whigs. As in the past, the lack of formal party machinery
was compensated for by the incredibly taxing efforts of the
candidates and by the ability of the leadership cliques to
arrange matters through consultation and correspondence.
Certainly there were no signs down to 1844, at least, of any
democratization of party management. Voter interest, however, remained consistently high. Between 1839 and 1847
voter participation in both gubernatorial and presidential
elections usually exceeded 85 per cent and after that period was
normally around 80 per cent, except for a dip to 73 per cent
in the presidential election of 1852. Although both parties
were strongly represented in all sections of the state, there was
a tendency for the principal commercial towns and their en-

virons to lean toward the Whigs and the rural areas toward the Democrats.

GEORGIA

Georgia's peculiar political behavior, which before 1834 featured violent contests in state politics between parties that had no remote connection with national parties and no discernible philosophies to differentiate them, had no counterpart in the older political communities. The only national problem in which Georgians were intensely interested was that of Indian removal, and on that question there was unanimity of opinion. But agreement on, or indifference to, national politics did not result in political apathy. On the contrary, the Georgia frontiersman and farmer indulged himself in a hectic brand of politics that dealt not so much with issues as with personalities and which focused on the efforts of two competing personal cliques—the Troupites and the Clarkites—to obtain place and power. Not until after 1832 did the indigenous state parties begin to align themselves with the new national parties, and the identification remained tenuous for yet another decade.

Georgia early in the nineteenth century was a frontier area. In 1790 it had only 82,000 inhabitants settled in eleven counties, and most of its territory was occupied by Indian tribes. By 1840 the population had swollen to 691,000, the number of counties to over ninety, and the process of Indian removal had been completed. Here, obviously, was no well-ordered, stable society of the Virginia type. Although cotton, slavery, and the plantation system were to bulk increasingly large on the Georgia scene, most of the inhabitants were newly settled yeoman farmers, who had obtained their lands virtually without cost under the state's extremely liberal land policy.

If these conditions did not produce a thoroughly democratic political system, they did at least encourage democratic forms and institutions that acknowledged the role of the citizen in public affairs. The influence of a Georgia politician rested less on his inherited or acquired social position than it did on his ability to win the respect and affection of his constituents by exhibiting the virtues, and vices, that were admired in frontier communities.

Georgia's system of government, which underwent more alterations between 1776 and 1824 than that of any other state, reflected the potency of democratic influences. By 1810, to select an appropriate period of reference, all male taxpayers— which was equivalent to all adult white males—were privileged to vote. The legislature, elected annually on the first Monday in October, consisted of one senator and from one to four representatives from each county, depending on the federal population of the county. The legislature elected the governor, the superior court judges—there was no supreme court— and numerous other state officials. The election of inferior court judges, justices of the peace, and clerks of the court by the voters made for popular control of county government. Congressmen, except in rare instances, were elected from the state at large and presidential electors were chosen (except in 1796) by the legislature until 1828. The governor was made elective by popular vote for a two-year term beginning in 1825. In 1834 all property qualifications for members of the legislature were abolished, and a year later judges of the superior court were made elective. There were only two units of political activity in Georgia, the county and the state, a fact which greatly simplified the problem of party organization. The county, rather than the state was the principal center of political activity, and within each county there developed powerful cliques that ran party affairs.

Campaigns and elections in Georgia tended to be boisterous occasions. Voting was by ballot and access to the polls was facilitated by the creation of election districts within counties.

Candidates were informally nominated and usually conducted their own campaigns, making use of personal canvasses, stump speeches, and handbills but relying as well on barbecues, gander-pullings, shooting-matches, pole-climbings and, not infrequently, duels with their opponents, to enliven and amuse the electorate. Politics was a combination of sport and drama, played before a crude, semi-literate audience that preferred action to dull prose.

Georgia had given prompt and unanimous ratification to the federal constitution, motivated by an acute awareness of its need for a strong government that would be capable of dealing with the Indian problem and with the Spanish menace on its borders. For a brief period there was a loose alignment of parties under Federalist and Republican banners, but orthodox Federalism never became rooted in Georgia. By 1798 James Jackson, who left his seat in the Senate to return to Georgia and denounce the fraudulent Yazoo grants, had crushed political opposition and had created a personal machine that dominated state affairs even after his death in 1806. By 1815 the remnant of Jackson's coterie, now rallied around Robert M. Troup and William H. Crawford, were meeting opposition from another personal faction led by John Clark. Although the Troupites represented the continuation of an aristocratic type of leadership and the Clarkites depicted themselves as the friends of the common man, there was actually little to distinguish the two parties in philosophy or in following.

Interest centered on the governorship, which was often a stepping-stone to the Senate, and on congressional seats. Although neither party possessed a formal organization, the rival leadership groups customarily met each year at the commencement exercises at Franklin University (later the University of Georgia) to perfect their alliances, lay their plans, and determine how offices should be distributed. The word was then passed along to lieutenants in the counties and to members of the legislature. On occasions, especially after 1825, the legislative caucus was employed in making nominations for the governorship. The legislature, which elected the governor, was usually fairly evenly divided between the two parties.

Clark won the governorship in 1819 and was reelected in 1821. In 1823, however, Troup was the victor by the slim margin of four votes. The Clarkites then sponsored the change to popular election, relying on the people to return Clark to office. But in an epic struggle in 1825 Troup bested Clark by 683 votes out of more than 40,000. In the contests for control of the congressional delegation, party regularity often gave way before preferences for local sons and colorful personalities. In 1820, for example, the votes received by the six successful candidates ranged from 7,560 to 10,486. In 1828 the victorious candidates had votes ranging between 16,118 and 23,403. Contributing to the dispersion of votes was the practice of casting "plumpers," or "bullet votes," for one or two of the several men on the party ticket.[35] A detailed analysis of voting in individual counties demonstrates that only a small proportion of the electorate actually voted for the full quota of congressional candidates.

The available evidence, confusing as it is, suggests that there was a consistently high level of voter participation. Analysis is complicated by the practice of bullet voting and also by the fact that because of various technical irregularities perhaps as much as one-fourth of the actual vote cast often was not counted in the official returns. Reasonably precise returns, however, show that in the congressional election of 1803 some 50 per cent of the adult white males voted; in 1810 voter participation was 56 per cent and in 1812 it was 62 per cent. Individual counties, of course, rose considerably above the averages cited. In the climactic battle for the governorship in 1825, which was doubtless marked by considerable frauds, the returns indicate that 82 per cent of the adult white males voted. The parties—if such they may be called—were devoid of issues and almost entirely lacking in formal organization,

35. Niles' *Register*, XI, 178-79.

but the voter nevertheless turned out at the polls to vote for his favorites.

The presidential elections of 1824 and 1828 had a negligible impact on Georgia politics. Over the opposition of the Clark contingent, the Troup majority in the legislature in 1824 chose electors favorable to Crawford, who had long been identified with the Troup party. Looking to 1828 both parties expressed loyalty to Jackson but each ran its own slate of electors in what amounted to a popularity contest between the two parties. After deducting defective returns, the Troup-Jackson ticket received about 9,600 votes and the Clark-Jackson ticket about 7,300.[36] Calhoun received only two of the state's nine electoral votes for the vice-presidency. He was unpopular in Georgia, among other reasons, because of his long-standing hostility to Crawford. Two venturesome Adams electors received 603 and 605 votes. This somewhat farcical election brought little more than a third of the adult white males to the polls, whereas four-fifths had voted in the 1825 gubernatorial election. It demonstrated that Adams had no support in Georgia and implied that the Troupites were stronger than the Clarkites.

The presidential election of 1832 found Georgians still absorbed in the partisan warfare between Troupites and Clarkites, although there were signs that new influences were operative on the political scene. John Clark had moved to Florida, and his departure occasioned some shifting of party loyalties. In 1829 rival Troup factions contested over the governorship, and in 1831 the former Clarkites, now labelled the Union party, elected Wilson Lumkin to the governorship over George R. Gilmer, the Troup candidate. Attention then turned to the approaching congressional elections, to a determined movement within the state to secure the calling of

36. The 1828 election provides an illustration of the difficulties involved in using Georgia election data. The returns from nine counties were rejected, no returns were received from eight counties, and those from several districts in other counties were declared to be invalid. (Milledgeville) *Georgia Journal,* Nov. 24, 1828.

a convention to amend the constitution, and to agitation of the tariff issue. In the prevailing excitement, the presidential election attracted little notice. No Clay ticket was run, but, as in 1828, the Troup and Union parties again sponsored separate electoral slates pledged to Jackson. The Unionists offered Barbour as their vice-presidential candidate and were defeated by nearly a two-to-one margin. Only 32 per cent of the adult white males voted; a month earlier 73 per cent had participated in the congressional election.

The first real effort to relate Georgia parties to national politics was undertaken by John M. Berrien late in 1832. Berrien, who was associated with the Troup party, had been born in New Jersey, was educated at Princeton, and rose to prominence in Georgia through his legal talents. He served as attorney general in Jackson's cabinet until the upheaval that developed out of the Peggy Eaton affair, when he was asked to resign. Returning to Georgia, he found himself—like John Branch of North Carolina—in an awkward position. Although he endorsed Jackson for re-election in 1832 he was understandably cool toward the administration and, feeling the need to rehabilitate his position in Georgia politics, launched an attack on the tariff of 1832. At the usual gathering of Georgia politicians in August, 1832, at the Franklin University commencement, Berrien was instrumental in having the group—drawn from both parties—issue a call for an Anti-Tariff Convention, to be composed of delegates from all counties chosen at the October election. When the convention met at Milledgeville in November, the nullification issue was raised by some extremists, and a large minority faction, led by John Forsyth, withdrew. Berrien, who was not sympathetic to nullification, remained and played a leading role.

The effect of this convention was to occasion some redefinition of parties. Forsyth and William H. Crawford, previously associated with the Troup party, now moved over to the Union party. A warm friend and admirer of Van Buren, Forsyth became the titular leader of the Union-Democratic party and its outstanding luminary. Berrien and nullification leader Augustin S. Clayton assumed positions of leadership in the old Troup party. The remodelled parties soon tested their strength in the election of delegates to the state constitutional convention, and while that body was in session—in May, 1833—they employed the occasion to solidify their ranks. The Union delegates, together with members of the legislature and other party figures, met and adopted resolutions denouncing nullification and approving the conduct of Senator Forsyth and President Jackson.[37] Their opponents held a similar meeting at which they nominated Joel Crawford for the governorship. Crawford was defeated in a bitter contest that brought 90 per cent of the adult white males to the polls. Soon after this defeat, the Berrien forces held a caucus and instituted plans for a thorough organization of the party—now renamed the "State-Rights Party of Georgia"—with a central state committee and permanent corresponding committees in each county.

The tightening of party lines was clearly evident in the congressional election of 1834. All nine Union candidates were elected, and the detailed returns for each county show that straight-ticket voting was the rule. The high man on the Union ticket received 32,934 votes and the low man 32,312. This was in sharp contrast to 1832, when there was a spread of more than 12,000 votes between the high and low man on the victorious Troup ticket. Although the parties were closely balanced on a state-wide basis, there was a pronounced tendency for many counties to be heavily partial to one party. Taliaferro County, for example, gave 403 votes for the State-Rights ticket and only 12 for the Unionists. Union county, on the other hand, cast 162 votes for the Unionists and not a single vote for the opposition. Clusters of adjacent counties often exhibited similar political tendencies, but there was no simple sectional pattern evident in the voting. This tendency for counties to be extremely lopsided in party preference, it

37. Niles' *Register*, XLIV, 224, 258.

might be observed, was doubtless encouraged by the unusual emphasis given to state-wide elections under the Georgia system, but the same condition was characteristic of other "new" political communities before the establishment of highly institutionalized parties.

Despite their new orientation, the Georgia parties had continued to be essentially state parties, with only a remote identification with national parties. The presidential election of 1836, however, which confronted the parties with the necessity of choosing a candidate to support, had the effect of establishing a closer relationship between state and national party identities. Both parties could back Jackson in 1832, but Van Buren was controversial.

The Union party, with no discernible enthusiasm, fell in line with the nominees of the Baltimore convention, in which it had been represented by a three-man delegation. The State-Rights men at first advanced George M. Troup as their candidate at a state convention in June, 1835, but ultimately named an electoral ticket pledged to White and Barbour at a mixed legislative caucus in December, 1835. The Union electoral ticket was nominated by similar machinery.[38]

Although the Union party had won both the gubernatorial election of 1835 and the congressional election held in October, 1836, Van Buren was defeated by 1,700 votes. Participation had been over 80 per cent in the gubernatorial and congressional contests, but it fell to 65 per cent in the presidential election. The inference would seem to be that the substitution of Van Buren for Jackson had destroyed the unity that had been characteristic of Georgia in the preceding presidential elections. With both parties now committed, perforce, to support or oppose the national administration, a new dimension was being impressed on Georgia politics.

The transition from a state-centered to a nationally-oriented politics was advanced by the presidential election of 1840. The

38. *Ibid.*, XLV, 331; (Washington) *National Intelligencer*, July 1, Dec. 29, 1835.

Union-Democratic party had little alternative but to adhere to Van Buren, although his prospects in the state were admittedly poor. A legislative caucus in December, 1839, named an electoral slate as well as candidates for Congress. Only two delegates represented the party in the Democratic National Convention in May, 1840.

The State-Rights party, still avoiding the name Whig, initially advanced Troup again as their preferred candidate. Even after Harrison had been nominated by the Harrisburg convention, in which Georgia was not represented, a party caucus resolved that neither Van Buren nor Harrison was entitled to the party's support. But the caucus did issue a call for a state convention to be held in Milledgeville on June 1 for the purpose of agreeing on a presidential nominee and naming a congressional ticket. By the time the convention met, the faction of the party led by John M. Berrien had waged an effective campaign in behalf of Harrison, and he was accepted as the party's standard bearer.

Never before had the state witnessed such interest in a presidential election. The theatrical campaign techniques that the Whigs used everywhere with such effect were extremely congenial to the Georgia scene. The Union-Democratic party sought to accommodate itself to the new era by holding a state convention at Milledgeville on July 3 and 4 that was attended by over fifteen hundred delegates. But they were no match for their opponents, who staged a two-day festival at Macon in mid-August that attracted, it was said, twelve thousand delegates from every county in the state. The Unionists had won the governorship in 1839, but in October, 1840, their congressional ticket was defeated and in November Van Buren was overwhelmed, securing less than 45 per cent of the popular vote. Nearly 90 per cent of the adult white males voted, a level that had previously been exceeded only in the 1837 gubernatorial election. That the defeat of the Democrats was largely attributable to the weakness of Van Buren as a candidate is

suggested by the fact that the party easily won the gubernatorial election in 1841.

For a decade after 1840 the Georgia parties continued to
battle on fairly even terms, until the events associated with
the Compromise of 1850 produced a major reorganization of
parties.   The State-Rights party, which finally adopted the
name Whig in 1843, won the governorship in that year, repeated in 1845, and carried the state for Taylor in 1848.   The
Whigs, originally anti-tariff and even tainted with nullification
sympathies, became under Berrien's leadership increasingly
nationalistic in outlook and gave Clay such strong backing that
he lost the state by only two thousand votes in 1844.   Interest
in presidential elections remained high, reaching a new peak
in 1844 when 94 per cent of the adult white males voted and
declining only slightly to 90 per cent in 1848.   Indeed, during
the 1840's, in contrast to other decades, presidential elections
drew more voters to the polls than gubernatorial elections.
Georgia parties had at last become aligned with national
parties.

Party formation in Georgia obviously followed a course
that was highly unusual.   What most distinguished the Georgia
situation, of course, was the fact that for nearly a decade before
1824 politics had been conducted on the basis of contests between two state-centered parties led by rival personal cliques,
the Troupites and the Clarkites.   These parties continued
to vie for dominance after 1824 but not on the grounds of differences over national issues or presidential preferences.   Indeed, presidential politics aroused little interest in 1828 or
1832 because both parties endorsed Jackson and there were no
Adams or Clay parties in the field.   After Jackson's second
election national politics, and especially "the presidential question," began to exert an influence on Georgia parties.

In Virginia and North Carolina, where there had been no
established party alignments, the presidential question provided the basis for the formation of parties around 1834.   In
Georgia, however, although there were shifts in loyalties after

1832, what happened essentially is that the pre-existing parties began to identify themselves with the national parties. The new orientation did not take place so abruptly nor so completely as in Virginia and North Carolina. Because of the tradition that had been established, Georgia parties remained state-centered down to 1840. To put it another way, Georgia had a dual system of politics down to 1832. Politicians and voters were Clarkites or Troupites in state elections but Jacksonians in presidential elections. After 1832 there was a difference of opinion about the succession to the presidency, the state parties had to accommodate to this factor, and, with some reshuffling of allegiances, they did so.

CONCLUSIONS

The first party system, which had shaped partisan loyalties in all of the northern states, had but a slight impact in the Old South. Only in Virginia and North Carolina were elections fought out between Republicans and Federalists over a period of several years, and the contest was soon so one-sided as to render unnecessary the types of party apparatus created in northern states. Many explanations might be offered for the failure of competitive parties to form. Possibly the fact that there was no disposition to oppose the succession of Virginians to the presidency lies at the root of the matter. If George Clinton, rather than James Madison, had been put forward in 1808 as the regular Republican candidate, the effect might have been comparable to that produced by the nomination of Van Buren in 1836. In any event, presidential elections occasioned little division of sentiment in the Old South, and party development there was arrested after 1800. The Republicans in Virginia and North Carolina had the rudiments of a party apparatus, vestiges of which survived until 1824 in the form of the legislative caucus. Elsewhere the party had no formal machinery; where all were nominal Republicans, partisanship need not be disciplined. Throughout the Old South, the management of politics was informal rather than institutional.

In the absence of divisions related to national politics, there was some tendency for "parties" to form for the purpose of contesting state elections. In Georgia there was the curious Troup *versus* Clark alignment and in Kentucky the brief struggle between the Old Court and New Court parties. In Tennessee around 1820 there were some signs of polarization behind the rival Overton and Erwin factions. But even in Georgia, where the tendency was most evident, the term "party" can be applied only in a very weak sense.

It has been observed that in new political communities it was common for a single clique, or faction, to exercise a dominating influence on political affairs on the state level. Then, characteristically, an opposition faction would form and enter into competition for the major offices. Thus, in Georgia, the old Jackson faction in time gave way to the rival Troup and Clark factions, and in Tennessee the Blount faction was succeeded by the Overton and Erwin factions. In Georgia this factionalism could operate with peculiarly wide effect because the state's congressional delegation was elected at large and—until 1825—the governor and the presidential electors were chosen by the legislature. In such circumstances, relatively little management was required. The Tennessee factions never approached the status of parties. Whether the Georgia factions should be regarded as parties is doubtful, for their scope was restricted essentially to competing for state-wide offices, they had no distinctive philosophies or programs, and they lacked any formal structure of authority. Some of the same deficiencies can be attributed to the Kentucky parties, although they did at least represent opposing views on matters of public policy.

Despite the lack of competitive, organized parties, and the general absence of "issues" in elections, voter participation was at a relatively high rate. Indeed, except for Virginia, where the suffrage was drastically limited, participation compared favorably with that in states where the parties were highly developed and was markedly higher than in those states—like Connecticut—where one party reigned supreme. It was not uncommon for three-fifths of the adult white males to go to the polls in Georgia and Kentucky and for even larger proportions to turn out in Tennessee and North Carolina. The voters were not inspired by a sense of party loyalty nor were they brought out by aggressive campaign committees. Presumably they were responding to the appeals of candidates, to the urgings of men of influence, and to a desire to participate in an exciting—and often entertaining—contest. Everywhere, of course, interest in state elections was greater than in presidential elections.

The most vital arena of politics in the Old South was the county. In all of the states the county was the unit of representation in the legislature and it constituted as well the basic unit of local government. Earlier than 1824 there were statewide elections for governor only in Tennessee and Kentucky, for presidential electors only in Virginia and (after 1816) North Carolina, and for congressmen only in Georgia. In Tennessee the governorship was rarely the object of intense competition, and even in Kentucky it was not the focal point for political activity. The most critical elections, then, were those fought out at the county level for seats in the state legislature. Comparable interest was frequently aroused by congressional contests.

So long as politics remained essentially a localized concern, political leadership could be exercised directly and personally by prominent individuals, allied groups, and candidates. No party machinery was required. Candidates were self-nominated, negotiated for support from men of influence, and conducted their own campaigns. In the legislature they might identify themselves with a faction, but such ties were usually very flexible. In most states the legislator was more dependent on the support of local personages, usually members of the county court, than he was on the patronage of the leader of a state faction. The county politicians, it would seem, were both independent and provincial, and even after 1834, when elections came to be fought on the basis of parties, they were reluctant to exchange old ways for new. But as the states assumed increased importance as units for electing presidential electors and governors and the contest for the presidency both divided and aroused the electorate, the exigencies of party competition made discipline and organization essential at all levels.

For a decade after 1824 politics in the Old South underwent little change. State elections were conducted as they had been in the past; presidential elections stirred little interest and created no lasting alignments, except in Kentucky. In 1824 Crawford was the favored candidate of the political leaders in Virginia, North Carolina, and Georgia, but after the election his followers moved easily into the Jackson camp. Tennessee was solidly behind Jackson; Kentucky was partial to Clay. By 1828, confronted with the choice between Jackson and Adams, every state went for the Old Hero. In Virginia and North Carolina there were organized efforts in behalf of Adams, but he was overwhelmed and his party soon disintegrated. Georgia and Tennessee were all but unanimous for Jackson. Only in Kentucky was there a genuine contest, conducted by well-organized parties that operated in the state elections as well as in the presidential contest. The election of 1832 was even more one-sided than that of 1828. Clay carried Kentucky, but his best showing elsewhere was in Virginia, and there he polled only one-quarter of the total vote.

The deviant behavior of Kentucky, where party alignments were stable between 1832 and 1836, can readily be accounted for on the basis of Clay's local popularity as a native son. The remainder of the Old South preferred Jackson because he was regarded as more truly representative of the section than Clay. So clear was this preference that those political leaders who were unsympathetic to Jackson's policies—or hostile to the dominant pro-Jackson factions in their states—would not take the risk of attempting to form opposition parties in behalf of Clay.

The monolithic character of southern politics underwent a profound change after 1832, with the result that in 1836 there were competitive parties in every state, and Van Buren won only Virginia and North Carolina. Some forecast of the cleavage that lay ahead could be seen in the movement to displace Van Buren as Jackson's running mate in 1832, especially in Virginia, North Carolina, and Georgia. The precise strength of this movement is difficult to assess, but it was formidable. It is even more difficult to decide the extent to which anti-Van Burenism was motivated by political opportunism and to what extent it reflected either sheer southernism or genuine concern about governmental policies.

In any event, parties were formed in each state; in Virginia as early as the state elections of 1833, in North Carolina and Georgia in the congressional elections, and in Tennessee in 1835 during the preliminaries to the presidential campaign. In Virginia, North Carolina, and Georgia the opposition initially laid heavy stress on the broad issue of state rights, but this emphasis became less pronounced by 1836, when the attack focused directly on Van Buren. In North Carolina and Georgia, however, and in Tennessee as well, the new parties can best be related to rival factions within the ranks of the Old Jacksonians, factions that were probably as much concerned with competing for power and place as they were with defending particular causes or interests. The opposition in Virginia was conspicuously lacking in unity, either in leadership or in sentiments, and was held together by common antagonisms to the Junto and to Van Buren. Whatever may be deemed to have been responsible for the cleavages in each state, it was surely Van Buren's candidacy that provided the opposition leaders with an opportunity to build popular support. In much the same way, the elimination of Adams from the political scene had vastly enhanced the prospects of the Jacksonian leaders in New England.

The party alignments that began to form around 1834 remained unstable until 1840, after which time they were increasingly reinforced and disciplined by party organizations. There had been some use of the state convention in Virginia, North Carolina, and Georgia before 1839, but it was more common for state-wide political arrangements to be made either informally or through some type of legislative caucus. It was in 1839 and 1840, in preparation for the presidential campaign, that the convention system was fully accepted in those states and in Tennessee as well. Generally the Whigs took the initiative in building a strong party apparatus, especially in North Carolina and Tennessee. Kentucky, of course, had embraced the convention system in 1828. The convention technique was employed not only in connection with presidential elections but also found increasing favor in state and congressional elections, although it does not seem to have been so widely adopted below the state level in the South as it was in New England and the Middle States.

The formation of organized, institutionalized parties meant that the voters now acquired partisan identities; they identified themselves as Whigs or Democrats and responded more or less habitually to the appeal of their party. Candidates, too, sought election less on the basis of their personal merits or popularity and more on the strength of their party affiliation. Thus voters and candidates alike developed vested interests in the parties as institutions, perceived public issues from partisan perspectives, and derived satisfactions from the dramatic election competitions with the rival party. Such attitudes had taken hold in New England and the Middle States in the early years of the century, but they did not become pervasive in the South until the Van Buren era.

From 1836 through 1852 the balance between the two parties remained close. The Whigs, aided by the fact that they had Van Buren for a target in 1840 as well as in 1836, built up such strength that they became dominant in North Carolina, Kentucky, and Tennessee and offered a serious challenge in Virginia and Georgia. Only Virginia voted consistently for Democratic presidential candidates; Kentucky and Tennessee were uniformly in the Whig column. As was true of New England and the Middle States, the Old South tended to swing as a unit in presidential elections. In every state, except Tennesse, the Democrats suffered losses in 1840, gained behind Polk in 1844, declined with Taylor as their opponent in 1848, and came back strongly in 1852. This was the same pattern followed by the Middle States and by the nation as a whole.

The parties were more evenly matched in the Old South than in New England; the average differential between the percentages of the votes obtained by the presidential candidates narrowed from 56 in 1828 and 64 in 1832 to 9, 14, 5, 8, and 9, in the succeeding elections. Party alignments in state elections corresponded with those in presidential elections, although there was some tendency for the Whigs to make their strongest showings in the presidential contests. Unlike the northern states, those of the Old South adhered rigorously to the two-party system; third party candidacies were unknown.

In the Old South as elsewhere the formation of competitive parties had a remarkable effect on voter participation, especially in presidential elections. Before 1836 it was exceptional for more than one-third of the adult white males to vote in presidential elections, but in 1836 participation exceeded 50 per cent in all except Virginia and in 1840 it ranged from 55 per cent in Virginia up to nearly 90 per cent in Georgia and Tennessee. In Kentucky, where party formation had occurred earliest, participation jumped from 25 per cent in 1824 to 71 per cent in 1828. Voting in state and congressional elections, which had always been enlivened by personal and factional contests, had been at a fairly high level before 1836, and after that date it kept pace with the rate achieved in presidential elections. Indeed, in North Carolina and Kentucky, where governors were elected in the same years as presidents, the gubernatorial contests usually produced slightly higher turnouts of voters than did the presidential race. Regardless of the fact that its parties were never so intensively organized as those in the northern states, the Old South sustained a far higher rate of voter participation down to 1860 than did New England and compared favorably with the Middle States.

The development of organized parties in the Old South had the effect of broadening the scope of politics. Formerly the counties or the congressional districts had been the largest units of political activity; now, with heated party competition extended to include governorships and presidential electors, campaigns had to encompass the entire state. This consideration, among others, induced changes in the traditional campaign techniques. Networks of committees, headed by a central committee, came into existence to stimulate and mobilize the electorate.

In their endeavors to attract the maximum numbers of voters to their standards, these committees utilized extremely popular appeals; they invested politics with a dramatic quality. The parties concocted creeds, slogans, emblems, and songs; staged festivals; enshrined their heroes and martyrs; promised rewards to the faithful and threatened the wayward with excommunication. Personal appeals by the candidates, long a feature of southern politics, became appeals to stand by the party as well as solicitations of individual support. By the 1840's the old custom of personal canvassing had become transformed into the intensive speaking tour, often highlighted by joint debates between the candidates or by the appearance of well known political figures from other states.

Parties are made by leaders. In each state, in each party, there were towering figures who filled such a role. Among the Jacksonians the outstanding were Thomas Ritchie in Virginia, Amos Kendall and Francis P. Blair in Kentucky, James K. Polk in Tennessee, John Forsyth in Georgia, and Romulus Saunders in North Carolina. Notable among the early Whig leaders were John M. Berrien of Georgia, John Bell and

Ephraim Foster of Tennessee, and Henry Clay of Kentucky. It was these men, together with their associates, who took the initiative in defining opposing positions on public questions, creating organizations capable of maintaining harmony and discipline, and appealing in the most effective possible ways for the support of the electorate. Despite the semblance of democratization of control of party affairs that came with the introduction of the convention system, leadership remained an element of crucial importance and was exercised by men of varied backgrounds and official status. Behind the paraphernalia of conventions and committees, which all too often performed what was essentially a cosmetic function, decisions were made by individual chieftains and their lieutenants.

The most striking aspect of party formation in the Old South was the suddenness with which parties emerged between 1833 and 1836. Equally remarkable was the persistence of the two-party system into the decade of the 1850's. For more than twenty years the section had closely balanced parties, a condition that had never previously maintained and that was never subsequently restored.

In the South, as elsewhere, it was the contest for the presidency that exerted the decisive influence on party formation. Parties did not form earlier than 1833—except in Kentucky— because Jackson was so clearly preferable to his opponents. It was the prospect that Van Buren would succeed Jackson that encouraged opposition elements to form and to contest both state and national elections with those who remained loyal to Jackson's heir. Well established by 1840, the new parties acquired such institutional characteristics that they could maintain themselves as competing electoral machines long after the specific issues and presidential personalities that had conditioned their formation had receded into the past. Even the political upheavals of the pre-Civil War decade did not destroy the two-party system in the Old South. Indeed, in no other section did the party alignments that had formed by 1840 so long endure.

CHAPTER VI

Party Formation in the New States

It is appropriate to group together for purposes of political analysis those states which entered the union between 1800 and 1824—Ohio, Indiana, Illinois, Louisiana, Alabama, Mississippi, and Missouri. Although these states may not seem to constitute a section in the same sense that we can consider New England, the Middle States, and the Old South to be sections, they were in fact remarkably alike in their political behavior. Their strongest common characteristic, of course, was that they were all new political communities.

Largely because they became states after the first American party system had lost its vitality and the presidency had ceased to be contested, their politics had never—except in Ohio—been organized on the basis of a cleavage beteen Republicans and Federalists. Neither had state oriented parties developed, as in Georgia or, to a degree, Kentucky. Instead politics was conducted essentially on the Tennessee model of factionalism and personalism.

All of the new states were nominally Republican in allegiance, but in actuality they can most accurately be described not as one-party states but as "no-party" states. The history of party formation in these states, then, does not really begin until after 1824. Once under way, the transition from factionalism and personalism to a partisan type politics went through a similar course of development in almost every state.

In general, vague and unbalanced party alignments appeared first in presidential elections, but these alignments did not for many years greatly influence other elections. The result was a period of "dual politics" in each state. Increasingly after 1834 political identities came to have the same meaning in all elections—national, state, and local—and parties became relatively well balanced and acquired elaborate organizations.

OHIO

With a population drawn from New England, the Middle States, and the upper South at a time when the first American party system was still vigorous, Ohio in its early years acquired some familiarity with party politics. In this respect it was not entirely representative of the other new states. Settlers arriving from the older states brought with them their recently acquired party identities, together with the political styles and organizational techniques of their particular regions. But perhaps in part because of the very heterogeneity of these backgrounds, as well as because of the general decline of parties throughout the nation, Ohio did not for long conduct its politics within the framework of the old parties.

Moreover, the development of any state-wide political organization was rendered extremely difficult because of the astonishing rate at which the population expanded. Between 1800 and 1820 the population grew seven fold, and it tripled between 1820 and 1840. Along with this rapid growth, which was of course characteristic of all new states, went a multiplication of congressional districts, counties, townships, and other units of representation. Such expansion obviously complicated the task of party building.

The Ohio constitution of 1802, which was to serve the state for half a century, established a highly democratic government.

The franchise was extended to all who were liable to taxes or who worked on the roads, which was nearly equivalent to adult white male suffrage. State elections were held annually on the second Tuesday in October and were conducted by ballot with the township as the polling unit. The governor was popularly elected for a two-year term and was a weak executive, having no veto on legislation and scant appointing power. The two-house legislature, apportioned among the counties on the basis of adult white male inhabitants as determined by a quadrennial census, was the dominant branch of the government. Members of the lower house were elected annually and senators served two-year terms. The legislature by joint ballot chose the principal state officials and elected judges for seven-year terms. There was no property qualification for office-holding. Township and county officials were popularly elected. Congressmen were elected from districts and presidential electors from the state at large. Because of its importance as an election unit, the county was the major center of political activity and there was consequently a tendency in Ohio for political organization to be relatively weak at the state level.

Early partisan divisions in Ohio can be traced to antagonisms between the territorial legislature and Governor Arthur St. Clair over issues that involved both personalities and policies. There was a tremendous influx of settlers after 1795, when the Treaty of Greenville facilitated the removal of the Indians from much of the region, and in December, 1798, the first territorial legislature was elected. St. Clair, an ardent and outspoken Federalist, together with his small coterie of appointive officials, soon clashed with the legislators over the choice of a territorial delegate and manifested coolness toward the general sentiment in favor of statehood at the earliest opportunity. When in 1802 Congress authorized the holding of a convention to decide the matter of statehood, the opponents of the governor and his Federalist supporters created Republican corresponding societies. These in turn sponsored county nominating meetings to assure united support for Republican candidates. The Federalists resorted to similar organizational activities in at least one county.

The ensuing election gave the Republicans an overwhelming majority in the convention, which proceeded to vote for statehood and draft a constitution. The Federalist minority, which was restricted to certain townships that were predominantly New England in origin, was soon so outnumbered that it could offer no real resistance to the Republicans. Lacking an effective opposition, the Republicans fell prey to factionalism. A so-called Virginia wing, led by Thomas Worthington, Edward Tiffin, and Nathaniel Massie, contested with a New England faction, which was often aided by the Federalist remnant and was directed by Samuel Huntington and R. J. Meigs, Jr.

These two cliques alternated in control of politics at the state level until after the War of 1812. Tiffin, Meigs, Huntington, and Worthington all served as governor and were usually elected in opposition to one of the leaders of the rival faction. Although party machinery remained rudimentary, the legislature served as a clearing house for political negotiations and some use was made of caucuses and committees of correspondence to manage factional affairs. In many counties the convention apparatus that had come into existence in 1802 survived and was employed in making nominations for county offices.

Some months before the state election of 1810 a network of Tammany Societies was established to support the candidacy of Worthington against Meigs, and for the next few years the voters of the state were arrayed into Tammany and anti-Tammany parties. So bitter was the strife that in 1812 each party ran opposing electoral slates pledged to Madison. The societies, which aroused considerable popular hostility because of their semi-secret character, soon declined, and political contests after 1816 were between personalities rather than between parties or factions. Some semblance of national political identification survived only because of the necessity of nominating a slate of Republican electors every four years. This task was performed in 1816 by an assemblage of legislators, judges, and influential citizens meeting at Chillicothe. In 1820 the electoral ticket was prepared by a similar conclave at Columbus during a session of the legislature.

On the basis of the size of the vote cast in presidential and gubernatorial elections, it would not seem that politics aroused much interest in Ohio before 1824. The peak participation in a presidential election occurred in 1812, when 20 per cent of the adult white males voted. Gubernatorial elections usually brought about one-third of the electorate to the polls, although a three-man race in 1822 occasioned a record participation of 47 per cent. Frontier democracy, Ohio style, did not produce elections that were either particularly exciting or well attended.

The impending revival of the contest for the presidency in 1824 stimulated a flurry of activity among the partisans of Clay, Jackson, and Adams. There were at the time no discernible partisan or factional alignments in the state that could provide the base of support for any of the leading contenders. Instead, parties pledged to one or another of the candidates had virtually to be created in their entirety. Much, then, was to depend on the initiative and ability of individual politicians as they sought to advance both their own interest and that of their favorite candidate. The party building activities, interestingly enough, were confined exclusively to the presidential election; the gubernatorial election of 1824 was conducted without any relationship to the presidential election that was to be held two weeks later.

In the early stages of the pre-election maneuvering, Clay and De Witt Clinton seemingly enjoyed the greatest support among politicians and newspaper editors, but the Clinton movement had collapsed by March, 1824. Meanwhile the Clay adherents, including most of the Ohio congressional delegation, sought to induce the legislature to nominate their champion. A caucus was accordingly held on December 10, 1822, but by a close vote it decided to make no nomination. Subsequently, on January 3, 1823, a second caucus, from which over thirty legislators absented themselves, nominated Clay for the presidency. The movement thus initiated by members of the legislature continued to develop. In March, 1824, a Clay electoral ticket, apparently arranged informally by some legislators and other supporters, was published and a central committee was designated. This committee stimulated the organization of county committees of correspondence and arranged for a primitive kind of state convention which met in Columbus on July 15, 1824, and dutifully ratified the previously announced electoral slate.

There was little exertion on behalf of Jackson until late in 1823, although Moses Dawson, editor of the Cincinnati *Advertiser* had begun to champion the general's cause early in that year. There were seemingly spontaneous meetings in Wayne and Adams counties in February and March, 1824, at which local organizations pledged to Jackson were created, but his campaign made little headway until Elijah Hayward, editor of the Cincinnati *National Republican* and erstwhile backer of Clinton, switched to Jackson and assumed the leadership of the movement. A meeting of Cincinnati Jacksonians in April, 1824, was followed a month later by a Hamilton County meeting, which urged men of similar sentiments in other counties to establish committees and on May 29 proposed that a state convention should be held. The "convention," which met in Columbus on July 14, was attended by only seventeen delegates, but it boldly proceeded to publish an address, name a central committee, and form a full electoral ticket. Hayward, who served as secretary of the extremely active Hamilton County committee and as a member of the state central committee was apparently the leading spirit in the organizational drive.

The Adams cause was severely handicapped by lack of effective state leadership and possessed little organization. A meeting of his supporters in Cincinnati in April, 1824, appointed committees to work in his behalf and their example was followed in several counties. Later, on July 15, a small assemblage in Columbus named a state committee of correspondence. As the campaign progressed, Clay's early advantage over his opponents was reduced, and on the eve of the election no man enjoyed a commanding position.

Despite the efforts of the three parties to create organizations, relatively little had been accomplished, and the election turned out to be a mildly interesting popularity contest, devoid of issues and even remote from local political concerns. Only 35 per cent of the eligibles went to the polls, although 53 per cent had voted two weeks before in the state election. Clay was the victor with a plurality of the total vote; Jackson was a very close second and Adams a distant third. A minute analysis of the election returns does not reveal any significant differences in the composition of the support for each of the three candidates, nor did the voting pattern forecast ultimate party alignments. Perhaps the most interesting aspect of the election was the evidence it afforded that Ohio politicians were readily inclined to use delegate conventions and committees of correspondence to organize their parties.

The organizations that had been formed in 1824 were exclusively concerned with the presidential election, and they ceased to operate in most counties after that election. The gubernatorial election in 1826 was conducted without reference to national politics, as in the past, and the victor—Trimble—scored an easy five-to-one victory over three opponents. In 1827, however, politicians turned their attention to the presidential question. The Jacksonians, with leadership again provided by Elijah Hayward's Hamilton County machine, held numerous county conventions preparatory to a state convention on January 8, 1828. The Adams supporters were no less energetic and made similar preparations for a convention that met at the Court House in Columbus on December 18, 1827.

The Adams convention might properly be regarded as the first full-fledged state party convention in Ohio, for the meetings that had been held during the 1824 campaign hardly merited that designation. With delegates in attendance from all but two of the state's sixty-seven counties—many of them members of the legislature, which was in session at the time—the convention was efficiently organized. An electoral ticket was formed, an address and resolutions were adopted and published, and a state central committee of fourteen was appointed to direct the campaign. No nominations were made for state offices.[1]

The Jacksonian state convention, in which fifty-four counties were represented by 160 delegates, also named an electoral slate, adopted an address, and set up a 32-man central committee, which was empowered to call a future convention. After the convention had adjourned, many of the delegates, together with Jacksonian legislators and prominent citizens assembled to nominate Campbell to oppose the incumbent, Trimble, for the governorship. The fact that the nomination was made in this fashion suggests that the formal party organization was still regarded as having national politics alone as its proper concern.

The campaign between the two newly mobilized parties was carried on with considerable vigor. Both parties held district conventions to nominate candidates for Congress, and in some areas "young men's" conventions met to stimulate enthusiasm. Both parties had extensive newspaper support and both used printed tickets, distributed by poll committees, to facilitate balloting. In the gubernatorial election early in October, which was not conducted strictly on party lines, Campbell was defeated by a small margin. But in the presidential election, Jackson gained an equally close victory over Adams. The Jacksonians also elected eight of fourteen con-

1. *Proceedings and Address of the Convention of Delegates, That met at Columbus, Ohio, Dec. 28, 1827*...[Columbus, 1827]; Niles' *Register*, XXXIII, 316.

gressmen. Most interesting was the fact that voter participation in the presidential election soared to 76 per cent, greatly exceeding the 61 per cent participation in the state election.

This election undoubtedly contributed greatly toward the establishment of enduring party identities in Ohio. It revealed a close balance of parties that was to be characteristic of Ohio politics down to the Civil War and it brought to a high stage of development the techniques of party organization that had been employed on a modest scale in 1824. Yet it would be inaccurate to conclude that the process of party formation in Ohio was completed in 1828. For the next several years, the tendency already noted for state politics to remain somewhat divorced from national politics persisted. Too, the organizational apparatus that was elaborated in presidential years was not fully maintained in the interim periods. Furthermore, when Clay succeeded Adams as Jackson's opponent, and even more influential, when Van Buren replaced Jackson as the Democratic standard-bearer, there were obviously significant shifts in party loyalties. But despite these important qualifications, the election of 1828 must be regarded as the beginning of a new era in Ohio politics.

After 1828 the political situation was muddled by the emergence of the Antimasons and by the uncertain future of the former Adams party, which, until the emergence of Clay in 1831, lacked a figurehead. The Jacksonians, oddly enough, were unable to capitalize on their advantage. The formidable organization they had built in 1828 languished, despite the sustenance provided by federal patronage. A state convention in 1830 attracted delegates from only half of the state's counties, and its nominee for governor, Robert Lucas, was subsequently defeated in a light vote. In the same year the Jacksonians elected only six congressmen.

Party spirit was revived with the approach of the 1832 elections. The Jacksonian state convention in January, 1832, named an electoral slate, appointed delegates to the national convention, nominated Lucas again for the governorship, and overhauled the party machinery. The Antimasons at first put an electoral ticket pledged to Wirt in the field but withdrew it late in the campaign and urged support for Clay. Just as in 1828, then, attention was focused on the contest between Jackson and his adversary, and both major parties conducted vigorous campaigns. Jackson was the winner, again by an extremely narrow margin in an election that brought three-fourths of the voters to the polls. In the state elections, in which only 63 per cent of the electorate voted, Lucas was victorious over the Antimason candidate who was also supported by the Clay party. The Jacksonians gained eleven of the state's nineteen congressional seats. The party alignment was similar to that which had appeared in 1828, but there was now a closer identity between national and state politics.

In 1834 the Democrats retained their supremacy over the Whigs, who were still weak in organization and again were without a national leader. There were, however, signs of discord among the Democrats over who should succeed Jackson. At the state convention in January, 1834, delegates were appointed to the national convention and, over the opposition of a small faction that sought to advance the candidacy of John McLean, a native son, were instructed to vote for Van Buren. Meanwhile, the Whigs took up McLean's candidacy, and in January, 1835, the Whig members of the legislature and other prominent members of the party announced their support for him. In August, however, McLean withdrew from the race, and the Whigs began to turn their attention to William Henry Harrison, who had served ably as Ohio's first territorial representative and still enjoyed wide popularity in the state.

The Democrats approached the 1836 elections with a party organization that was vastly superior to that of their opponents. By 1835 the party was using the convention system to nominate candidates at all levels and was energetic in state as in national politics. The Whigs, on the other hand, had largely to reconstruct their party apparatus. In July, 1835, the party leaders met in Columbus to lay plans for strengthening their forces and announced that a state convention would be held on February 22, 1836. In August a committee of general correspondence was created, apparently to stimulate organization at the county level. Months of intense party activity culminated in the holding of a highly successful convention attended by over a thousand delegates. Harrison was enthusiastically put forward as the party's presidential candidate and the convention took the additional step of naming Joseph Vance as the gubernatorial nominee.[2] The Democrats, who convened according to custom on January 8, 1836, were noticeably less enthusiastic in reasserting their support for Van Buren, but they, too, gave every indication of being well mobilized to contest both the state and presidential elections.

Perhaps because both parties had at last determined to conduct the state election on a straight party basis, the vote in the gubernatorial election exceeded any previously cast for that office. With two-thirds of the eligible voters participating, Vance won by the close margin that had by now come to be traditional in Ohio. The Whigs repeated their success in the presidential election, in which three-fourths of the electorate participated. With Jackson on the sidelines and with a military hero heading the opposition, the Democrats labored under a handicap that even their superior party organization could not surmount.

The 1836 election marked the completion of the transitional period in Ohio politics that had been inaugurated in 1828. Thereafter, elections at all levels were fought out between Whigs and Democrats, usually on a remarkably even basis. After 1836 the most significant developments were in campaign techniques.

Whig preparations for the presidential election of 1840 were begun in July, 1837, when a state convention nominated Harrison again and proposed that a national Whig convention should be held. This proposal was repeated in May, 1838, at a state convention, which asserted the party's confidence in

2. Niles' *Register*, XLVIII, 395; L, 81.

Harrison but pledged its "cordial support" to Clay or Webster if either should become the party's standard bearer.

Indicative of the political excitement generated by the new party system was the large attendance—over three thousand—at this convention.[3] In the same year a Democratic Young Men's convention reportedly attracted over four thousand delegates. Although the point would be difficult to establish, it is possible that Ohio may have set the pattern in 1838 for the "monster rallies" that were to be such a conspicuous feature of the 1840 presidential campaign. Along with the huge conventions came campaign oratory, slogans, parades, and many other features that were to transform politics in Ohio into a great dramatic spectacle.

In an effort to preserve party harmony, which was threatened by differences of opinion on the presidential question, delegates to the Whig national convention were chosen in 1839 not by a state convention but by conventions in each congressional district.[4] After Harrison had been nominated, the party took up his cause with a degree of enthusiasm that probably had never been equalled. The "Ohio Harrison State Convention," as it was called, that assembled in Columbus on February 21, 1840, broke all records for attendance, as well as for flamboyance. Ross County alone appointed 950 delegates, and the total attendance ran to several thousand. Tom Corwin was nominated for governor together with a Harrison slate of electors, but these routine proceedings were all but obscured by the festivities that enlivened the occasion. Most delegations arrived with log cabins, forts, barrels of hard cider, or other props, as well as hundreds of banners and emblems, emblazoned with all sorts of devices, and vied with one another in the popular appeal of their performances.[5] The Democratic convention, although it included some two thousand delegates, was by comparison a relatively tame affair. The

3. *Ibid.*, LIV, 240.
4. *Ibid.*, LVI, 259.
5. *Ibid.*, LVIII, 21-22.

mood that had been established by the Whigs in February persisted, and grew even more rambunctious as the campaign proceeded. The state, it would seem, was transformed into one huge circus ground, and never had the voters been treated to such entertainment.

Harrison, who in 1836 had made the first campaign tour ever undertaken by a presidential candidate, again took to the stump and made several speeches in Ohio at Columbus, Dayton, Chillicothe, Fort Meigs, Fort Greenville, Lebanon, Carthage, and elsewhere. On each occasion he was greeted by enormous throngs. Richard M. Johnson, the unconventional Democratic vice-presidential candidate, also addressed numerous campaign rallies in Ohio in the course of a tour of the West, but he could not counteract the rising Harrison sentiment.

The result was foreordained. The Whigs swept the state and inspired such an outpouring of the electorate as had never before been approached. The gubernatorial contest attracted 85 per cent of the electorate to the polls, and the presidential vote was only slightly under that mark. Harrison received 54 per cent of the total vote, the highest percentage of any presidential candidate in Ohio down to the Civil War.

After 1840 the party balance in Ohio remained close until 1848, when the Free Soil party threatened to disrupt old alignments. Democratic governors were elected in 1842, 1850, 1851, and 1853 and the state's electoral vote was cast for Democratic candidates in 1848 and 1852. Voter participation remained high, usually ranging between 75 per cent and 80 per cent in presidential elections but falling some fifteen points below that level in gubernatorial elections. In a very pronounced degree, Ohio political interest seemed to focus on national politics. The convention system, introduced successfully at the state level in 1827, continued to provide the universal pattern for party management.

Ohio in many respects stood midway between the Middle States and the new states in its political behavior. Like the former section, it tended to be evenly divided between the major parties, resorted readily to the use of the convention system, and achieved at an early date a fairly stable relationship between the parties. On the other hand, party formation after 1824 in Ohio did not involve a reordering of pre-existing party loyalties nor did it occur as abruptly as in certain of the Middle States. Rather, there was the tendency, observable in several of the new states, for parties to form first to contest presidential elections and for state politics to be conducted with little regard to national parties.

INDIANA

If Ohio exhibited in only a limited degree those characteristics that can generally be associated with the political behavior of the new states, Indiana can be regarded as typical of such communities. Not until 1840 was politics to be conducted on a party basis in that state, although a restricted type of party development took place every four years in connection with contests for the presidency. Meanwhile, state politics remained under the management of a powerful clique that successfully avoided identification with national parties. In Indiana we have yet another, but especially intriguing, illustration of the rule that parties did not form over state matters, that state politics could be conducted without political parties, and that parties were formed chiefly to contest for the presidency.

When Ohio was set off as a distinct territory in 1800, most of the remainder of the Northwest Territory was erected into the territory of Indiana. Later, in 1809, Illinois was given separate status, and Indiana acquired its present dimensions. Down to 1830, settlement was largely restricted to the western and southern portions of the state, initially because most of the remaining area was still occupied by Indian tribes and also because of the pioneer's predilection for hilly, timbered country. Immigration into Indiana came overwhelmingly from the southern states, but the settlers were relatively poor yeomen farmers rather than plantation owners of the type that figured prominently on the southern frontier. In 1820, four years after its admission to statehood, Indiana had a population of 147,000, which grew rapidly to 685,000 by 1840.

In the early years especially, the population was widely dispersed, communication was extremely poor, educational facilities were negligible, and governmental affairs were simple and limited in scope. Land speculation was less of a factor in Indiana than in most other new regions. Landholdings tended to be small, and there were few men in the state who could make any pretentions to aristocracy. Consequently, Hoosier society was notably democratic and, in the eyes of cultured observers, extremely crude.

During the early territorial period, political cleavages developed over several issues, the most serious of which was slavery. One faction, strongest in the Wabash area, first sought to have Congress suspend the antislavery provisions of the Northwest Ordinance and when this effort failed succeeded in persuading the territorial officials to promulgate a code that provided for the virtual legalization of slavery. By 1810, however, the antislavery faction, led by Jonathan Jennings, had secured the ascendancy and repealed all legislation safeguarding slave property. During the course of the controversy, political excitement was frequently at a high level and there were some election contests in which Republican societies, on the Ohio model, were organized to support the anti-slavery candidates. Governor Harrison and many of his associates were identified with the slavery faction, and Jennings portrayed himself as the leader of the popular forces against the Vincennes "aristocracy." Once this major issue had been settled, politics became largely devoid of issues and, except for personal contests, aroused little interest.

The transition to statehood in 1816 was accomplished smoothly. A liberal constitution, much like that of Ohio, continued the democratic procedures that had come to prevail in Indiana, especially after Congress extended the suffrage to white male taxpayers and made both the legislative council and the territorial delegate elective by popular vote. The legislature, apportioned on the basis of adult white male population, was made up of an annually elected lower house and a senate, one-third of whose members were elected each year. The governor, popularly elected for a three-year term, was given a veto and had important powers of appointment but could not serve more than six years in any nine. There was also a popularly elected lieutenant governor. Members of the judiciary were appointed for limited terms; local officials, including sheriffs, were elective. State elections were held annually on the first Monday in August and were conducted by ballot under the supervision of judges and with the township as the polling unit. All adult white male citizens were given the franchise. Congressmen were elected from districts in the odd years. Presidential electors, chosen by the legislature in 1816 and 1820, were elected by popular vote on a general ticket beginning in 1824.

Politics in the new state was firmly controlled by a triumvirate made up of Jonathan Jennings, William Hendricks, and James Noble. Jennings became the first governor, Henricks the first congressman, and Noble was sent to the Senate. These skilled office-holders, who had played important roles in the territorial era and commanded wide respect, guided state affairs so successfully that no challenging faction arose and state elections were devoid of partisanship. Customarily at the end of each legislative session a caucus would be held at which political matters would be discussed and informal arrangements made with respect to the distribution of offices, appointive and elective. At the county level, candidates were self-nominated and independent of party ties, relying on their personal popularity and their stump-speaking prowess to secure election.

On the eve of the presidential election of 1824, the harmony that characterized Indiana politics was ruffled by differences of opinion about the merits of the leading candidates. Sentiment among the most influential politicians was divided, some favoring Adams and others Clay. Adherents of each contender in the legislature met in caucus to formulate slates of electors, but the issue did not generate much excitement. Meanwhile, during the summer of 1824, a few popular meetings were held to express support for Jackson.

Finally, late in July, Elihu Stout, editor of the lone pro-Jackson paper in the state, the Vincennes *Western Star,* assumed leadership of the movement. He outlined in his newspaper a plan that called upon the friends of Jackson to hold county meetings at which committees would be named, and these in turn would name delegates to attend a state convention at Salem on September 16. Stout's ambitious scheme, for which there was no precedent in Indiana, was realized only in part. Seventeen delegates representing only thirteen of the state's fifty-one counties convened to choose candidates for electors and to draft an address and set up a three-man central committee. Only one or two of the delegates had any standing as politicians; the office-holders were cool to Jackson.

With little in the way of formal organization, the three parties conducted modest campaigns in behalf of their candidates. Only 37 per cent of the electorate, a proportion well below that in previous state elections, turned out to vote. Jackson received a plurality of the vote, with Clay second and Adams third. As in Ohio, the election was a popularity contest, to which little of significance could be attached. When it had ended, politics in the state returned to normal, and in 1825 James B. Ray, explicitly disavowing any connection between state and national politics, was elected governor. Ray, incidentally, broke with precedent by stumping the state, although candidates for lesser offices had long engaged in the practice.

The Jacksonians revived late in 1827, attacking the ring of politicians that had for so long held sway in the state and demanding that the people liberate themselves from such vassalage. County meetings were held preparatory to a state convention that assembled in Indianapolis on January 8, 1828. Attended by delegates from some twenty counties, the gathering also included the Jacksonian legislators. Once again, in addition to nominating electors, the party leaders put forth an extremely elaborate plan for organizing the party under a "committee of general superintendence." The friends of Adams, who included many prominent state political figures, also convened, but they made little effort at creating an organization.

With the field reduced to two candidates, popular interest in the contest was much greater than it had been in 1824. Nearly 70 per cent of the electorate went to the polls and they gave Jackson 56 per cent of the total vote. In the state election, held the previous August, Ray had been opposed by two candidates, one bearing the Jackson label and the other identifying himself with Adams. Ray won with a plurality and after the election published a letter that is revealing of his attitude toward parties.

Pointing out that before the election he had declared his complete neutrality on the presidential question, he expressed his repugnance "to *partyism,* and to the anti-republican modern practice of electing state officers upon the merits and popularity of other men." He asserted that he owed his election to no party. "In some instances, counties decidedly Jacksonian, gave me majorities. In other cases, counties known to be undoubtedly for the [Adams] administration, gave me majorities."[6] Ray's stand commanded considerable popular approval, and down to 1840 gubernatorial elections were kept separate from national party politics.

6. Niles' *Register*, XXXV, 147.

After 1828 the rudimentary party organizations, which had never taken root in the townships and counties, again evaporated. In 1830, A. F. Morrison, through his *Indiana Democrat,* sought to revive the party and brought together a group of leaders who decided to appoint a standing central committee, which would name correspondence committees in each county. This resort to an appointed party apparatus is suggestive of the lack of interest in party organization at the local levels. Although the plan was not effectuated, the usual state convention was assembled in December, 1831, to prepare for the presidential election. The Clay forces also held a state convention in November. The personally popular Noble, a member of the old triumvirate, defeated the Jacksonian-allied candidate for the governorship in 1831, but Jackson carried the state in 1832 by a two-to-one margin in a relatively dull contest that attracted only three-fifths of the voters to the polls.

Party spirit again languished in the state. In the 1834 gubernatorial election both candidates were vague about their national party identification, and Noble was again elected over James G. Read, who had been nominated by a Jacksonian state convention. In this campaign the candidates had entered into a written agreement for a series of joint appearances throughout the state.

The emergence as a presidential candidate of William Henry Harrison, successful governor of the territory and hero of Tippecanoe, revived partisan feelings and gave special interest to the impending presidential contest. The Democrats again strove to reconstruct a party apparatus, according to a plan whereby the state committee appointed committees in each congressional district and each county. The Whigs were equally zealous in their preparations for the campaign although, like the Democrats, they had little in the way of local party organization.

Harrison's popularity carried him to an easy victory. With voter participation rising to 70 per cent, the hero of Tippecanoe received 56 per cent of the total vote. This crushing defeat so demoralized the Democrats that in 1837 they did not even nominate a candidate for governor, and they won only one of seven congressional seats. The sudden alteration in party fortunes is indicative of the weakness of party discipline and organization in the state.

The 1840 elections were of unusual importance. For the first time since 1828, the gubernatorial and presidential elections would occur in the same year. The Whigs began their mobilization with a state convention in 1838 at which they named delegates to the national convention, instructing them to vote for Harrison but pledging support to Clay if he should gain the nomination. The Democrats, recovering from the debacle of 1837, held conventions in some districts in 1839 to nominate congressional candidates and won three seats, together with a majority in the legislature. Both parties at their state conventions nominated not only electoral slates but also candidates for governor and lieutenant-governor. For the first time, a state election was to be fought almost entirely on national issues and on the basis of national party alignments. The result was another easy victory for the Whigs. In the August election, with voter participation soaring to the unprecedented figure of 86 per cent, the Whig candidate secured 54 per cent of the vote.

The campaign frenzy continued at a high level through to November. As was the case elsewhere in the nation, virtually the whole population, women as well as men, threw themselves into the spectacular rallies, cabin raisings, processions, and other diversions that enlivened the contest. Perhaps the outstanding event was the encampment of veterans at Tippecanoe on May 29, which attracted an attendance of Whig enthusiasts estimated, no doubt exaggeratedly, at fifty thousand. In November the outpouring of voters equalled that in the state election, and Harrison, with 56 per cent of the total vote, repeated the triumph he had won in 1836.

The elections of 1840 completed the process of party formation in Indiana. Thereafter, contests for offices at all levels were fought on a party basis and both parties built durable organizations. The intense loyalties, instilled especially by the memorable 1840 campaign, persisted, although when Harrison had passed from the scene the Whigs lost their initial margin of supremacy over their adversaries. After 1840 the Democrats won every presidential and gubernatorial election until 1860, when the Republicans scored their first successes. But the party balance was usually close and political interest remained at a high level. Only once after 1840 did participation in a presidential election drop below 80 per cent; state elections were somewhat less well attended.

The most difficult aspect of Indiana politics to explain is the slowness with which national party identifications became operative in state politics. Doubtless many factors were involved. The dominant faction—headed by the old triumvirate—could retain power locally without the risk of involving itself in presidential politics. The rapid expansion of the state's population made the task of the would-be party organizer extremely difficult. The fact that gubernatorial elections coincided with presidential elections only once in twelve years and that congressional elections were held in the odd years also complicated the problem. Had presidential, gubernatorial, and congressional elections all been held at the same time it would hardly have been possible to maintain the kind of dual politics that persisted from 1824 almost until 1840. It would seem to be the case that issues, as such, did not divide the Indiana electorate so much as did differences over presidential personalities. And as the major personalities changed down to 1840, so too did the loose alignments in presidential elections.

ILLINOIS

Illinois provides in an extreme form an illustration of the slowness with which politics in a new state became adjusted to the party system. From the territorial period until near the end of Jackson's second administration, political leadership was exercised by individuals, often combined in shifting alliances, without reference to parties and without formal organization. Ultimately, around 1835, parties formed behind opposing presidential candidates and at the same time successful efforts were made to establish the convention system as the basis for organizing and managing the parties. Within the next few years, politicians exchanged their former independence for the rewards that went with the acceptance of party discipline and voters, similarly, adopted partisan identities, responding to campaign appeals as Whigs or Democrats.

Like Indiana, Illinois was a rapidly growing frontier state. Its population multiplied three-fold between 1820 and 1830 and nearly trebled again in the following decade. Over the same twenty-year period the number of counties increased from nineteen to eighty-eight and the congressional districts from one to three. Because of such extraordinary expansion, the task of party organization was to be carried forward only under great difficulties. But the very magnitude of the movement of new settlers into the state doomed the early system of informal management of politics by individuals who, with a relatively small personal following, could exert large influence in public affairs. The new arrivals were disposed to give their allegiance to parties rather than to old leaders who could no longer remain on familiar terms with even a fraction of the electorate.

Illinois was set off as a separate territory in 1804, was authorized to have its own popularly-elected legislature in 1812, and was empowered to draft a constitution in 1818, preparatory to its admission as a state late in the same year. Borrowing heavily from the constitutions of Kentucky, Ohio, and New York, the predominantly southern members of the constitutional convention produced a document that assured a high degree of popular control of government at all levels. The governor, elected for a four-year term but ineligible to succeed himself, was a weak executive, sharing a modified veto power with a council of revision. Extensive legislative and appointive power was conferred on the legislature, which was apportioned roughly on the basis of white population. Members of the lower house, elected from each county, served two year terms; senators, elected from one or more counties, served for four years. County officials—three commissioners, a sheriff, and two coroners—were popularly elected. Before 1848 there was no provision for township government. Elections for all state and county officials, as well as for congressmen, were held on the first Monday in August and, with the exception of some years before 1829, were conducted *viva voce* with precincts in each county as the voting unit. Congressmen were elected from districts after 1831. Presidential electors were chosen from districts in 1820 and 1824; thereafter they were elected at large. The suffrage was liberally conferred on all adult white male inhabitants who had resided six months in the state.

During the territorial period loose factional groupings had developed, essentially for the purpose of contesting for positions of power and influence. At the head of one faction stood Ninian Edwards, former Chief Justice of Kentucky, who had been appointed territorial governor. Associated with him was his son-in-law, Daniel Pope Cook, numerous other relations, and various appointive officials. Prominent anti-Edwards leaders, who on occasion formed combinations to advance their personal political fortunes, were Jesse B. Thomas, Shadrack Bond, John McLean, and Elias Kent Kane. Aside from these factional struggles, the territory was divided over the issue of slavery, which remained a subject of controversy until August, 1824, when in a popular referendum the voters refused to approve the holding of a convention to alter the anti-slavery provisions of the state constitution.

In the first state elections, a complex series of deals resulted in the choice of Bond for the governorship, while Edwards and Thomas went to the Senate. In 1822 there was a

three-way contest for the governorship, with factional alignments so blurred that they offered no clue to the relative
strength of the contending groups. Meanwhile Cook had been
elected to Congress in 1819 and in subsequent elections held
the seat against the challenges of such anti-Edwards stalwarts
as McLean, Kane, and Bond. Such political management as
was practiced was informal in character. Candidates relied on
their personal followings and on arrangements for support
from other influential figures. Direct appeals were made to
the voters in campaign speeches, and political interest was
sufficiently stimulated by these methods to inspire more than
half of the electorate to vote in state elections.

The contest for the presidency in 1824 aroused no excitement in Illinois and contributed nothing to the clarification of
political alignments. In each of the three electoral districts
candidates pledged to Adams, Jackson, Clay, and Crawford
entered the lists, and all that can be said of the outcome is that
no one of the presidential candidates was able to establish his
dominance. Jackson won two electoral votes and Adams one
in this dull and confusing election in which only one-fourth of
the eligible voters participated. For the next decade, there
was no tendency for parties to polarize around the presidential
question. Instead, the loose factionalism inherited from the
territorial period persisted. Most of the leading political figures in the state professed to be friendly to Jackson, but they
were divided into two shifting groups. One element, known
as the "whole hogs," enjoyed some official favor from the
national administration after 1830 and included among its
leaders Elias Kent Kane and William Kinney. The other,
called the "milk-and-cider" men, was headed by Edwards.

These factions were neither well organized nor stable and
were not distinguishable on doctrinal lines. Moreover, many
politicians retained their independence of factional ties, like
the personally popular Joseph Duncan, who defeated Cook for
Congress in 1826. Such anti-Jacksonian sentiment as existed
was mobilized in 1828 and 1832 by men of little political

prominence and did not constitute an important factor in state politics. There was, in brief, no Jackson party in Illinois in any proper sense, nor was there an anti-Jackson party, earlier than 1835. The political scene has been effectively described by Theodore C. Pease in a single word—chaos.

The gubernatorial elections after 1824 exemplified the vagueness of political alignments. In 1826 Edwards, who had resigned from the Senate after his ill-advised attacks on the integrity of William H. Crawford, barely defeated a little-known opponent who had no strong factional ties. During his four years in the governorship, Edwards adopted an ambiguous position on national politics, although he belatedly signified mild support for Jackson in 1828. He retained sufficient influence to secure the election as his successor of John Reynolds, a "milk-and-cider" man, over the "whole hog," William Kinney. In 1834 Joseph Duncan, who was only nominally a Jacksonian, easily defeated two candidates, each of whom had been nominated by rival Jacksonian elements in what purported to be state conventions. Shortly after his election Duncan revealed himself as a decided opponent of the national administration and in time became a leading figure in the Whig party. Similarly, congressional contests down to 1836 bore little discernible relationship to national political rivalries, and elections to the state legislature continued to be fought on the basis of personalities.

In 1828 and 1832 modest efforts were made by the oddly assorted Jacksonians and their equally miscellaneous opponents to rally support for their favorites. Early in 1827 the lower house of the legislature had resolved to recommend Jackson for the presidency and subsequently public meetings were held in some counties to endorse his candidacy. Nothing is known of the movement that developed in behalf of Adams, but it had its most substantial support in the northern counties. Jackson easily won a two-to-one victory in an election that brought 52 per cent of the voters to the polls.

Organizational activity was more in evidence before the

1832 campaign. The initiative was taken by a meeting of citizens from Fayette and adjacent counties at Vandalia in December, 1831, during a session of the supreme court. This gathering named a committee to prepare an address in behalf of Jackson, appointed delegates to the national convention, and proposed that meetings should be convened in each of the three congressional districts to nominate electors. Subsequently, a faction that preferred Richard M. Johnson to Van Buren as Jackson's running mate met in Vandalia in January and set in motion arrangements for a state convention that met in March and named five electors pledged to Jackson and Johnson.

These maneuvers are of some interest because they suggest the existence of the antagonism to Van Buren that was to burst forth with considerable vigor in 1835. They also reveal the fumbling attempts to introduce the convention system into state politics. The five Jackson–Van Buren electors were victorious in the presidential election, in which voter participation sagged to 46 per cent, and Jackson's total vote was more than twice that of his rival. That national politics had not as yet succeeded in arousing the interest of the voters was demonstrated by the fact that the turnout in both presidential elections was below that in state elections held in the same period.

The political situation in the state underwent drastic alteration in 1835, when the Democratic party began to acquire structure and discipline and the opposition found a basis for uniting against Van Buren. Closely associated with the presidential contest was an interesting controversy over the propriety of using the convention system as a means of uniting and managing parties. The convention issue was raised when a meeting in Morgan County urged that a state convention be held at Vandalia on April 27, 1835, to appoint delegates to the Democratic National Convention. Taking a prominent role at this meeting was the youthful Stephen A. Douglas, who had arrived in Illinois late in 1833 and who soon became the outstanding advocate of organizing the Democratic party on the efficient model that he had observed during his brief sojourn in New York. The Vandalia convention was held, but it was attended by delegates from only a few counties. Meanwhile, the Democrats in Cook County were engaged in building a convention-type organization and urged that their example be followed by other counties. As the movement spread, the Morgan County Democrats were encouraged to propose that another state convention should be called to meet on December 7 and form an electoral ticket.

In the months before the convention assembled, meetings to appoint delegates were held in numerous counties, and in some counties the organizing efforts were carried down to the precinct level. In many areas, however, the convention proposal encountered strong opposition on the ground that it was anti-republican and operated to restrict the freedom of both candidates and voters.

When the convention met in Vandalia for a two-day session, twenty-three of the state's sixty counties were represented. The delegates had no difficulty in agreeing on a slate of electors, but they became involved in heated debate over a resolution that called upon the party to use the convention system to nominate candidates for all county and state offices. In the course of the debate Douglas argued that conventions afforded the only means of managing elections successfully and pointed to the experience of other states. His opponents contended that "old-fashioned Democrats," especially in the southern part of the state, did not like the system, especially when applied to county and district offices, and that independent men would not submit to being controlled by the decisions of a convention. After the chairman of the convention had resigned in protest against the introduction of the controversial issue, the resolutions were not adopted.[7] Despite this setback the

7. On the efforts of Douglas to introduce and justify the use of the convention system in Illinois, see Robert W. Johannsen, ed., *The Letters of Stephen A. Douglas* (Urbana, 1961), especially pages 24-30, 39, 47-50. Douglas was a

proponents of the convention system continued their activities, and by the end of 1836 in certain of the northern counties, and especially in the third congressional district, the Democratic party had acquired elaborate organization.

The dispute over the convention system was carried on also in the legislature, where the supporters and the opponents of Van Buren took differing positions on the issue. Late in 1835 the anti-Van Buren members of the state senate endorsed Hugh L. White for the presidency and went on to declare that "every man who is eligible to the office of president has an undeniable right to become a candidate for the same without the intervention of caucuses and conventions." They further defined their position by resolving: "That we approve of the democratic doctrines as laid down by Jefferson in 1801 and Jackson in 1829, and that we disapprove of the convention system attempted to be forced upon the American people by the Van Buren party, and believe it to be destructive of the freedom of the elective franchise, opposed to republican institutions, and dangerous to the liberties of the people.[8] Subsequently the lower house responded by adopting resolutions in support of Van Buren and Johnson and defending the convention system as an instrument for uniting the Democratic party. In no other state was the convention brought under heavier attack nor made such a direct issue between the emerging parties.

After the adjournment of the legislature, leaders of the anti-Van Buren movement held a meeting in Springfield at which an address to the people was authorized and arrangements were made for a White electoral ticket made up entirely of erstwhile Jacksonians. Most of White's supporters, indeed, insisted that they were as loyal to Jackson as the Van Buren adherents. The situation became confused in 1836 as sentiment developed for Harrison, particularly among those who

---

member of the committee that drafted the address of the convention, which was largely devoted to a defense of the convention system.

8. Niles' *Register*, XLIX, 384.

had never espoused Jackson's cause.   Finally, in September, 1836, a Harrison gathering in Edwardsville endorsed the slate of White electors that had been named earlier but expressed the hope that, under certain conditions, the electors might give their votes to Harrison.

Thus Van Buren was opposed by a loose fusion of former Democrats and new Whigs under the Janus-like White-Harrison emblem.   Despite the best efforts of the developing parties to arouse enthusiasm, and the prospect that the race would be a close one, only 44 per cent of the electorate went to the polls. Van Buren received 55 per cent of the popular vote, a far smaller proportion than that which Jackson had secured.

Building upon the foundations that had been laid in 1835, the Illinois Democrats carried forward the work of organizing their party while the Whigs continued to view the convention system with hostility.   In July, 1837, Douglas and other Democratic leaders, including members of the legislature, conferred at Vandalia and decided to hold a state convention late in the year to nominate candidates for governor and lieutenant-governor.   A central committee of fifteen was appointed to correspond with the county committees.   When the convention met in December it was well attended and efficiently organized, and its nominee—Thomas Carlin—was elected by a small margin in 1838.   Conventions were also used to nominate candidates for Congress and—in some areas—for county and legislative offices.

By 1838 the resistance to the convention system had largely ended.   The southern counties lagged behind those in the north, which had many transplanted politicians from New England and the Middle States who were intimately acquainted with advanced types of party organization, but no section of the state was immune to the innovation.   The party had by 1840 become well-disciplined and used its machinery to register an unbroken series of victories over the Whigs until 1856, when it lost the governorship.

The Whigs in Illinois never succeeded in developing an

effective organization. In 1839, after considerable vacillation, a Whig state convention was held at Springfild, October 7-9, which appointed delegates to the national convention and created a state central committee, of which Abraham Lincoln was a member. This committee endeavored to strengthen the party by appointing committees in each county, which in turn were supposed to appoint subcommittees. The plan was useful for campaign purposes, but it lacked permanence and did not establish discipline within the party as did the convention system. However, with these modest efforts and with the popular Harrison as their candidate, the Whigs put on a spectacular campaign in 1840 and lost by only two thousand votes. So intense was the excitement that voter participation soared to 86 per cent, almost twice as high as in 1836 and far above any level previously reached in state elections.

But the organization disintegrated after the campaign, and the party never again offered a serious challenge to the dominant Democrats. In 1842 plans for a Whig convention were abandoned and former Governor Duncan was accepted by general agreement as the party's candidate. After his defeat, Duncan expressed the view of old-time politicians when he denounced the convention system as "nothing more nor less than a contrivance of government officers, of office seekers, and men who make politics a trade, to take the selection of all public agents from the people, leaving them nothing to do but vote as their leaders and drillmasters tell them."[9]

Lacking an elaborate organization, the Whig party relied for its leadership on a "Springfield Junto," of which Lincoln was a member. This "Junto" influenced the selection of candidates for state-wide offices and rallied the party every four years for the presidential contests. But in the counties and congressional districts, where organization was generally lacking, the party frequently either ran no candidate or else

9. C. M. Thompson, "Attitude of the Western Whigs Toward the Convention System," *Proceedings of the Mississippi Valley Historical Association*, V (1911-12), 181.

was weakened by the entry of several independent Whigs into competition against a single Democrat. The Democratic party, which for several years after 1843 was effectively managed by the congressional delegation, was by contrast a model of efficiency.

Party formation in Illinois, in brief, took place in 1835 with the determined efforts of the supporters of Van Buren to organize the Democratic party on a disciplined basis. The opposition, initially loosely aligned behind White and Harrison, was distinguished by its antipathy both to Van Buren and to the convention system. Before 1835, although the overwhelming majority of the politicians and voters professed to be Jacksonians, there was in fact no organized Jackson party nor were elections contested on a party basis. The Democrats after 1835 perfected their organization and secured complete dominance over their rivals, who never succeeded in creating an effective party apparatus. Why the Illinois Whigs remained so peculiarly opposed to the convention system is far from clear, but the explanation may be sought in an investigation of the character of the early leadership of the party.

One of the interesting effects of the unusual party situation in Illinois was the wide variation between voter participation in state and presidential elections. Between 1840 and 1852, participation in presidential elections was usually from fifteen to twenty percentage points above that in gubernatorial elections. The Whigs, in effect, were able to rouse themselves for a presidential contest but not for other elections. In no state was this phenomena more pronounced than in Illinois.

ALABAMA

Alabama and Mississippi were—like Indiana and Illinois— new political communities in 1824. Like the states on the

northwestern frontier, they were growing rapidly in population and therefore lacked the social and institutional stability
of the older states. Both entered upon their careers as states
with extremely democratic constitutions. Neither had any
experience in conducting politics on a party basis. Party
formation, then, was destined to be a slow and difficult process
for many of the same reasons that have been discussed in connection with other new communities. But Alabama and Mississippi were further distinguished by their extraordinary commitment to a cotton economy, with all that this implied in
terms of the slavery-plantation system. They were also, especially before 1840, strongly influenced in their political attitudes
by their dependence on the federal government for solutions
to such problems as Indian removal, land disposal, and the
improvement of transportation.

Because of their peculiar characteristics as new, expanding
cotton states, combining in a special way the frontier and the
plantation, they developed an unusual kind of party system,
which differed from that of the northern frontier and also
from that of the Old South. In both states politics lacked
strong organization and discipline, national party alignments
were unstable, and there was a decided tendency for party
alignments to assume one form in state elections and another
in presidential elections.

In the years after the War of 1812 there was a surge of
population from the states of the Old South into the Gulf
region where conditions of soil and climate were ideal for the
large-scale cultivation of cotton. Migrants by the thousands,
the more affluent accompanied by groups of slaves, poured into
the valleys of the Tennessee, Tombigbee, Warrior, and Alabama rivers, setting off a speculative land boom that reached
fantastic proportions by 1819. The areas of settlement were
at first widely dispersed. Not until the late 1830's, when the
Indians had been removed from eastern Alabama and when
initial prejudices against the treeless Black Belt region had
been overcome, did the internal frontiers disappear. The

population, drawn largely from Georgia, the Carolinas, and Virginia, amounted to about 125,000 in 1820, of whom one-third were slaves. By 1840 there were nearly 600,000 people in the state, two-fifths of them slaves. The major strongholds of the plantation system were in the Tennessee valley and in the vast Black Belt, stretching across central Alabama; in between were the so-called "white" counties. In a loose way, political differences occasionally reflected conflicts between the "white" and the "black" counties.

Alabama's constitution was markedly more liberal than those of the states of the Old South. There was a popularly elected governor, a two-house legislature apportioned on the basis of federal population, and locally elected county officials. At the annual state elections on the first Monday in August the voters chose the lower house of the legislature, one-third of the senate, and—in the odd years—a governor. Congressmen were elected from districts and presidential electors from the state at large. All elections were by ballot, and the suffrage was conferred on all adult white males. Whereas in the states of the Old South, constitutions were framed with a view to protecting the privileged position of some particular groups or sections, the Alabama constitution was produced by a new community that had not yet had time to organize itself into hostile or apprehensive elements. It was, therefore, based on the necessary assumption that each white man was politically the equal of every other.

As in other dynamic frontier communities, politics in Alabama went through a phase that featured contests between personalities and, on occasion, loose factions for power and place. For more than a decade there was to be no semblance of organized parties, and there was no preponderant faction, as in Tennessee, to exercise control over political affairs through informal methods. There was for a time some tendency for politics at the highest level to become a contest between two rival power groups—the "Georgia Machine" and the "Champions of the People"—but by 1824 even this weak polarization had broken down, and there seem to have been no durable alignments of any kind.

The first gubernatorial election, which saw the candidate of the Georgia Machine defeat his rival in a close contest, produced a vote equal to 97 per cent of the adult white males—a highly suspicious figure. At the second election in 1821, which was essentially a two-man popularity contest, participation was again at a very high rate—85 per cent. Thereafter interest declined. In 1825, 1827, and 1829 there was only a single candidate in the running, and voter participation fell below 30 per cent. In 1829, however, 73 per cent of the eligible voters participated in a referendum on a proposed amendment to the constitution, and legislative contests frequently inspired very large turnouts.

The presidential elections of 1824 and 1828 had no significant effect on party formation in Alabama. On both occasions Jackson was the overwhelming popular choice, receiving 70 per cent of the vote in 1824 and 90 per cent in 1828. Slightly more than half of the electorate voted in each election. By 1832 there were signs of a developing cleavage. Controversy within the state over the attitude that should be adopted toward the failure of the federal government to expedite the removal of the Indians from eastern Alabama produced a highly vocal and belligerent state-rights movement. In the gubernatorial election of 1831, a champion of moderation had been opposed unsuccessfully by a spokesman for those who favored defiance of federal authority, and the issue served to emphasize a division of opinion that was later to array "unionists" against "state-rights" men. In addition, there was the sentiment, common in the South, that Van Buren was unacceptable as a candidate for the vice-presidency.

The state-rights, anti-Van Buren attitudes found expression in 1832 in the form of a Jackson–Barbour electoral ticket. With no Clay ticket in the field, the contest was entirely between the regular Jackson–Van Buren slate and the dissident faction, and in a dull election in which only one-third of the eligibles voted, the regulars secured a six-to-one majority. Judging from the bare election returns, Alabama was 100 per cent for Jackson, but in fact there was no organized Jackson party, nor was the anti-Van Buren opposition prepared to undertake united action. In 1833 the incumbent governor was re-elected without opposition and legislative contests bore little or no relationship to national party identities.

With the approach of the presidential election of 1836, politicians and voters began to divide into rival camps. Those Jacksonians who for various reasons had become strongly identified with the national administration saw the necessity of attempting to hold the state for Van Buren, and in 1834 they began to sponsor public meetings to demonstrate support for this candidacy. It was this faction that backed C. C. Clay for the governorship in 1835 against a candidate who was regarded as representing the Whig-state-rights-anti-Van Buren opposition. Clay scored an easy victory, but the vagueness of party alignments at the time is apparent from the fact that the legislature chosen at the same election was hostile to Van Buren. Shortly before they adjourned, both houses by large majorities nominated Hugh Lawson White for the presidency and opposed the holding of a Democratic national convention.[10]

Having lost control of the legislature, the Van Buren faction decided, virtually out of necessity, to hold a state convention for the purpose of giving some kind of sanction to an electoral ticket. Meetings were called in the counties to choose delegates to attend the convention in Tuscaloosa on the first Monday in December. This move was severely condemned by the pro-White editor of the Huntsville *Southern Advocate*. "The caucus [convention] plan of party operations, pursued as it has been, and as it continued to be, is a sure, gradual, and corrupting usurpation of the right of self government," he fulminated. "The friends of Mr. Van Buren in this State, having long since despaired of the Legislature, are now resort-

10. Niles' *Register*, XLVII, 378.

ing to this especial favorite, for the purpose of overruling the choice of Alabama."[11]   When the convention met, it named a slate of Van Buren electors but prudently gave no indication of its preference for the vice-presidency.[12]

The White forces, carefully avoiding the use of the term "convention," arranged for "highly respectable meetings of citizens" at the Capitol on December 22, at which resolutions were adopted, electors were nominated, and a small standing committee to promote White's candidacy was appointed.   Like the Democratic convention, this meeting took place while the legislature was still in session and was largely attended by pro-White legislators.[13]   At the state election, held in August, 1836, the "presidential question" was not a decisive factor; politics at the county level remained on what was essentially an individualistic basis.   So vague were political allegiances that opinions differed as to whether the new legislature had a majority favorable to White or to Van Buren.   Furthermore, the pro-White forces, most of whom claimed to be loyal Democrats, generally eschewed the use of the Whig label.[14]   Confronted in November with a choice between Van Buren and White, two-thirds of the electorate went to the polls and gave Jackson's designated heir a comfortable majority.

By 1836 Alabama had ceased to be politically monolithic, but the alignment that had appeared in the presidential contest was not a stable one, especially in state elections.   The awkward Whig-state-rights alliance supported a candidate in the 1837 gubernatorial election against the regular Democratic nominee, but two years later the Democratic incumbent was re-elected over negligible opposition, although the Whigs did contest legislative and congressional seats.   There were, in general, three weakly organized parties in the state: the regular Democrats, the Whigs, and the extreme state-rights men.   The last group was loosely bound by party loyalties and might sup-

11. (Huntsville) *Southern Advocate*, Dec. 1, 1835.
12. *Ibid.*, Dec. 22, 1835.
13. *Ibid.*, Jan. 5, 12, 1836.
14. *Ibid.*, Aug. 2, 9, 16, 23, 1836.

port either Democratic or Whig nominees, depending on which was least objectionable. Both the Democrats and the Whigs took moderate unionist positions and were indistinguishable in their attitudes toward many national issues. After 1837, however, the Whigs developed cohesion by attacking "locofoco" financial policies and the incompetence of the Van Buren administration.

Partisan feelings had developed sufficiently by 1840 to promise a vigorously contested election. Both parties sent delegations to their respective national conventions, and both held state conventions to nominate electors. The Whig affair was in the new style, with over a thousand delegates in attendance at Tuscaloosa on June 1, 1840.[15] For months the state was saturated with political oratory and pageantry, and although local party organization was not well established, every voter must have been made to feel the urgency of the choice between Van and Old Tip. On election day, 90 per cent of the adult white males flocked to the ballot boxes, and the Democrats succeeded in overcoming the Whig enthusiasm by a safe margin.

For the next decade the balance that had been reached between the parties in 1840 was fairly stable. The Whigs, polling usually about 45 per cent of the total vote in state-wide elections, remained in a competitive position but were always the minority party. They offered no candidate for the governorship in 1843, and in 1845 they supported a dissident Democrat, but they won sufficient seats in the legislature and in Congress to sustain their hopes. They made a weak showing in 1844 in support of Clay against Polk, who had a strong personal following in Alabama. Their closest approach to victory came in 1848. Taylor lost by only a few hundred votes to Lewis Cass, whose "squatter sovereignty" doctrine and northern background made him a weak candidate in Alabama.

Indeed, 1848 marked the high point in the career of the Alabama Whig party. Within the next two years the excite-

15. Niles' *Register*, LVII, 216, 245, 311.

ment engendered by the Wilmot Proviso and the California issue had disrupted the old party alignments and had led to a fusion of unionist Whigs and Democrats in a short-lived Union party. By 1852 the old parties attempted to regain their identities for the presidential elections, but the Whigs had become so demoralized that they never recovered their previous strength.

During the decade that the two parties contested for supremacy, both endeavored to build effective organizations. The Democratic apparatus, headed by the state convention that met biennially to nominate a gubernatorial candidate and every four years to name presidential electors, was the more effective, but the Whigs also utilized the convention system. As was generally true in the South, party machinery—and party discipline—did not acquire the hold on candidates and voters that was observable in the northeastern states. Because the parties were largely defined by their positions on the presidency, voter participation in presidential elections was considerably higher than in state elections, ranging from 90 per cent in 1840 down to 73 per cent in 1848. In 1852, because of the collapse of the Whigs, it plummeted to 48 per cent.

The Alabama parties, and the same was true of those in the other states in the Cotton Kingdom, were both strongly pro-southern and could not disagree widely about issues that affected the South, and most particularly the institution of slavery. As long as controversy could be confined to such matters as fiscal policy or "executive usurpation," the parties could contend against one another on a fairly even basis. But the emergence after 1848 of the question of the status of slavery in the territories completely upset the balance that had been reached between 1836 and 1840. From this perspective, the brief emergence of a nationally oriented two-party system in Alabama was the result of exceptional circumstances. The state had been politically monolithic before 1836, and it was never to have a well balanced two-party system after 1848.

MISSISSIPPI

Party formation in Mississippi was retarded by the same influences that operated generally in the South and was also affected by the frontier conditions that prevailed until 1840 and by the strong sectional feelings that developed in defense of the slavery-plantation system. Because Adams and Clay aroused no enthusiasm as alternatives to Jackson, the contests for the presidency through 1832 did not produce durable alignments; instead, politics was conducted on a non-party basis even though nearly all political figures claimed to be partisans of Jackson. When, after 1833, parties began to coalesce, the situation remained confused and unstable, for there were actually three distinct parties in the state, and this division obviously created complications, especially in national political affairs. By 1840 some semblance of a two-party system had been established, but its survival was soon threatened by the emergence of issues connected with the security of slavery.

Mississippi acquired statehood in 1817 under a moderately liberal constitution that was replaced in 1832 by a document that gave the state a form of government as democratic as any in the nation. Initially the franchise had been restricted to taxpayers or those who performed militia duty, substantial property holding had been required for office-holders, and there had been a limited number of popularly elected officials. The new constitution gave all adult white male citizens the privilege of voting, removed the property qualification for office-holders, and made judges and other principal state officials elective. The two-house legislature was apportioned on the basis of white population, the members of the lower and upper houses serving terms of two and four years respectively. State elections were held biennially on the first Monday and

Tuesday in November in the odd years, at which time not only were legislators, county officials, and a governor chosen but also members of Congress from the state at large. This method of electing congressmen operated to increase interest in state elections and enhanced the influence and importance of party organization at the state level. Presidential electors were also elected on a general ticket. All elections were conducted by ballot.

As in Alabama, the rapid expansion of the population—from 75,000 in 1820 to 375,000 in 1840—militated against the development of strong party organizations, especially at the county level. In 1840, for example, over one-half of the white population in the state resided in counties that had not even existed as recently as 1830. Party formation was also impeded in the early years by the dispersed pattern of settlement, which tended to produce sectional, rather than broadly partisan, interests.

Mississippi politics in the years before 1834 exhibited the same characteristics common to other new communities. At the state level rival cliques schemed to secure the principal offices while in the counties individual politicians and their connections battled for seats in the legislature. Colorful personalities, such as Franklin Plummer, the spokesman for the piney-woods settlers of East Mississippi, commanded strong local support. In the legislature, groupings tended to be regional rather than partisan or factional. Candidates, even for such offices as the governorship and Congress, were self-nominated and conducted their own campaigns without any semblance of party organization but with the endorsement and assistance of such local leaders as they could enlist.

Elections aroused considerable interest. In the 1820's it was not uncommon for more than three-fourths of the adult white males to cast their ballots. In 1823 and 1827, when there were three-man races for the governorship, voter participation approached 80 per cent. Campaigning was done in the ebullient style common to the frontier; intensive speaking tours brought the candidates to the most remote hamlets. The voter then made a choice between men rather than parties.

Presidential contests contributed little to party formation in Mississippi until after 1832. In 1824 many leading public figures, and most newspapers, were partial to Adams, but when Jackson emerged as a serious candidate, he quickly became the popular favorite and won a two-to-one victory. In 1828 modest organized efforts were made by the partisans of both candidates. The Adams men held a large public meeting in Natchez on January 23, 1828, to frame an electoral ticket and then sponsored meetings in several counties to secure endorsement of the slate. The Jacksonians held a poorly attended state convention on January 7, made up of delegates from several counties, to nominate their electors. Subsequently, on May 22, a group of Jacksonian leaders met to endorse a candidate for Congress. Once again Jackson was an easy winner, polling more than four times the vote received by Adams.

Clay's support was negligible in 1832, and such interest as developed in the election centered on the contest between two rival slates of Jackson electors. The "regular" ticket, which was pledged to Van Buren for the vice-presidency and had been formed by members of the state constitutional convention, defeated a Jackson–Barbour ticket by a three-to-one margin. Voter interest in these three presidential elections was low. Only one-third of the electorate voted in 1832; the proportions in 1824 and 1828 had been 42 per cent and 57 per cent. Except for the meetings held to nominate electors, there was little in the way of party organization. Moreover, state elections continued to be contests among personalities, factions, and regions.

Serious attempts at party formation got under way in 1834, when the State-Rights Association, the Whigs, and the Democrats all undertook to organize their forces. Numerous issues— Indian policy, the tariff, the Force Bill, the removal of the deposits, and the question of Jackson's successor—had aroused interest in national affairs and had produced distinct cleavages of opinion.

Antagonism to Jackson's policies, particularly to his destruction of the bank and his firm opposition to nullification, became vocal as the Old Hero entered upon his final years in office. Also involved was hostility toward Samuel Gwin, register of the land office at Clinton, who had been recognized by the national administration as its chief dispenser of patronage in Mississippi and who headed a clique of federal office holders that sought to control the Jackson party in the state. The immediate occasion for the acceleration of political activity was the state election to be held in November, 1835, with not only the governorship and the two congressional seats at stake but also a legislature that was to elect a senator. Beyond that was the prospect of 1836, when the "regular" Democrats would be handicapped by the substitution of Van Buren for Jackson as their presidential candidate.

First to organize were the proponents of nullification, who were outraged by the Force Bill. On January 11, 1834, during sessions of the state courts in Jackson, numerous judges, lawyers, and citizens convened and adopted resolutions calling for the formation of a State-Rights party and proposing that a state convention be held in May. Later in the same month the group met again to adopt a lengthy address in which the doctrine of state sovereignty was elaborated. The convention, attended by about fifty delegates from eight counties, assembled in Jackson on May 19 and spent three days approving a plan to organize a "State-Rights Association," expounding nullificationist views, and praising Senators Poindexter and Black and Congressman Cage for their refusal to support the Force Bill. It was agreed to form state-rights associations in each county and hold semi-annual meetings of the central association in Jackson. No candidates were nominated, but it was expected that the association would use its influence in opposition to the regular Democratic nominees. Taking the leadership in this extremist movement was John A. Quitman, who was to be the foremost exponent of nullification doctrines in the state down to the Civil War.

The Democrats launched their effort at a meeting of party leaders and citizens in the Capitol on May 1, 1834, at which it was agreed to issue a call for a state convention to meet on June 9, "for the purpose of investigating the present condition of public affairs and adopting appropriate action in relation thereto."[16] Soon public meetings were arranged to appoint delegates to the convention, in which ten of the twenty-seven counties were ultimately represented.

The three-day session was extremely productive, with Samuel Gwin and his associates guiding the deliberations. In addition to the customary resolutions applauding Jackson, the convention authorized the appointment of a state committee and provided for the appointment of county committees, which in turn were to call meetings to elect committees of vigilance and correspondence. Delegates were named to attend the national convention in Baltimore. Finally, it was decided to hold a second convention in November for the purpose of nominating candidates. That the session was not entirely free of discord is suggested by the defeat of a resolution that the meeting should be officially styled "the convention of the States rights Union and Democratic party of the State of Mississippi."[17]

At the November convention, in which every county was represented, it was first deemed to be necessary to offer some defense of the convention system. After observing that in the past candidates had run as Democrats who subsequently displayed hostility to the party's principles—an unambiguous reference to Poindexter, Black, and Cage—the session resolved: "That nominations by a convention of delegates elected by the people themselves, representing the democracy of the various counties, are in accordance with the established usages of the democratic party in other States and constitute the only

16. (Jackson) *Mississippian*, May 2, 1834.
17. *Ibid.*, June 13, 1834.

method by which those important objects, the union and success of the party and its principles, can be achieved, and cannot be opposed by any sincere friend of democracy." It was
also laid down that nominees must pledge themselves to abide
by the decisions of the convention and support its choices.

No dissension developed over the nomination of candidates
for the governorship and the two congressional seats nor over
the recommendation that Van Buren should be supported in
the Baltimore convention. But there was a major controversy
over the endorsement of a senatorial candidate to replace
Poindexter. Ultimately Robert J. Walker, who had moved to
Mississippi from Pennsylvania in 1826 and had become an influential member of the "Natchez Junto" that dominated party
affairs, was favored over Franklin Plummer, the picturesque
demagogue from East Mississippi who never enjoyed the favor
of the party leaders.[18] Walker's candidacy was motivated in
part by his desire to forestall an investigation—launched by
Senator Poindexter—into the land speculations of Walker and
other Jackson adherents.

Meanwhile, the Whig party was also assuming form. As
the furore over the Force Bill subsided, opposition elements
coalesced on the basis of their condemnation of Jackson's fiscal
policies and their distaste for "executive usurpation." A preliminary meeting at Natchez in June set in motion plans for
a state convention, December 1-3, 1834, at Jackson. Candidates were nominated for the governorship and for Congress,
but no stand was taken in the senatorial contest. Every effort
was made to conciliate the State-Rights Association, which
was expected to hold the balance of power, and the candidates
selected did, in fact, receive the joint support of the State-
Rights adherents and the Whigs.

Thus, a year in advance of the state elections, the parties

18. *Ibid.*, Nov. 7, 1834; Niles' *Register*, XLVII, 200. This was the first
time, to my knowledge, that a candidate for the United States Senate was
nominated by a state party convention. Priority has sometimes been given to
Lincoln's nomination in Illinois in 1858. See Don E. Fehrenbacher, *Prelude to
Greatness: Lincoln in the 1850's* (Stanford, Cal., 1962).

prepared for a major contest. Plummer, previously a loyal supporter of Jackson in Congress, campaigned for the Whig nominees because of his disappointment at not receiving the Democratic backing for his senatorial ambitions. Walker stumped the state for months, advancing his own candidacy for the Senate, and other candidates were equally zealous. It was in this campaign that the interesting custom originated of sending political "runners" throughout assigned districts to arrange speaking appointments, circulate documents, and make political speeches at every crossroads and barroom. In their campaign, the Whigs, among other charges, denounced the Democrats for having used a convention to "dictate" nominations, and Plummer was especially voluble on this issue, even though he had taken a leading role in the first convention held in the state in 1828.[19] At the county level there was little party apparatus except for campaign purposes; nominations as in the past were arranged informally or candidates were self-announced.

The election gave the Whig-State-Rights alliance a victory by a narrow margin in the races for the governorship and in one of the two congressional seats. The new legislature, in which party alignments were not sharp, ultimately elected Walker to the Senate over Poindexter and Plummer. This election signalled the emergence in the state of loosely knit parties for the first time. Although alignments were far from stable, especially because of subsequent shifts by the state-rights element, the partisan identifications formed in 1835 were influential both with political leaders and with the masses of voters.

The presidential election was less exciting than the 1835 state election but just as closely contested. Because the convention system had been so severely attacked in the state campaign, both the Democrats and the Whigs chose other means of nominating candidates for presidential electors. The Democrats held a meeting of legislators and other party adherents at

19. (Jackson) *Mississippian*, July 3, 1835.

the Capitol on February 3 to announce their slate, and the Whigs and other supporters of Hugh L. White adopted a similar procedure a month later.[20] The Democrats recognized that Van Buren was not a popular figure in the state and sought to emphasize loyalty to Jackson as the major consideration. The champions of White, who included the State-Rights Association as well as the regular Whigs, appealed to sectional loyalties but were embarrassed by the charge that their candidate could not possibly receive an electoral majority. In a relatively light turnout (63 per cent), Van Buren carried the state by the slender margin of about five hundred votes.

The seemingly firm alignments that had appeared in these two crucial elections wavered after 1836. A severe banking crisis in Mississippi in 1837 weakened the Democratic cause. At the same time, however, the Whig opposition was split into unionist and state-rights wings. The result was that the Democrats were able to regain the governorship in 1837 because the opposition divided its strength between two candidates, but they suffered reverses in congressional contests and in their efforts to control the legislature.

By 1839 the situation was clarified by the movement of the bulk of the state-rights element into the Democratic party. During the legislative session in January, 1839, a Democratic-State-Rights convention was held in Jackson to complete the alliance. In addition to nominating candidates for the governorship and the two congressional seats, the convention acknowledged the state-rights faction by paying tribute to Calhoun and moving generally toward a state-rights position. The Whigs, now making their stand on fiscal issues, held a similar convention on January 28 to name their candidates. Strengthened by their new allies, the Democrats scored a sweeping victory in an election that brought 90 per cent of the adult white males to the polls. But the Whigs were not yet driven from the field. In 1840, with the vulnerable Van Buren as their target, they rallied behind Harrison and after a spec-

20. *Ibid.*, Feb. 5, Mar. 11, 1836.

tacular campaign won a clean-cut victory. The militancy of the two parties attracted voters to the polls in unprecedented numbers for a presidential election; 88 per cent of the adult white males voted.

The Whigs remained in a competitive position for the next decade, although they never obtained a state-wide majority. Their strength declined steadily in state elections, but they made better showings in presidential contests. In 1848, with a southern candidate and military hero heading their ticket, they lost by less than a thousand votes. The sectional crisis that developed in 1849 placed a severe strain on the old parties in Mississippi and a modified alignment—pitting Unionists against Southern Rights parties—appeared. Subsequently most Democrats resumed their old allegiance, but the Whigs never recovered their former strength, even though the solid core of the party retained a sense of identity under various labels until 1860. Voter participation remained at an extremely high level, rarely dropping below 80 per cent and not uncommonly rising above 85 per cent. Through 1848 participation was usually higher in presidential than in state elections; thereafter the reverse was true.

In Mississippi, as throughout most of the South, the contrast between the party situation in 1832 and 1836 is striking. In 1832 Jackson carried the state by an eight-to-one majority; in 1836 Van Buren barely edged out White. While Jackson was a candidate, the state supported him so overwhelmingly that there was no opportunity for an opposition party to form. Politics remained essentially unorganized and non-partisan in character. But in 1834 many factors, not the least of which was the prospect of a genuine contest over the presidential succession, led to the formation of parties, chiefly with reference to national issues. Thereafter, although the alignments were generally less stable than in the older states, elections became contests between moderately well-organized parties, rather than between individuals or factions.

MISSOURI

Missouri bore many resemblances to both Illinois and Kentucky, yet there were distinctive features about its political behavior. Like Illinois it was a western, frontier community, growing at such a rate that its population increased six-fold between 1820 and 1840. Its constitution was patterned after that of Kentucky, and it was a slave state, but slavery played a relatively minor role in its economy. Party formation took place much later than in Kentucky, and when parties formed the Democrats assumed a pre-eminence that was never seriously threatened. In contrast with Illinois, national elections generally aroused less interest than state elections, and voter participation never attained high levels. But beyond all conventional influences, Missouri bore the imprint of the personality of Thomas Hart Benton, who for three decades dominated political affairs in the state to a degree that has rarely, if ever, been equalled.

The structure of government in Missouri was such as to make the counties important political units. Members of the lower house of the legislature, elected biennially, were apportioned among the counties on the basis of free white male population. Senators were elected for four-year terms from districts made up of one or more counties. County electorates also chose a sheriff and coroners. The governor was given a four-year term and had extensive powers of appointment, but his effectiveness as a political leader was weakened by the provision that he was ineligible to succeed himself. The franchise was extended to free adult male citizens. State elections were held biennially on the first Monday in August, with the township as the voting unit. Congressmen, as well as presidential electors, were elected from the state at large.

The background for the history of party formation in

Missouri can be sketched largely in terms of the rise to prominence of Thomas Hart Benton. Arriving in Missouri in 1815, after a tempestuous early career in Tennessee that was climaxed by his famous brawl with Jackson, he allied himself economically with the prosperous, conservative element in St. Louis and in territorial politics became associated with the dominant "junto" faction. A zealous advocate of Western development, he championed the admission of Missouri to statehood with protection for slavery and was elected with David Barton to represent the new state in the Senate. Together with Barton and Congressman John Scott, he was an early supporter of Henry Clay for the presidency and endorsed Clay's nomination by a legislative caucus in November, 1822. With such formidable backing, Clay carried the state easily in 1824, with Jackson a distant second and Adams scarcely in the race. Politics was still conducted on an entirely informal, personal basis, with no vestiges of party organization. Interest in the presidential contest was so slight that only one-fifth of the eligible voters cast their ballots. More than three times that number had voted in the August state elections.

After the election, when it became apparent that Clay was out of the running, Benton declared his preference for Jackson while Barton—whose re-election to the Senate Benton had opposed in 1824—came out for Adams. In the House of Representatives, Scott, under heavy pressure from both sides, cast the vote of Missouri for Adams. Having committed himself to Jackson, Benton never wavered thereafter, and he became *the* Jackson party in Missouri. So great was his influence and so enormous was his energy that he could stand forth without a rival as the Jackson leader in Missouri. But the very fact that he was so potent a figure had the effect of perpetuating the old, personalized, informal style of political management and retarding the transition to the new-type of convention-structured party. Consequently partisan identities, and party discipline, remained vague until after 1836. Although there was, strictly speaking, no Jackson-Democratic party in Missouri, there was a Benton faction, and its candidates were usually victorious in state-wide elections.

Benton's prestige and personal authority were enhanced in 1825 when the candidate whom he favored won the governorship in a special election over three rivals, and in 1826 he was easily reelected to the Senate. There was no tendency, however, for parties to form. In 1826, for example, the victor in the congressional election, Edward Bates, specifically denied any party affiliation.

The presidential election of 1828, although it stimulated some organizational activity in behalf of each candidate, had no lasting effect on the political situation. Senator Barton assumed the leadership of the Adams forces, and at a meeting in St. Louis on November 27 it was agreed to call a state convention of the "Friends of the Administration" on March 3 in Jefferson City. Eighteen counties were represented by fifty-four delegates at this convention, which nominated three electors and set up a correspondence committee to promote Adams' campaign. The Jackson men, meanwhile, had held a similar convention in Jefferson City on January 8, 1828, to name their electors and issue an address. Neither convention made any nominations for state offices nor was there any serious attempt to build local party organizations.

Benton worked with his customary energy throughout the campaign, making stump speeches, organizing public meetings, arranging for newspaper support and for the distribution of handbills and pamphlets, while Barton and his associates engaged in similar activities. Jackson triumphed easily, winning 70 per cent of the popular vote; voter participation was 54 per cent. Significantly, the state election in August had been conducted with no relationship to the presidential contest and the incumbent governor was elected without opposition.

The Barton-Adams party promptly collapsed after the election, and politics in Missouri continued to revolve around personalities and factions. In 1830 Barton's prestige suffered a fatal blow when he failed to secure re-election to the Senate.

His successor, however, was not chosen on a party basis and was not, in fact, a Jacksonian. To add to the confusion, Benton's choice for Congress in 1831—nominated by a so-called convention at Columbia in October—was defeated by William H. Ashley, a nominal Jacksonian whose support came from the anti-Jacksonians.

Some attempts were made late in 1831 and early in 1832 to organize a Clay party, but they do not appear to have been successful, and a Clay electoral ticket, not arranged by a convention, was merely announced in the *Missouri Republican*. The Jacksonians held a convention in November, 1831, to nominate their electors and—for the first time—candidates for governor and lieutenant-governor. The August election was closely contested, with the candidates of the convention winning by small margins. The presidential election, in which only 41 per cent of the electorate participated, produced a very different alignment, for Jackson secured a two-to-one majority over Clay.

The Jacksonians were seemingly possessed of overwhelming strength in presidential elections, but because they lacked a disciplined organization, and because the electorate still voted for personalities rather than for parties, alignments remained indistinct. Ashley, who can best be classified as an independent Whig without organized support, was re-elected to Congress in 1833 and 1835 over his Jacksonian opponents and in 1836 nearly won the governorship. On the other hand, the Democrats made considerable preparations for the presidential election of 1836, beginning with a state convention on January 8, 1835, and carried the state for Van Buren by a very substantial margin over a White-Harrison fusion ticket that was not completed until September, 1836. Again, the presidential election brought little more than a third of the voters to the polls, whereas more than half had voted in the gubernatorial election.

Party alignments grew increasingly clear after 1836, as the Democrats strengthened the organization that they had created by 1835, and the Whigs saw the necessity of solidifying their ranks. At first the Missouri Whigs were divided—as were their colleagues in Illinois—over the propriety of adopting the convention system. Late in 1837 plans were made at a Whig meeting in St. Louis for a convention to be held early in 1838 for the purpose of organizing the party, but so strong was the opposition that the matter was dropped. The proposal was revived in 1839, following another defeat, and by this time sentiment had altered.

In that year John Scott had declined to run as a Whig candidate for Congress on the grounds that it would be "like fighting regular troops with undisciplined militia." He was referring, of course, to Benton's Democratic machine. "Until the late movement in reference to a state convention," he added, "the whigs had never attempted anything like union of action."[21]

The Whig members of the legislature took the initiative in urging that meetings should be held in each county to elect delegates to a convention that was to meet in Jefferson City on October 21, 1839. The response was good, and most of the counties were represented at the session. Nominations were made for state offices as well as for Congress and presidential electors and delegates were also appointed to attend the Whig national convention.[22] The Democrats engaged in similar preparations, with the result that the 1840 state and presidential elections were to represent a real trial of strength between two parties.

Missouri indulged in the theatrics that everywhere distinguished campaigning in 1840, with the Whigs outdoing the Democrats in the imaginativeness and enthusiasm of their performance. But the Democrats met the challenge and both in August and November won by large margins. Voter participation rose to new highs. In the state election 73 per cent of the eligibles participated, a proportion never again reached

21. Niles' *Register*, LVII, 138.
22. *Ibid.*, LVII, 167-68.

before 1860. The presidential contest brought out 74 per cent of the electorate. Only on this occasion, and in 1848—when participation reached 75 per cent—did the presidential vote exceed that cast in the state election.

For a decade after 1840 party alignments remained fairly stable in both state and national elections. The Democrats customarily received over 55 per cent of the total vote cast, but the Whigs remained a determined minority. Benton continued to dominate the Democratic party until 1849, when his vigorous stand against the extension of slavery was repudiated by the legislature. In the ensuing intraparty conflict, Benton lost his seat in the Senate, and the pro-slavery faction gained control of the party. Benton's downfall occasioned some shifts in party loyalties, but the Democrats retained their majority position until 1860. Oddly enough, voter participation declined after 1848; it was exceptional when as many as three-fifths of the adult white males voted.

There were unusual aspects to the Missouri political scene. It is somewhat remarkable that parties were so late in forming, especially in view of the fact that the Benton-Jackson faction was always confronted by an opposition of sorts after 1827. Yet there was hardly an effective Democratic party until 1835 and the Whigs did not become organized until 1839. Before 1835 Jacksonians competed against one another for the same offices and an anti-Jacksonian, like Ashley, could win three successive terms in Congress in state-wide elections. Part of the explanation for this situation lies in the general slowness with which new political communities moved from a personalized type of politics to a party system. But involved also would seem to be the attitudes of Benton, who successfully used old-fashioned methods to maintain his personal position and to carry the state for Democratic presidential candidates.

The strong fidelity of Missouri to the Democratic party is also noteworthy. It ranked second only to New Hampshire in producing consistently large majorities for the party after 1832. The state did not succumb to the strong state-rights, anti-

northern, anti-Van Buren feeling that so threatened Demo-
catic ascendancy in the southern states, nor did it develop the
enthusiasm for Harrison that occurred in other western states.
Most puzzling of all, however, is the low level of voter participation in the state, even after 1840 and especially in presidential elections. Outside of New England—and excluding
Virginia and Louisiana, which had limitations on the franchise
—Missouri had the poorest record of any state for attendance at
elections. Such apathy is hardly consistent with the lively
scene in Caleb Bingham's charming portrayal of "The County
Election."

LOUISIANA

Louisiana is a peculiarly difficult state to classify, for although it was, like Mississippi, a frontier state strongly committed to slavery, it differed significantly in its political behavior both from the older and the new southern states. Its
distinctiveness can be attributed to a unique combination of
factors. There was, foremost of all, the division of the population culturally into two antagonistic groups—the French and
the Anglo-Saxons—who identified themselves in politics as
"Creoles" or "Americans" to such a degree that party identities
often were reduced to secondary influence. Secondly, the state
was governed by a minority under a constitution that drastically limited suffrage privileges and made for a most inequitable
system of representation. Finally, the presence of the largest
metropolis in the South—New Orleans—and a powerful sugar-
growing interest differentiated Louisiana from other southern
states. These circumstances all influenced party formation in
the state, and they were responsible for the early lack of
identity between state and national political alignments, the

persistent strength of the Whigs, and the conspicuously low voter participation.

Cultural and sectional tensions formed the background for Louisiana politics until the 1830's. During the territorial period the old French population had become resentful of American dominance and had developed an acute political self-consciousness. After 1812 state politics involved struggles for control between the French and the Americans. Because of the pattern of settlement, the contests had also a sectional aspect. The French predominated in southwestern Louisiana, the Americans in the Florida and Red River areas. New Orleans, which often held the balance of power, was the scene of bitter conflicts between the French of the Old City, who controlled the municipal government, and the Americans of the newer wards, who resented their subordination.

Neither the French nor the Americans were firmly united; on the contrary there were within each group personal factions or, especially among the French, rival family clans. Consequently there were often two or more French or American candidates for the same office. Even after 1824, the French continued to be primarily interested in local and state offices, leaving federal politics largely to the Americans. So strong was this French *versus* American feeling in state politics that long after party distinctions had begun to form in presidential elections, state elections continued to be fought on the basis of old rivalries. The result was a kind of dual politics, in which voters assumed party identities in presidential elections but retained their old ethnic loyalties in state elections. The situation was to be confused further by the fact that although Jackson enjoyed considerable personal popularity, his policies had little appeal to those who held political privileges in the state.

The Louisiana constitution of 1812—which survived until 1845—was a product of the determination of the Creoles to secure and retain control of the government. It was cleverly drafted to favor the old settlers and in operation discriminated against New Orleans, the American settlements, and the mass of the adult white male inhabitants. A key feature was the suffrage provision. Voting privileges were confined to those who paid state taxes. Because of the nature of the tax legislation, more than half of the adult white males were disfranchised.[23] Periodically a census of electors was made, which revealed, for example, that only 40 per cent of the adult white males could vote in 1815; 47 per cent in 1825; and 51 per cent in 1840.[24] In New Orleans, where the proportion of state taxpayers was less than half that of the state as a whole, only about one man in five could vote.

These restrictive suffrage provisions affected the system of representation in the legislature, both houses of which were apportioned on the basis of number of qualified voters. Southwestern Louisiana, with 35 per cent of the population in 1820, had 45 per cent of the seats in the lower house and 47 per cent in the upper house. New Orleans, which had approximately the same population, had only 17 per cent of the seats in the lower house and 12 per cent in the upper house. Because there was no reapportionment of the legislature between 1826 and 1841, when the American settlements north of the Red River were growing rapidly, representation became increasingly inequitable.

The governorship in Louisiana, unlike in most states at that period, was an important office. The chief executive had

23. No person whose name was not on the tax lists could vote. Taxes were levied on slaves, merchants, retailers, taverns, peddlers, brokers, auctioneers, lawyers, doctors, cattle (when more than twenty-five), horses (when more than ten), four-wheel carriages, two-wheel carriages, billiard tables, bank stock, insurance companies, other incorporated commercial companies, and real estate. There was no poll tax. *Acts of the State of Louisiana*, 1st leg., 2nd ses. (New Orleans, 1813), 218-44.

24. The censuses were supervised by the sheriffs in each parish. In addition to enumerating the free persons by sex and color, slaves by sex, and white males by age groupings, the census had a separate category for the enumeration of voters. *Ibid.*, 162-68. The census data was usually printed in the legislative journals, although the census of 1825-26 is not to be found in any official source. Dr. Joseph G. Tregle kindly supplied me with the unofficial copy of that census as reported in the (New Orleans) *Louisiana Advertiser*, May 16, 1827.

a strong veto and vast powers of appointment. In theory he was chosen by the legislature from among the two candidates receiving the highest popular vote; in practice the victor in the popular election was always chosen. The term of office was four years and the incumbent was ineligible to succeed himself. In 1812 an informal agreement had been reached to the effect that the governorship should alternate between the French and the Americans, but after the Americans broke the understanding in 1824 by electing one of their men to succeed another American, the French retaliated by holding the office from 1828 to 1846.

Elections were held biennially in the even years on three days in July. Voting was by ballot and the parish was the polling unit, although it might be divided into three districts with the poll open one day in each district. Members of the lower house, elected for two-year terms, were apportioned among the parishes; members of the upper house, who served for four years, were apportioned among fourteen fixed districts. Congressmen, elected from districts, were chosen at the July elections. Presidential electors were appointed by the legislature until 1828, when they were made elective in November from the state at large. Parish government was not democratized until 1845.

Interest in national politics, which had been negligible in Louisiana, was awakened by the contest for the presidency in 1824. Clay was at first the overwhelming favorite because of his nationalistic views and his strong family ties in the state. His son-in-law, Martin Duralde, was an influential leader among the French politicians. When in 1823 Jackson's candidacy became a serious reality, a host of his personal friends rallied to his support and undertook to direct sentiment in his favor. By 1824 the legislature was fairly evenly divided between adherents of Clay and Jackson and attention centered on the election in July of a new legislature that would choose the state's electors.

Although the presidential question was not involved in the election of the governor or members of Congress, candidates for the legislature were pressed to declare themselves, and, at least in New Orleans, organized efforts were put forth in behalf of rival slates. When the legislature met in November, the balance was so close that the decision rested with a small pro-Adams group. A bargain was arranged whereby the Jackson and Adams men coalesced to choose three electors pledged to Jackson and two pledged to Adams. Subsequently, in the House election, two of Louisiana's three congressmen cast the vote of the state for Adams. These maneuvers did not give rise to parties, but they did array many political leaders—especially among the Americans—into rival camps behind Jackson or Clay-Adams.

This cleavage had little effect on politics until 1827, when the prospect of a contest between Adams and Jackson stimulated both camps to action. Friends of Jackson purchased the New Orleans *Advertiser* and installed as editor the aggressive P. K. Wagner, who portrayed the Old Hero as the victim of an outrageous bargain perpetrated by cunning professional politicians. The Adams press engaged in personal attacks on Jackson, whose high-handed actions in 1815 had so alienated many prominent French citizens as to dispose them to place little confidence in the "military chieftain." Because electors were to be chosen for the first time by popular vote, some machinery was needed to produce agreement on slates of candidates. Leaders of both parties attempted to convoke legislative caucuses, but popular sentiment against the caucus was so strong that this tactic was abandoned, and resort was had instead to state nominating conventions. During 1827 public meetings in behalf of each candidate were held all over the state, local committees of correspondence were created, and delegates were appointed to the state conventions.

The Adams convention, attended by forty-seven delegates from half of the state's thirty parishes, met at Baton Rouge,

November 5-6, 1827.[25] Electors were nominated, an address and resolutions were adopted and ordered to be published, and the delegates were exhorted to rouse their parishes for Adams. The Jackson convention met in New Orleans on January 15, 1828, shortly after the general had paid a four-day visit to the city to observe the thirteenth anniversary of his greatest victory. Twenty-seven parishes were represented by 127 delegates, who named an electoral slate and adopted the customary address and resolutions. Some attempt was made to have the delegates endorse gubernatorial and congressional candidates for the July election, but no agreement could be reached. When the state election was held, a pro-Adams French candidate won the governorship over three opponents, and the Jacksonians lost the legislature and two of the three congressional seats. The result was not interpreted as presaging a victory for Adams, however, for old ethnic and factional rivalries, rather than the presidential question, dominated the contests.

After the state election, the presidential campaign was conducted with great vigor; no previous election had ever occasioned so much excitement. Although only 36 per cent of the adult white males went to the polls, this was the highest proportion that had yet voted in the state and represented over 70 per cent of the eligible voters. Jackson won with 53 per cent of the popular vote, running decidedly behind Adams only in the French region south of the Red River. In all of the other states south of Maryland, except Kentucky, Adam's vote had been extremely small; his respectable showing in Louisiana is a measure of that state's deviation from the normal southern pattern. Despite the apparent emergence of closely balanced and moderately organized parties in the presidential election, political alignments had not yet become stabilized. The powerful cross-current that operated in state poli-

25. *Proceedings of the Delegates of the Friends of the Administration of John Quincy Adams, Assembled in Convention at Baton Rouge* [New Orleans, 1827].

tics had not yet been channeled into the two streams that represented the Jackson and anti-Jackson parties.

For the next six years, the political situation remained extremely confused. After Jackson assumed office, Martin Gordon, the wealthy and power-seeking owner of the Orleans Navigation Company, was appointed collector of the Port of New Orleans and was made the chief dispenser of federal patronage in Louisiana. Gordon thereupon took over the leadership of the Jackson party, but his crude tactics involved him in continual difficulties. In his distribution of patronage he slighted the claims of the Creoles and of the Jacksonians in the Florida parishes, and his domineering manner aroused widespread resentments. His ineptitude was revealed in 1830, when the death of the incumbent necessitated the election of a new governor. He arranged for a state convention to meet, intending that it should nominate his hand-picked choice for the governorship, but so strong was the antagonism to Gordon that only a handful of delegates turned up. His candidate then withdrew, leaving the field to a dissident Jacksonian from the Florida region. Meanwhile the Creole-Clay party had united behind a French candidate, who won over the feud-ridden Jacksonians. In the same election Clay men won all three Congressional seats.

In 1832 the Clay supporters were lethargic because of their conviction that their candidate's prospects were hopeless, and they accordingly put forth little effort. The Jacksonians temporarily abandoned their internecine battles and met in New Orleans in January to nominate electors and appoint delegates to the Baltimore convention. With only one-fourth of the adult white males voting, Jackson defeated Clay by a greater than two-to-one majority. The previous July, however, supporters of Clay had again captured all the congressional seats. Quite obviously, partisanship still had a very limited meaning in Louisiana.

The weakness of the Jacksonians in state politics was again exposed in 1834. Still restive under Gordon's domination, the party lacked unity. Hoping to crush French power in the state, the Gordon machine advocated the abolition of the suffrage restrictions, reduction of the governor's powers, and equitable apportionment of the legislature. This threat served to solidify French support behind the Whig gubernatorial candidate—who was French—and the Democratic candidate was overwhelmingly defeated. The Democrats were equally unsuccessful in the congressional election. After 1834, Gordon having lost his post as collector, the party acquired new leaders, the chief of whom was to be John Slidell, and began to cultivate support among French politicians. As the ethnic cleavage became blurred, national party identifications grew stronger.

The presidential election of 1836 did relatively little to advance this tendency, for there was no enthusiasm for either Van Buren or White. Both Whigs and Democrats held state conventions to nominate electors, but no great exertions were put forth in the ensuing campaign. Voter participation reached an all-time low when only one-fifth of the adult white males cast ballots. Once again, the Democrats were victorious in a presidential election, this time by a margin of less than three-hundred votes.

Perhaps the most significant aspect of these years was that the strong state-rights, anti-Van Buren feeling that contributed so substantially to party formation in other Southern states was of minor importance in Louisiana. Outside of the Florida parishes, state-rights doctrines had little currency. Furthermore, the state had never been so monolithic in its support of Jackson as its neighbors; the basis for an anti-Jackson party had existed since 1824. But what was most distinctive about the Louisiana situation was the ethno-cultural basis for party formation; Creoles vied with Americans, and this conflict long transcended other considerations.

After 1836 state politics came increasingly under the domination of the major parties, which had adapted themselves with fair success to the ethnic forces in the state. The Democrats in 1838 shrewdly nominated a Creole as their candidate for governor, and although he was defeated by the Whig nominee—also a Creole—the margin was close. As in 1834, each party was united behind a single candidate; there were no independents in the race. The Whigs followed up this victory with intensive preparations for the presidential election of 1840. In true Whig style, they mounted a spectacular campaign, which the Democrats sought to emulate. The wave of enthusiasm carried Harrison to a stunning victory; he received nearly 60 per cent of the popular vote. The outpouring of voters—39 per cent of the adult white males, or nearly 80 per cent of the qualified voters—surpassed all previous records.

Down to 1840 the Jacksonians had never lost a presidential election, but they had never supported a winning gubernatorial candidate and were almost equally unsuccessful in congressional and legislative contests. This curious pattern resulted in part from the fact that the French had become closely identified with the Adams-Clay forces, whom they backed strongly in state elections. The Creoles, however, remained relatively indifferent to national politics and did not turn out to vote heavily in presidential elections, a circumstance that operated to the advantage of the Jacksonians. Moreover, Jackson's personal popularity doubtless affected the outcome of the contests in which he was a participant.

After 1840, the pattern was reversed. The Democrats won the governorship in 1842—when a Creole Democrat defeated an American Whig—and never relinquished it thereafter. On the other hand, the Whigs displayed their greatest strength in presidential elections, winning in 1840 and 1848 and losing in 1844 only because of the notorious frauds perpetrated by the Democrats in Plaquemines parish, which they colonized with boatloads of illegal voters from New Orleans. The Whigs retained their strong identification with the French element, invariably offering a Creole as their candidate for governor after 1842. It is conceivable that this tactic lost them some of the "American" support that they had in presidential elections. In any case, interest in presidential elections after 1840—as evidenced by voter participation—was much greater than it was in state elections.

The balance between the parties remained remarkably stable until after 1856. Neither the controversies over the slavery issue in national politics nor changes in the state constitution in 1845 and 1852—including liberalization of the suffrage—greatly affected the relative strength of the two parties. After 1852 the Whigs moved generally into the American party; the Democrats retained their old identity. Both parties held to similar moderate positions on the grave sectional questions that played havoc with the party system elsewhere.

In 1845 suffrage privileges were extended to all adult white male citizens who had resided in the state for two years.[26] The residence requirement was reduced to one year in 1852. These changes had only a modest effect on the proportion of adult white males who were eligible to vote. According to the censuses of electors made in 1847, 1853, and 1859, the proportions were 52 per cent, 61 per cent, and 53 per cent respectively. Whereas 39 per cent of the adult white males had voted in 1840, participation rose to 47 per cent in 1848 and reached a peak of 52 per cent in 1860. This increase in voter participation may have augmented slightly the strength of the Democratic party, but the fact is not clearly apparent from the election returns.

In summary, Louisiana moved from an ethnocentric type of politics that featured struggles among rival factions to a party-based politics in two stages. Party alignments are discernible after 1827 in contests for the presidency, but these alignments did not operate strongly in state elections until

26. In the course of a discussion of the liberalization of the suffrage in the 1845 constitutional convention one delegate explained that under the old system "each party purchased property of little value, which they divided out among a numerous batch of voters, whose suffrages in that way they secured. This was carried so far that the true intention of the Constitution becomes a dead letter." *Proceedings and Debates of the Convention of Louisiana . . .* (New Orleans, 1845), 105. Another delegate recalled that during the presidential campaign of 1844 one tax collector had issued 1,500 false tax receipts. *Ibid.,* 107-9.

1834. Alone among the states of the lower South, Louisiana was never overwhelmingly committed to Jackson nor did it experience an abrupt formation of parties on the issues that produced such cleavages elsewhere around 1834. The Louisiana parties, once they had become aligned and balanced, were more stable and durable than those in the neighboring states.

CONCLUSIONS

The seven states that have been grouped together in the category of "new states" shared much in common in their political development and are readily distinguishable from the three regions previously considered. All of them were still new political communities in 1824 in the sense that they had little or no experience with conducting politics on a party basis. Candidates for elective office and those who voted for them did not behave as partisans, except for a perfunctory display of fidelity to the Old Republican party in presidential elections. In state-wide elections, sectional and ethnic rivalries were often influential.

At the highest level of state politics, small leadership cliques—like the "triumvirate" in Indiana, the Edwards and and Thomas factions in Illinois, or the Benton junto in Missouri—sought to acquire power and offices, and in the counties or parishes loose alliances were formed for similar purposes. But it is a striking fact that no state-oriented parties, even of the crude Georgia type, were formed and there was accordingly little use of formal devices of political management, such as caucuses, conventions, or committees. The absence of parties in these states gives added weight to the observation that party formation is directly related to the contest for the presidency. Without the stimulus of such a contest, parties were not formed. Not until the contest for the presidency was revived after 1824 did party formation begin.

The new states were similar, too, in their governmental structures. Except in Louisiana—where there were restrictions on the suffrage, inequitable representation, and undemocratic parish institutions—the constitutions were of a liberal type. Virtually all adult white males were eligible to vote; legislatures were equitably apportioned on a population basis; governors, presidential electors, local officials, and—in some instances —even judges were popularly elected; and polling procedures were designed to facilitate voting. Whereas the original constitutions of the older states had embodied many unique features and therefore differed widely, those of the new states conformed to the same broad pattern and contained little that was novel or distinctive.

The fact that these were, indeed, new political communities, expanding at a rapid rate in population and areas of settlement and lacking the more or less stable social relationships that had become established in the older states, affected the conduct of politics. The building of durable, highly organized parties had to be done completely—from top to bottom—and in the midst of dynamic change. What was truly remarkable was the rapidity with which techniques of party organization that had been perfected in the Northeast were successfully applied in the new states, especially after 1832. It is not apparent that the new states made any significant contributions to the machinery of politics, but they may be credited with popularizing and reinforcing the campaign style that swept the nation in 1840.

Party formation in the new states did not occur so abruptly as in New England or the Old South. Moreover, the problem is complicated by the fact that in certain states several years intervened between the formation of parties in presidential elections and the establishment of similar alignments in state elections. In Ohio national party identities were fairly well fixed as early as 1828, but it was not until 1836 that state politics became fully integrated with the new party system. Presidential elections occasioned cleavages and minimal organization in Indiana, but not until 1840 were the Whig and Democratic parties fully mobilized to operate effectively in both state and national elections. There was little semblance of partisanship on an organized and continuing basis in Illinois before 1835, when the Democratic party began to take shape, and the Whigs never matched their rivals in discipline and vigor. In Mississippi party organization dated from 1834, when intensive preparations were made for the 1835 state election. The Democratic party in Alabama assumed form in 1835, but not until 1841 were the Whigs organized to contest a state election. Louisiana is a very special case. There was some continuity in alignments in presidential elections from 1828, but state and congressional elections produced very different alignments down, at least, to 1836. In Missouri the peculiar type of political authority wielded by Senator Benton inhibited genuine party development; although the Democratic party may be said to have originated with Benton's decision to support Jackson in 1825, it had little organization before 1835 and the Whigs did not organize until 1839.

With the exceptions, then, of Ohio and Louisiana, there was little semblance of party formation in the new states until after 1832. It is true, of course, that in most states some organizational activity took place before each presidential election, but the identities assumed in these elections were not lasting and they were not influential in state or local politics. In certain states—Indiana, Illinois, and Missouri are notable examples—politics continued to be managed in the old informal style by factions and individual leaders. Because partisanship did not extend beyond the presidential elections, it becomes difficult to interpret what Jacksonism signified. Although Jackson carried every state both in 1828 and 1832, most of them by very large majorities, it was common—especially in Indiana, Ohio, Louisiana, and Mississippi—for men who were hostile or indifferent to Jackson to win elections to governorships and to seats in both houses of Congress. The situation became even more confusing after 1832 when candidates would profess admiration for Jackson but would denounce his heir-apparent, Martin Van Buren.

The critical years of party formation in the new states, as in the Old South, were 1834 and 1835. In the presidential election of 1832 Clay had been in a competitive position only in Ohio; Jackson's majorities in the other states ranged from 66 per cent of the total vote in Missouri up to 100 per cent in Alabama. The average of the differences between the percentages of the popular vote secured by Jackson and Clay was forty-six points. In 1836 the margin had narrowed to nine points. Van Buren lost Ohio and Indiana and secured over 60 per cent of the popular vote only in Missouri. The amorphous Jackson party of 1828 and 1832 had shrunk in size and had assumed disciplined form behind Van Buren; the opposition, made up of erstwhile Jacksonians as well as former supporters of Adams and Clay, had coalesced behind White or Harrison and found a common ground in their hostility to Van Buren. The shift in sentiment in the new states was only slightly less dramatic than in the Old South but was very much more pronounced than it had been in New England and the Middle States. In those two sections the process of party formation had been largely accomplished before 1830, with the result that no extraordinary upheaval marked the election of 1836.

The convention system was instituted in each state as the standard device for party management as soon as parties began to form. Except in Ohio, where some use had been made of them at the county level since the early 1800's, conventions were introduced chiefly to nominate electors and mobilize the parties for presidential contests. Subsequently, as party competition was extended to state and congressional elections, it became common practice for delegate conventions to make nominations for most elective offices.

In Ohio and Indiana crude state conventions were held for

the first time in 1824, and those that met to make preparations for the 1828 campaign were well developed. Conventions were not used to nominate gubernatorial candidates in Ohio until 1830, and in Indiana, although the Jacksonians nominated a candidate for governor in 1834, the practice was not firmly established until 1840. State conventions met before the 1828 campaign in Missouri and Louisiana and began to exercise some authority in state politics in Missouri in 1831 and in Louisiana in 1834. The Jacksonians in Mississippi sponsored a poorly attended state convention in 1828, but it was in 1834 that both the Democrats and the Whigs embraced the convention system. Alabama witnessed its first convention in 1835, and by 1840 both parties had committed themselves to the device. In Illinois the Democrats held their first full-fledged conventions in 1835 to perfect their organization and prepare for the congressional and presidential elections; in 1837 their gubernatorial candidate was named by a state convention. The Illinois Whigs held a state convention in 1839, but they continued to rely primarily on informal methods of party management.

The construction of a party apparatus in the townships, counties, parishes, and districts usually followed considerably behind the establishment of the state convention, especially in the southern states. The parties, in other words, were organized from the top downward, and characteristically they competed first in presidential elections for some years before engaging in contests for state and local offices. In general it was the Jacksonians who were most energetic in introducing and developing the convention system in all the states.

The political behavior of the seven states followed a similar pattern, but close analysis reveals individual differences. Ohio, which was almost evenly divided in party preferences from 1828, could in many respects be classed with the Middle States. Alabama and Mississippi, on the other hand, were exceptional for their solidarity behind Jackson in 1828 and 1832 and therefore resembled the states of the Old South.

Louisiana, with its peculiar brand of ethno-politics and its distinctive economic concerns, occupied a special category, as did Missouri, the political fief of Senator Benton. Indiana and Illinois had much in common, although the candidacy of Harrison in 1836 and 1840 operated to give the Whigs in the former state an advantage that they never secured in the latter.

The party alignments that had been formed in each state by 1836 remained fairly stable until after 1850. The balance between the parties was not so close as in the Middle States, but it approximated that of the Old South and was decidedly more even than in New England. In the presidential elections from 1836 through 1852 the averages of the differences between the percentages of the popular votes obtained by the major party candidates varied between five points in 1848 and eleven points in 1852. There was a distinct bias toward the Democratic party; out of forty-nine contests between 1828 and 1852 the Democrats lost only eight. No section was more uniformly committed to the Democratic party.

All seven states tended generally to shift in the same direction in presidential elections. Jackson in 1832 was stronger in every state, except Missouri, than he had been in 1828. In 1836 and again in 1840 the Democrats suffered losses in every state, but in 1844 they gained everywhere. In 1848 there was a mixed reaction. The Democrats gained in Ohio and Indiana but suffered sharp declines in the other five states. This trend was reversed in 1852, when the Democrats registered advances in every state.

The most interesting and significant shifts between 1844 and 1852 occurred in Alabama and Mississippi. In both states the Democrats scored lopsided victories in 1844, won by the barest of margins in 1848, and came back to overwhelm the Whigs in 1852. A similar, though less extreme, pattern is observable in Louisiana. The explanation for the marked revival of Whig fortunes in those three states in 1848 would seem to lie in their decided preference for the southern favorite, Zachary Taylor of Louisiana. Similarly, the deviant behavior of Ohio and Indiana can be related to the candidacy of Lewis Cass of Michigan.

Voter participation in the new states was on the whole above the national average, except in 1832. Louisiana, because of restrictive suffrage practices, was a conspicuous exception to this generalization, and Missouri was also well behind the other states. More than 60 per cent of the adult white males voted in presidential elections in Ohio and Indiana from 1828, in Alabama and Mississippi from 1836, and in Illinois from 1840. The most spectacular rise in voter participation occurred in 1840, when in five states 85 per cent or more of the adult white males went to the polls. From this high peak, participation declined slightly in 1844 and again in 1848, fell sharply in 1852, and then rose again in every state in 1856 and 1860. Alabama registered the highest turnout among the seven states in 1840, Mississippi was foremost in 1844 and 1848, and Indiana led not only the section but also the entire nation in 1852, 1856, and 1860. Participation in presidential elections was usually much higher than in state elections after 1836, except in Mississippi and Missouri. This condition was not unrelated to the fact that in most states the Whigs put forth their best efforts, and made their strongest showings, in the presidential contests.

CHAPTER VII

THE SECOND AMERICAN
PARTY SYSTEM

It has been a major thesis of this study that the process of party formation which produced the second American party system can best be understood by examining developments within each of the states over the years between 1824 and 1840. It is quite clear that the new parties did not emerge suddenly and at one time throughout the nation. Rather, they were formed by able leaders at different times from state to state. With some notable exceptions, party formation took place at intervals in each of four definable regions —New England, the Middle States, the Old South, and the New West. The dominant impetus to party formation was supplied by the contest for the presidency, and the circumstance that most affected the sequence of party formation was the sectional identification of the presidential candidates.

Having viewed the course of party formation in some detail from the perspective of the several states and regions, it now becomes possible to deal comprehensively with the subject in order to make explicit certain patterns and relationships. The first problem, essentially, is to consider when and why parties formed and also to observe when and how the new alignments became operative in both state and national elections. The starting point for the inquiry must be the presidential election of 1824, which hastened the final break-up of

329

what remained of the first party system and initiated the formation of new parties.

The election of 1824 was of unusual importance because it involved the revival of the contest for the presidency. It was peculiar, however, in that the contest was not conducted on a party basis, for all of the rival candidates regarded themselves as adherents of the old Republican party. There was, fortuitously, no notable Virginian to continue the Virginia dynasty. In this situation the Republican party was confronted with the problem of deciding among several aspirants. The machinery available to perform this function—the congressional caucus—had never previously been tested by such a difficult choice, and it was unequal to the task. Party discipline was weak, the authority of the caucus was negligible, and the consequence was that the caucus candidate—William H. Crawford— was opposed by Adams, Jackson, and Clay, each with strong local bases of support.

This unprecedented array of candidates was symptomatic of the disintegration of the old party system. The Federalists, who had put forth their last presidential candidate in 1816, retained some semblance of identity in most of the northern states, but were dominant only in Delaware and were in no condition to attempt a revival in national politics. As Federalist opposition had become ineffectual from state to state, there was a tendency for the Republicans to lose their militancy and their unity and succumb to internal factional disputes. Outside of New England, where the Republicans generally maintained their centralized apparatus, party organization deteriorated. In the South interparty competition had long since declined, and the machinery for maintaining party discipline, which had never been elaborate, was little used. The first party system had never really become established in the new states of the West, and politics in that region was conducted largely on a non-party basis, even though most politicians and voters there identified themselves nominally as Republicans.

As the presidential campaign evolved, political leaders in each state had to make choices among the recognized candidates. In part, at least, their decisions were influenced by their calculations as to the effect their commitments would have on their own political fortunes. In many states the decision was easily made because of the overwhelming appeal of a particular candidate. But in other states the choice was difficult, for popular sentiment might be divided or confused.

In New England, which had for so long endured political frustration, Adams was the all but unanimous favorite. There was no substantial support for any other candidate, and Adams carried every state with ease in a dull election that brought less than one voter in five to the polls.

The Middle States, which had no favorite son in the race, were divided in their allegiances. In New York and Delaware, where electors were chosen by the legislature, it would appear that Adams and Crawford were nearly equal in strength. New Jersey favored Jackson by a small margin over Adams, and in Maryland, Adams received a plurality of the popular vote, with Jackson in second place. Pennsylvania went for the Old Hero by a landslide over Adams and Crawford.

The pattern was only slightly less varied in the five states of the Old South. The legislature of Crawford's home state, Georgia, readily chose electors pledged to the caucus candidate. In Tennessee and Kentucky the voters responded enthusiastically for their respective native sons, Jackson and Clay. The Crawford forces carried Virginia easily, despite the opposition of Jackson and Adams tickets, but in North Carolina the Crawford regulars were defeated by a People's Ticket, representing a combination of Jackson and Adams supporters.

The newer states of the west present a picture of confusion. In Ohio, Indiana, and Illinois, Jackson, Adams, and Clay were all in contention, and in no state did one candidate secure a majority of the popular vote. Clay won a plurality in Ohio, Jackson in Indiana, and in Illinois the returns defied interpretation, although Jackson was probably the leader. Jackson

carried Alabama and Mississippi over weak opposition, chiefly
from Adams, but he lost Missouri to Clay. In Louisiana the
legislature divided its electoral vote between Jackson and
Adams, but Clay was probably as well regarded as either.

Except in New England, then, there was no strong sectional
preference for one candidate. Jackson was weak in New England and Adams in the South, while Crawford and Clay
showed little strength outside of selected states. Because in
most states either one candidate had overwhelming dominance or else votes were dispersed among three or four candidates, the election did not immediately give rise to the formation of a new two-party system. On the other hand, to the
extent that Republicans and Federalists took on, at least temporarily, new identities as Adams, Jackson, Crawford, or Clay
men, the old parties were increasingly demoralized.

Judging from the low degree of voter participation, the
campaign aroused remarkably little popular interest. In only
six states did more than one-third of the eligible electorate go
to the polls, and the average participation for all the states was
a meagre 26.5 per cent. Several factors account for this apparent apathy. In most states, as has been indicated, both the
political leaders and the voters were so heavily predisposed
toward one candidate as to foreclose any real competition.
Where genuine rivalry developed, there was commonly too
little time available to construct elaborate campaign organizations. Moreover, the voters in most states had not been
accustomed to participating in contests for the presidency, both
because such contests had been rare in the past and because in
several states electors had been chosen by the legislature, rather
than by popular vote. In strictly political terms, at least, the
presidency was not yet the dramatic object of contention that
it was soon to become.

After the election, and even after the exciting contest in
the House that gave Adams the presidency, there was no immediate recognition of the fact that the old party system had
come to an end. In those states where the Republican party

had retained its identity down to 1824, there was a general disposition to regard disagreement over the presidential question as a temporary rift and to proceed on the assumption that the party was still intact. But the approach of the election of 1828 occasioned rapid alterations in the political scene.

With Adams in the presidency, Jackson gained strength as his prospective opponent, attracting to his camp many who had previously been partial to Crawford, Calhoun, or even Clay. From state to state, then, political leaders were confronted with a choice between the two men. With the field thus narrowed, the consequence was the formation of Jackson and Adams parties. In some states these parties were to function only during the presidential contest and then disintegrate, but in other states they were to produce lasting alignments that were to be operative in both presidential and state elections.

The process of party formation occurred earliest in the Middle States. New alignments, identified with Jackson or Adams, were evident in New Jersey by 1826 and in Delaware and Maryland by 1827. In these three states the new parties were closely balanced from the outset, were similarly aligned in both state and national elections, and were durable. Except, perhaps, in Delaware they did not represent a continuance of the old parties under new names but instead amalgamated former Republicans and Federalists. In New York, Van Buren's Bucktails hoisted the Jackson banner in 1827, while most of the old Clintonians, perforce, supported Adams. Subsequently the Bucktail-Jacksonians were to become the Democratic party, but the opposition was not firmly united until after the Antimasons had passed from the scene. Pennsylvania is more difficult to categorize, for although there was continuity in the Jackson leadership from 1824, the opposition, especially in presidential elections, was weak and disorganized for many years.

There would seem to be two main reasons why party formation took place earlier in the Middle States than elsewhere. Unlike the West and much of the South, this region had long been accustomed to conducting its politics on a two-party basis. Further, the balance and alignment of parties was influenced by the fact that the region had no "favorite son" of its own in the contest and was therefore—unlike other regions—not heavily disposed toward one candidate. The occasion for the redefinition of parties was the presidential contest, even though the new formations first manifested themselves in state elections between 1826 and 1828.

In New England, the Jackson cause did not acquire leadership and support until 1827 and 1828. The new cleavage appeared first in the spring elections in 1828 in New Hampshire, Massachusetts, and Maine, following some preliminary activity in the preceding year. Subsequently, there were Jackson tickets in all of the states in the presidential election, although the Jacksonians did not contest state elections until 1829 in Vermont and Connecticut and 1830 in Rhode Island. Those who were to become the Jackson leaders recognized Adams' overwhelming popularity in his native region and did not launch their major effort until they saw some prospect that Adams might lose the presidency. The new parties came into existence generally over the presidential question. Both the Jacksonians and the Adamsites, however, soon welcomed old Federalists into their ranks.

In the presidential elections, the Jacksonians fared poorly in every state, although they were able to offer some semblance of a contest in New Hampshire and Maine. As soon as Adams had been removed from the national scene, however, the Jacksonians won control in New Hampshire and Maine and within a few years were offering severe competition to their rivals in Rhode Island and Connecticut. As in the Middle States, the new alignments that had been formed between 1827 and 1830 tended to be durable. But unlike the Middle States, the party balance from state to state was uneven. That is, the majority party usually enjoyed a wide margin over its adversary. Perhaps because of the unequal nature of the contest, voter participation in New England was generally much below that in other regions.

The election of 1828 had a negligible effect on party formation in the South, except in Kentucky. As between Jackson and Adams, sentiment was overwhelming for the regional candidate. There was organization and activity in behalf of Adams tickets, especially in Virginia and North Carolina, but once the election was over, the Adams party collapsed, and state elections were not fought out on the basis of national party identities. Kentucky was a special case, for there the formidable influence of Clay was thrown against Jackson. In 1827 new and durable parties were formed on the presidential question, and thereafter both state and national elections were contested heatedly.

In the newer states of the West the election of 1828 began a peculiar era of dual politics. Parties were formed to participate in the presidential elections, but state elections remained for many years on a non-party basis. Thus there were Jackson and Adams parties in every state in 1828, but they were temporary formations. None of these states, except Ohio, had acquired familiarity with managing politics on a two-party basis, and they were slow to adopt the party system. Jackson carried every state in 1828, winning by very wide margins in all but Ohio, Indiana, and Louisiana. Subsequently, however, these ostensibly Jacksonian states elected numerous governors, legislatures, and congressmen who were hostile to Jackson. It is, therefore, quite difficult to determine what Jacksonism meant in the region.

The contest for the presidency in 1828, then, stimulated the formation of parties in virtually all of the states. In most states, however, these parties were very unbalanced, and they were also unbalanced sectionally. Adams carried all but two states in the North, and Jackson won every state in the South and West.

The new party formation tended to survive and become durable in the North, whereas elsewhere it proved to be impermanent. The failure of the Adams party to sustain itself in the South and West can be explained in terms of a combination of several circumstances. To begin with, the party was very weak in 1828 in most of those states. Even where it possessed considerable strength, it was to suffer a serious blow when its figurehead, or standard bearer, Adams, was eliminated from the national political scene. Also of considerable importance is the fact that the states in these two regions did not have a background of competitive, two-party politics. Consequently they returned rather readily to the no-party, or vague one-party, kind of politics to which they were accustomed. In every state, of course, there were the rudiments of a Jackson party, but in the absence of vigorous opposition, this party had little organization, discipline, or cohesion and often did not function in state elections.

In the North, on the other hand, different circumstances prevailed. There the balance between the Jackson and Adams parties in 1828 had been relatively close, and in most states fairly elaborate organizations had been developed looking to the presidential contest. Even with Adams out of the picture, the "opposition" parties in most instances held on. In New England they possessed the advantage of being initially, at least, the majority party, and they obviously wished to retain power in those states. The Jacksonians, of course, continued in the field because they were sustained by the victory of their leader, as well as by federal patronage.

The anti-Jacksonians in the Middle States faced a somewhat more doubtful future, but in New Jersey, Delaware, and Maryland they had entered so vigorously into state politics on a highly organized basis that they could surmount even the handicap of the lack of a national leader. In New York and Pennsylvania, where the anti-Jacksonians were beset with special problems, Antimasonry served to fill a political void and provided the basis for sustaining an opposition party. In all of these states, too, long familiarity with two-party politics doubtless encouraged the early re-establishment of the party system.

The election of 1832, despite the fact that it ostensibly involved crucial issues of public policy, had remarkably little influence on party formation—except in New England—or upon existing party alignments. Throughout the South and West its effect was roughly similar to that of the election of 1828. That is, there were temporary formations in behalf of Clay to oppose the dominant Jacksonians, but except in Kentucky, Ohio, and Missouri the Jacksonians won by such tremendous margins that the Clay party was scarcely competitive and hardly survived the contest. Kentucky, as previously mentioned was a special case; there the two-party system had been firmly established since 1827. In Ohio, and to a lesser degree in Indiana, the election produced alignments reminiscent of those of 1828 and doubtless reinforced the evident tendency in those two states toward a full-fledged two-party system.

In the North, Clay polled a smaller proportion of the votes in every state than had Adams and lost four states that Adams had won in 1828. Understandably, the Jacksonians made their greatest gains in New England, which did not display the same enthusiasm for the Kentuckian that it had manifested for the son of Massachusetts. In the Middle States, the party balance from state to state was remarkably similar to what it had been in 1828.

The role of the Antimasons during these years deserves some special comment. They were strong in Vermont and Massachusetts but virtually non-existent in New Hampshire and Maine, formidable in New York and Pennsylvania, and insignificant in New Jersey. Vermont and Massachusetts were the two New England states where Jacksonian sentiment was weakest; New York and Pennsylvania were the two Middle States where Adams sentiment was weakest. What I am suggesting is that in each instance the Antimasonic party served to fill a particular kind of political void. Or, to put it differently, where for various reasons the contest for the presidency did not stimulate the formation of balanced parties oriented toward the presidential candidates, the Antimasons flourished.

Perhaps the most significant aspect of the election of 1832, in addition to what it revealed about New England attitudes, was the forecast it gave of the opposition in the South to Martin Van Buren. In Virginia, North Carolina, Georgia, and Alabama there were organized efforts by self-proclaimed Jacksonians to oppose Van Buren's election to the presidency, and there was noticeable restiveness in other states as well. Many of the dissidents were admirers of Calhoun and had deplored the sequence of events that had brought about their idol's downfall and the elevation of the "wily magician" from New York. Others, it would seem, simply were appalled at the prospect of a northerner in the presidency. Many, no doubt, had little real enthusiasm for Jackson, but they did not deem it prudent in 1832 to defy him with Clay as their only alternative.

With Jackson in office for his second, and presumably final term, and with Van Buren as his heir apparent, there soon began a second phase in the formation of parties. By 1832 parties that were fairly well balanced and that were similarly aligned in state and national elections had been formed in New England, the Middle States, and Kentucky. But elsewhere party formation had been retarded by factors that have already been discussed. The imminence of Jackson's retirement and the prospect of Van Buren as his successor, however, presented political leaders in the South and West with a radically new situation, for Van Buren was not the popular hero that Jackson was, and he could lay no special claim to the allegiance of those regions. The altered complexion of the contest for the presidency did not greatly upset alignments in those states where parties had already become well established, but it had a cataclysmic effect in the South.

From Virginia to Mississippi, there was tremendous ferment in 1834, out of which soon emerged two parties. The vague kind of one-party politics that had prevailed came to an abrupt end, and by 1836 there were competitive parties in every state. Although the new alignments did not become firm in some states until after 1837, the basic outlines of what were to be the Democratic and Whig parties had been delineated.

The "opposition" parties agitated a variety of issues—executive usurpation, the removal of the deposits, the tariff, and state-rights were especially prominent—but they all had in common antagonism to Martin Van Buren. Former Jacksonians, many of whom continued to express loyalty to the Old Hero and his policies, now broke with those "regulars" who were prepared to support Van Buren. The contending parties first clashed during the state and congressional elections of 1834 and 1835, and by 1836 they were well mobilized behind Van Buren and Hugh Lawson White. For the first time in the South, closely balanced parties were to participate in a presidential election.

The approach of the 1836 election had the effect of hastening the transition of the Western states—Ohio, Indiana, Illinois, and Missouri—to a durable two-party system. In each of these states, and most notably in Ohio and Indiana, there had been unstable alignments since 1828, but the parties possessed little permanent organization and they did not usually operate effectively in state elections. However in 1835 and 1836 more or less intensive efforts were made by both the supporters and the opponents of Van Buren to mobilize for the impending contest. In Ohio and Indiana, William Henry Harrison provided a popular figure around whom the anti-Van Buren sentiment could rally, while in Illinois and Missouri joint White-Harrison tickets were concocted. The alignments that emerged at this time tended to persist, although not until 1840 were the parties in Indiana, Illinois, and Missouri fully organized to contest state as well as national elections.

The relationship of the election of 1836 to party formation can be assessed by cursory examination of the election returns. In contrast to the overwhelming majorities that Jackson had received in the South in 1832, Van Buren polled slightly less than 50 per cent of the popular vote.[1] Georgia and Tennessee, which had been all but unanimous for Jackson in 1832, now went for White. In the West, Van Buren lost Ohio and Indiana and encountered stiff opposition in Illinois and Missouri. Understandably, New England was the one region where Van Buren showed far greater strength than had Jackson; only Vermont and Massachusetts denied him their electoral votes. The party balance in the Middle States showed little change from 1832, although Van Buren ran slightly behind Jackson.

Van Buren's candidacy was the crucial factor in stimulating party formation in the South between 1834 and 1836. Those politicians who for one reason or another were opposed to the "regular" Jacksonian leadership in any state but who had not dared to risk a break with Jackson could denounce Van Buren with considerable assurance. Their position was strengthened when they could offer as an alternative to the New Yorker a candidate from their own region, Hugh Lawson White. From another viewpoint, it might be said that Van Buren's candidacy provided the opportunity for political dissension in the South to manifest itself in partisan form.

What was perhaps most remarkable about the political complexion of the South at this juncture was that Van Buren lost only three states. Obviously there had developed in each state by 1834 a hard core Jacksonian leadership, which might be termed the "regulars," that saw possibilities of victory even with an unpopular candidate. They were doubtless influenced in their judgment by their appraisal of the fact that Van Buren could count on support throughout the nation, whereas the anti-Van Buren parties were unable to unite on a single candidate. However the situation may be analysed, the South had now entered a brief era of two-party politics.

The long process of party formation moved toward com-

1. I refer here to Virginia, North Carolina, Georgia, Kentucky, Tennessee, Alabama, Mississippi, and Louisiana. Van Buren received 173,278 votes to 174,346 for his opponents.

pletion between 1836 and 1840. In the South and West both the Democratic and the anti-Van Buren parties entered into contests in state politics. Some notable shifts took place in party allegiances, especially around 1837 in the South. But these defections are difficult to measure because at the same time the intensity of the party competition was bringing new voters to the polls in unprecedented numbers.

It still remained to be determined whether the Whig parties, as they may now be called, could be welded into a nationwide alliance, comparable to that of the Democrats. They might agree on opposing Van Buren and the Democrats and they could unite in blaming the nation's economic ills on the administration, but they would face a critical test when it came to selecting a candidate to oppose Van Buren in 1840 and adopting a statement of party principles. These tests were met successfully at the national convention in Harrisburg in December, 1839. There the party leaders, exhibiting amazing technical ingenuity, succeeded in producing agreement on William Henry Harrison and zealously avoided any semblance of a party platform. The Whigs were united for the contest for the presidency behind a candidate who could be inflated to the dimensions of a national hero. Stirred by the prospect of capturing the White House and, no less important, their state capitols, they returned home to launch the most spectacular campaign in which the whole nation had ever engaged.

In 1840, for the first time, two parties that were truly national in scope contested for the presidency. In every state, politics was now established on a two-party basis. The highly competitive party structures exerted every effort to arouse popular excitement, with the Whigs leading the way in inventiveness and enthusiasm. The Democrats were no match for their adversaries; Van Buren could carry only six states. But more significant than the Whig victory was the evidence it gave that the second American party system had come into being. It was now apparent that both parties could operate effectively in every part of the nation. Moreover, the result of this competitive party situation was an unprecedented out-pouring of the electorate. Nearly four-fifths of the eligible voters were inspired to vote in 1840, far surpassing the previous high of 56 per cent in 1828.

In the excitement of this memorable campaign, voters were moved to identify strongly with the symbols, personalities, organizations, and myths that taken altogether constituted *their* party. Once formed, these loyalties were not easily laid aside. The party leaders, and those who worked so actively to operate the party machinery, acquired a vested interest in the main-tenance of the party as an institution that could be for them a source of prestige, power, and even livelihood. Throughout the nation, then, the new order of politics was to be the politics of parties.

The second American party system can be understood not only in terms of the sequence of stages that marked its forma-tion but also in terms of some general characteristics that it exhibited as it reached maturity. From one perspective, the new party system reflected the fact that it had been formed to engage in the contest for the presidency. But it must also be viewed within the changing constitutional and legal environ-ment of the era. As the parties formed, they adapted to the altered environment, with the result that by the 1840's they differed greatly from the parties of the early 1800's.

What was most striking about the parties by the 1840's was that two-party alignments had been established throughout the nation and that within each region—and in most states—these parties were balanced and competitive. They were similarly aligned for contesting both state and national elections. They tended to adopt similar forms of organization, engage in similar functions, and employ similar campaign techniques. There was, indeed, a nationalization of institutional forms and po-litical styles. There was also a nationalization of political identities. Voters everywhere thought of themselves as either Whigs or Democrats. Everywhere, too, heightened interparty competition stimulated increased voter participation.

Several contrasts between the first and second party systems will be apparent. Before 1824, a wide variety of party situations—previously categorized as two-party, one-party, dual-party, and no-party—had prevailed. Competitive two-party alignments had been restricted to New England and the Middle States. Throughout much of the nation political identities were vague or non-existent. Even where parties flourished, forms of organization and political styles varied widely from state to state. In brief, politics was not conducted in conformity to a generalized national pattern.

Many factors might be adduced to account for the evident trend from diversity toward homogeneity, but considerable weight must be given to changes in the constitutional and legal environment. To put it somewhat crudely, the game of politics was played under many different sets of rules in 1800; by 1840 the rules had become *relatively* uniform from state to state. In another context, the tasks to be performed by party machinery in Jefferson's day were not the same in Massachusetts, North Carolina, and Ohio; by the time of the Log Cabin campaign the tasks were essentially similar in nearly all of the states. Between 1800 and 1840 what might be called a "hidden revolution" took place in the electoral environment, with significant consequences for the American party system.

The trend from diversity to uniformity affected almost every aspect of the electoral environment. Foremost, I would suggest, was the change in the method of choosing presidential electors. In 1800 electors were chosen by popular vote of the state-at-large in only two states; by 1832 all of the states except South Carolina had adopted this procedure. Elections of congressmen from a state-at-large or from multiple member districts was common in the early period, but by 1840 single-member districts prevailed and after 1842 they became mandatory. As late as 1824 governors were chosen by the legislatures in six states; after 1844 only Virginia and South Carolina still adhered to that practice. Voice voting and hand-written ballots gave way increasingly to printed ballots, polling units were reduced in area, and suffrage restrictions on white males, except in three states, were all but eliminated.

As state governmental structures were reformed through the adoption of new constitutions, they were brought more and more into conformity with a general pattern. Singular or unusual elements, such as semi-annual elections in Connecticut, the Council of Appointments in New York, or the electoral college in Maryland were discarded. Emulation rather than innovation was the rule. In general, there was a movement in the direction of making more officials elective by the people at more levels of government. In a sense, these reforms added greatly to the difficulties of party management, for they complicated the nominating and campaign functions enormously, not only by multiplying the numbers of officials to be elected but also by adding to the types of constituencies from which those officials were to be chosen. The important consideration, however, is that by the 1840's parties everywhere confronted broadly similar tasks. The trend toward uniformity within the electoral environment must not, of course, be exaggerated. Obvious variations still existed—and exist today—from state to state, but they were far less glaring in 1840 than in 1800.

Changes in the electoral environment affected parties in many ways. They might determine, for example, whether parties would have simple or highly elaborated organizations, whether the major focus of party activity would be at the county level or the state level, whether the minority party would remain competitive or lapse into hopelessness, whether parties would be balanced or unbalanced from county to county, and whether parties had identical alignments in state and national elections. In states where the election of presidential electors and governors was transferred from the legislature to the voters, parties had to undertake to mobilize a mass electorate—rather than small numbers of legislators—to secure victory. When the election of congressmen was altered from the state-at-large to single-member districts, new nominating devices had to be created and centralized party control might be weakened. As county officials were made elective, or as legislators were chosen from districts rather than from counties, or as powers of appointment were transferred from the legislatures to the governors, the structure of parties might be drastically altered. We cannot be concerned here with explaining in depth all of the possible relationships between various features of the electoral environment and party structures. The point to be made is simply that there was a very direct relationship and that changes in the environment account in part for the differences between the first and second party systems as well as for the general characteristics of the latter.

Again, without attempting to develop the theme, it would seem that there was a reciprocal relationship between constitutional and legal forms and party structures. That is, the emergence of parties and the exigencies of partisan competition doubtless operated to produce changes in the electoral environment. There were "party political" factors at work to make presidential electors elective by popular vote or to reduce the size of polling units or to sanction the use of printed ballots. Parties from a very early date discovered that by changing the "rules of the game" they might achieve advantages over their opponents, and this consideration, among others, was influential in stimulating change.

There were other factors, of course, that must be taken into account in describing the altered environment of politics. Gentry control, which had flourished when politics was local in scope, declined as social and economic conditions altered. Vastly improved means of communication and transportation facilitated the organization and direction of mass parties. The entrance of new states into the union and the rapid growth of population gave new dimensions to politics. The influence of all of these conditions was evident in the character of the second party system.

One of the most conspicuous evidences of uniformity in the second party system was in the realm of party management.

Early in the nineteenth century, as has been abundantly illustrated, there had been a great diversity of political practices. The manner in which variety gave way to uniformity
can best be studied in terms of the devices employed, particularly at the state level, for making nominations and directing
party affairs.

There were, before 1824, three generalized types of political
management. In two states, New Jersey and Delaware, the
delegate-convention system was firmly established. In most
of the other states where the first party system had at one time
flourished, the legislative caucus, or some variety of mixed
legislative caucus, was used to make state-wide nominations
and manage party matters. In New England and the Middle
States conventions were commonly employed to make nominations for other than state-wide offices. In some of the southern
states and in the newer states of the West the functions performed elsewhere by conventions or caucuses were often
handled by informal, self-constituted juntos, made up of men
possessed of considerable influence. In those states where at
particular times there was no evident management of politics
in a formal sense, there might be self-nominated candidates
and individual leaders who could command wide allegiance.

The adoption of the convention system proceeded gradual-
ly from region to region. After 1824 the state convention was
an established feature of party organization in the Middle
States, except in Maryland, where it first appeared in 1827.
It was generally adopted in New England between 1828 and
1832, although it did not entirely replace the mixed caucus in
Massachusetts and New Hampshire until much later. Rhode
Island, of course, had its own peculiar mixed conventions.
The state convention was slow in winning acceptance in the
South. It was introduced into Kentucky in 1827, but elsewhere it was rarely employed before 1839. Although there
were numerous conventions in Virginia after 1828, the Democrats continued to rely on a mixed caucus-convention even
after 1840. Practices varied widely in the West. There were

conventions in Indiana as early as 1824, and in Ohio, Mississippi, Louisiana, and Missouri by 1828, but they did not become regular features of party machinery generally until 1835 or later.

No adequate study has been made of the transition from the caucus to the convention. To the degree that the caucus represented an interior type of control, much might be made of the significance of the change. At the very least, the shift implies a considerable loss in the political authority of the legislatures. Whether it also implies the "democratization" of the parties is open to serious question.

The immediate reason for the substitution of the state convention for the legislative caucus in most states was a highly practical one. Where old party lines were blurred or violently shattered by the circumstances associated with the contests for the presidency, the old caucus arrangements broke down, both in Congress and in the states. Conditions varied from state to state. In New England, for example, where the Jacksonians initially had few representatives in the legislature, they turned to the convention as the only device that could give some kind of sanction to their nominations. In some states the Antimasons successfully adopted the convention for similar reasons. The convention also proved to be a convenient device for the "People's party" in New York in 1824, and for the Pennsylvania factions that endorsed Jackson in the same year. When the device had been adopted by one party, the opposing party —or parties—usually felt obliged to follow suit, for there was no doubt that the convention had the appearance of being more "open," and more "popular," than the caucus.

Having first demonstrated its efficacy in most of the northeastern states, the convention was widely copied elsewhere. Its sudden, full-blown emergence in Kentucky in 1827 suggests that some careful study had been made of the eastern models. In Illinois it seems quite clear that Stephen A. Douglas zealously promoted the convention system, presumably drawing upon his knowledge of party machinery in New

York. No particular party can be credited with special partiality for the convention. The Jacksonians and the Antimasons
were the chief innovators in New England, but in the South
it was often the Whigs who displayed the greater initiative.

Where the caucus system had long held sway, the convention was generally hailed as a desirable alternative. But in
those states where party organization of any kind had been
lacking, there was frequently resistance to its introduction.
To use Kentucky again as an example, both parties there in
1827 felt it necessary to justify their plans to hold conventions
on the grounds that the opposition was engaged in similar
projects. In Mississippi the Whigs denounced the Democrats
for using the convention to "dictate" nominations. Especially
notable was the controversy in Illinois, where the convention
system met stubborn resistance from a segment of the Democratic party as well as from the Whigs. Despite these instances
of hostility, the convention had become by 1840 the standard
device for making party decisions.

In addition to the immediate circumstances that prompted
the change from the caucus to the convention, there were other
considerations involved. The caucus system had long been the
object of popular suspicion in many states, and the operations
of the Republican congressional caucus in 1816, as well as in
1824, had further weakened respect for the device. Perhaps
the curtailment of the elective functions of the legislature—
evidenced by the trend toward the popular choice of electors,
governors, and other state officials—reflected a general loss of
confidence in that branch of government, which found expression in attacks on the caucus.

The fact that delegate conventions had long been in operation at the levels of the county, senatorial district, or congressional district in several states where the caucus was also
established meant that opponents of the caucus did not have
to look far for an alternative. Certainly improvements in
transportation facilities removed one of the major obstacles
to the holding of conventions, especially in the larger states.

Once the convention had acquired popularity in the eastern states, and especially after it had come into use for national nominations in 1832, its general acceptance was facilitated.

Probably the strongest argument in favor of the convention system was that it provided a means whereby party members, though elected delegates, could participate in the direction of party affairs at all levels. It was this consideration that gave such an authoritative sanction to convention nominations and thereby strengthened party discipline. But a full investigation might disclose that the conventions did not have precisely the functions that they appeared to have. Ostensibly they were decision-making bodies. In actuality they seem to have had a cosmetic function. That is, they gave the appearance of representing party sentiment whereas in fact they usually did little more than follow the dictates of party leaders. Made up in large measure of office-holders and party activists, they were readily susceptible to manipulation and control.

The convention system can also be viewed as the most conspicuous feature of the highly elaborated organization developed by parties in this era. Political tasks that had previously been carried out informally or by small, semi-secret committees now seemingly necessitated the involvement of enormous numbers of party activists. In addition to nominating conventions in all electoral units, there were central committees, poll committees, and various auxiliary organizations. Given the inordinately complicated nature of the American system of elections, it became evident that if politics was to be conducted on a party basis, an extraordinary amount of manpower was required. As competitive parties formed from state to state, therefore, the same process of elaboration of party organization took place. In general, parties in the Middle States were the most highly organized of all, with the lower South at the other extreme.

The second American party system also brought into vogue a new campaign style. Its ingredients can scarcely be described with precision, but they included an emphasis on dramatic spectacles—such as the mass rally, the procession, and the employment of banners, emblems, songs, and theatrical devices—and on club-like associations, colorful personalities, and emotionally charged appeals to party loyalty. Politics in this era took on a dramatic function. It enabled voters throughout the nation to experience the thrill of participating in what amounted to a great democratic festival that seemed to perceptive foreign observers to be remarkably akin to the religious festivals of Catholic Europe.

In their exciting election campaigns, the Americans of that generation found a satisfying form of cultural expression. Perhaps because there were so few emotional outlets available to them of equal effectiveness, they gave themselves up enthusiastically to the vast drama of the election contest. They eagerly assumed the identity of partisans, perhaps for much the same reason that their descendants were to become Dodger fans, Shriners, or rock-and-roll addicts. In this guise, at least, campaigns had little to do with government or public policy, or even with the choice of officials. For the party leaders, of course, the purpose of the campaign was to stimulate the faithful and, if possible, convert the wayward in order to produce victory at the polls.

The dramatic quality of the campaigns together with the intense efforts put forth by the elaborate party apparatus and the close balance of the parties produced measurable results in terms of increased voter participation. It is true that under the "old style" politics, in states as various as New Hampshire, Delaware, and Tennessee, as many as 80 per cent of the eligible voters had participated in elections. But in most states this high level was rarely approached, and presidential elections attracted relatively small turnouts.

The revival of the contest for the presidency did not have the immediate effect of stimulating maximum voter participation. In terms of national averages, only about a quarter of the eligibles voted in 1824, and in the three succeeding elections somewhat more than half went to the polls. Much more significant than the national average, however, are the rates of participation for particular states and regions.   These reveal an obvious correlation between the degree of voter participation and the closeness of the party contest.

In general, those states where parties were most evenly balanced achieved the highest voter turnout.   The most spectacular increases in voter participation in 1828, for example, occurred in Maine, New Hampshire, the Middle States, Kentucky, and Ohio.   These were all states in which competitive parties had been formed to contest the election.   Voter participation soared remarkably between 1832 and 1836 in states like Georgia, Tennessee, Alabama, and Mississippi for similar reasons.   By 1840, when party formation had taken place in every state and when the two national parties were fully mobilized to engage in a spectacular campaign, voter participation surged upwards to new levels in every state.   Throughout the nation nearly four-fifths of the eligibles voted.

There were some interesting regional differences in voter participation.   The New England states tended consistently to rank well below the national averages, especially after 1840. Moreover, it was common in that region for voter participation to be somewhat higher in state elections than in presidential elections, except in Connecticut.   In the new states of the West, on the other hand, participation was higher in presidential elections than in state elections, except in Missouri and Mississippi.   It is difficult to single out any one region as leading the way in voter participation, so high was the general level of voting outside of New England, but in the 1840's the three states with the most impressive records were Georgia, Mississippi, and Tennessee.   Whether the election returns may be accepted as accurate measurements of voter participation is, of course, open to some question, for there was undoubtedly considerable fraud in many states.

Among the influences that shaped the second party system, none is more difficult to evaluate than leadership.   Parties did not "emerge," neither did they "form," rather, they were formed by astute and energetic politicians. When the process of party formation is examined from state to state, it can be seen that at some appropriate opportunity rival leaders, or groups of leaders, took the initiative in creating parties.

It is, then, to men like Isaac Hill of New Hampshire, J. M. Niles of Connecticut, Thurlow Weed of New York, John M. Clayton of Delaware, Romulus Saunders of North Carolina, John M. Berrien of Georgia, Amos Kendall of Kentucky, Moses Dawson of Ohio, and Stephen A. Douglas of Illinois, and their counterparts elsewhere, that the new party system owed its existence. It was they who marked out the lines of battle, determined the strategy, built the organizations, and directed the campaigns. Aiding them were a corps of lieutenants and a vast army of those best described as party workers, or activists. Finally, of course, there were the voters who became identified with the party and the elected and appointed officials who owed their positions to the party.

It was in the early stages of party formation that the leaders played their most conspicuous roles and registered their most impressive achievements. The suddenness with which the politics of a state could be transformed by their efforts—when the proper circumstances prevailed—was nothing less than amazing. Almost invariably it was the "presidential question" on which they first based their drive to form a party, but the parties that they formed and led were soon engaged in contesting elections at all levels of government.

A full consideration of party leadership is beyond the scope of this study, although the subject is certainly one that merits far more attention than it has received. We should know who these men were, what motivated them, how they operated, and what rewards they received. Although they had their predecessors in the era of the first party system, they were essentially a new category of men, performing highly specialized functions in a new political environment.

The second American party system must be understood in terms of the conditions that stimulated its formation. It was formed, essentially, for the purpose of contesting for the presidency. It assumed the character that it did because political leaders in every state related their actions closely to the presidential contests. Between 1824 and 1840, the "presidential question," rather than doctrinal disputes was the axis around which politics revolved.

It is paradoxical that although the parties were initially shaped by strongly sectionalized attitudes toward particular candidates, the ultimate effect of the several contests was to produce two parties that were truly national in their dimensions. In a very particular sense it could be said that the parties of the 1840's were "artificial," in that they seemingly existed in defiance of the real sectional antagonisms that were present at the time.

The relatively brief duration of this party system can be explained in terms of its "artificiality." It could survive only so long as explicitly sectional issues could be avoided. This party system could expend great energy on presidential contests, usually involving generals of more or less heroic stature, and it could engage in interminable debates on the sectionally innocuous issue of fiscal policy. But it could scarcely cope with the tariff or internal improvements issues, and, of course, it foundered completely when it could no longer ignore territorial expansion and slavery.

Matters of doctrine, as well as sectional feeling, had been extremely influential in molding the first party system, and the first parties evidenced a strong sectional bias. After the disruption of the second party system, another reorganization of parties took place. The occasion for the upheaval of the 1850's was not the "presidential question" but rather the set of issues that focused on the status of slavery in the territories but, more broadly, reflected the forces of sectionalism. The new, or third, party system was highly sectionalized, and remained so into the twentieth century.

Although it foundered disastrously, the second American party system left an impressive inheritance to succeeding political generations. The national two-party system, with its continuing great absorption in the drama of the presidential contest, had become traditional. The marvellously intricate and elaborate exterior type of party apparatus, with the delegate convention as its distinctive feature, was to survive until modified by the direct primary system. Popular-style campaign techniques, so expressive of our folk culture, have endured even into the age of Madison Avenue and television. The highly professional party manager, with his army of workers, continues to be needed to operate the exceedingly vast and complex party machinery. Perhaps the voter had changed. At least he no longer responds as loyally, or as numerously, as he once did to the call of his party.

Most of all, a new institution, with its own vested interests, had been added to the political scene. The institutionalized political party was to be not merely a "mirror" of opinion nor a "medium" through which pressures were transmitted. It was to exert its own active influence in furtherance of its own special interests. Its leaders, activists, and those who held office in its name were to act on what are termed "partisan considerations." Decisions had to be made with the welfare of the party in mind, as well as the presumed welfare of those whom the party purportedly represented. Moreover, those who identified strongly with the party were influenced in their behavior by virtue of having assumed such an identity. They were no longer free to calculate objectively their own course of political action; as identifiers they reacted as partisans.

Here, in essence, was the difference between the unstructured, individualistic politics that had prevailed in most states before 1790 and in some as late as the 1830's. Politicians formerly consulted their own individual interest, or perhaps that of the junto or faction with which they were associated. Voters, in turn, acted on the basis of personal identification with the candidates, or of attachment to locality or social group. The establishment of institutionalized political parties, however, added a new ingredient to the forces that influenced political behavior.

The mature political parties were to bulk extremely large in the American political process, perform a variety of functions, and meet a number of obvious needs. But they were incapable of performing the one function most commonly associated with the idea of party. They could not govern.

Two related obstacles prevented the parties from realizing fully their potential. One was the constitutional structure of both the federal and state governments. The other was the ambivalent attitude of the American people toward parties; they came to accept them as necessary features of the political system but at the same time remained suspicious of them as agencies of power.

The manner in which American constitutions frustrate party government needs little explanation, but it does require emphasis. If one thing is clear about the intentions of those who framed the federal Constitution, from which few state constitutions have departed, it is that they consciously sought to make it extremely difficult for any section, class, numerical majority, or party to control the government. Among the more obvious devices instituted for this purpose were the establishment of three co-ordinate branches of government; the election of the two houses of the federal Congress by different constituencies and for different terms; the election of a president by indirect means for a term different from that of either body of Congress; and the division of sovereign powers between the states and the federal government.

It could be argued that after 1790 numerous detailed constitutional changes and revisions of election procedures diminished the possibilities of party government. The popular election of presidential electors, United States senators, and governors; the election of congressmen from districts, rather than from the state at large; the general extension of the principle of popular election of officials at all levels; and the direct primary system have all had the effect of adding to the frustrations of parties. They have greatly complicated the electoral tasks undertaken by parties and have resulted in the fragmentation of political authority.

The point is not that these constitutional impediments to party government were unwise or that party government is an ideal to be sought at any cost. It is, rather, that the functions performed by American political parties must be studied and appraised in the light of the constitutional environment in which they must operate. It would be fallacious to assume that the only function of parties was that of providing a government or an opposition to the government. American parties have flourished because they have had other functions.

BIBLIOGRAPHY
INDEX

BIBLIOGRAPHY

———•—•———

GENERAL STUDIES

The foremost work on the general subject of political parties in recent years is M. Duverger, *Political Parties: Their Organization and Activity in the Modern State* (New York, 1954), to which I gratefully acknowledge my indebtedness. The two classic studies of American parties are James Bryce, *The American Commonwealth* (2nd ed.; London and New York, 1889) and M. Ostrogorski, *Democracy and the Party System in the United States* (New York, 1910). The most imaginative attempt to present a comprehensive statement of the role of parties in the American political system remains H. J. Ford, *The Rise and Growth of American Politics: A Sketch of Constitutional Development* (New York, 1914). Among the standard histories of American parties, all of them sadly inadequate, are Wilfred E. Binkley, *American Political Parties: Their Natural History* (New York, 1943); Edgar E. Robinson, *The Evolution of American Political Parties* (New York, 1924); and James A. Woodburn, *Political Parties and Party Problems in the United States* (3rd ed.; New York, 1924). Other works of general relevance are E. H. Roseboom, *A History of Presidential Elections* (New York, 1957); Edward Stanwood, *A History of the Presidency from 1788 to 1897* (Boston, 1898); Frederick W. Dallinger, *Nominations for Elective Office in the United States* (New York, 1903); and Chilton Williamson, *American Suffrage from Property to Democracy, 1760-1860* (Princeton, 1960).

Three works upon which I have relied very heavily deserve special mention. For my descriptions of the constitutional environment in each state I have drawn upon Francis Newton Thorpe, *The Federal and State Constitutions* ... (7 vols.; Washington,

359

D.C., 1909), supplemented in many instances by references to the
sessions laws of particular states. I gleaned an enormous amount
of information from a thorough study of that extraordinary news
magazine, Hezekiah Niles' *Weekly Register*, Vols. 1-67 (Baltimore,
1811-1845), which I have cited throughout as Niles' *Register*.
Also extremely useful was Charles O. Paullin, *Atlas of the Historical Geography of the United States* (Washington, D.C., 1932),
especially on such topics as methods of electing congressmen and
presidential electors.

THE FIRST PARTY SYSTEM

The best general studies of the origin and development of the
first party system are the two admirable works by Noble E. Cun-
ningham, Jr., *The Jeffersonian Republicans: The Formation of
Party Organization, 1789-1801* (Chapel Hill, N.C., 1957) and *The
Jeffersonian Republicans in Power: Party Operations, 1801-1809*
(Chapel Hill, N.C., 1963). Cunningham's second volume, and
William N. Chambers, *Political Parties in a New Nation ... 1776-
1809* (New York, 1963) appeared too late to be of use to me.
Other indispensable recent monographs on the first parties are
Joseph Charles, *The Origins of the American Party System* (Wil-
liamsburg, 1956); Manning J. Dauer, *The Adams Federalists*
(Baltimore, 1953), and Stephen G. Kurtz, *The Presidency of John
Adams: The Collapse of Federalism, 1795-1800* (Philadelphia,
1957). Special studies of importance are Ralph V. Harlow, *The
History of Legislative Methods in the Period before 1825* (New
Haven, 1915); Eugene P. Link, *Democratic Republican Societies,
1790-1800* (New York, 1942); Shaw Livermore, Jr., *The Twilight
of Federalism: The Disintegration of the Federalist Party, 1815-
1830* (Princeton, 1962); Glover Moore, *The Missouri Controversy,
1819-1821* (Lexington, Ky., 1953); Samuel Eliot Morison, "The
First National Nominating Convention," *American Historical Review*, XVII (1912), 744-63; Charles O. Paullin, "The First Elections under the Constitution," *Iowa Journal of History and Politics*,
II (1904), 3-33; Charles S. Sydnor, "The One-Party Period of
American History," *American Historical Review*, LI (1946), 439-
51; and C. S. Thompson, *An Essay on the Rise and Fall of the
Congressional Caucus ...* (New Haven, 1902). The pioneer work
on early political practices, which, despite its shortcomings is still
valuable, is George D. Luetscher, *Early Political Machinery in the
United States* (Philadelphia, 1903).

THE SECOND PARTY SYSTEM

The most recent comprehensive treatment of the period is Glyndon G. Van Deusen, *The Jacksonian Era, 1828-1848* (New York, 1959). Among other standard references are Claude G. Bowers, *The Party Battles of the Jackson Period* (Boston and New York, 1929); Bray Hammond, *Banks and Politics in America from the Revolution to the Civil War* (Princeton, 1957); William MacDonald, *Jacksonian Democracy, 1829-1835* (New Haven, 1906); Charles H. Peck, *The Jacksonian Epoch* (New York, 1899); Arthur M. Schlesinger, Jr., *The Age of Jackson* (Boston, 1945); and Frederick Jackson Turner, *The United States, 1830-1850* (New York, 1935).

Works of a specialized character that are relevant to the political history of the era are Charles Francis Adams, ed., *Memoirs of John Quincy Adams* (12 vols.; Philadelphia, 1874-77); John Spencer Bassett, ed., *Correspondence of Andrew Jackson* (7 vols.; Washington, D.C., 1926-35); Samuel Flagg Bemis, *John Quincy Adams and the Union* (New York, 1956); Richard H. Brown, "Southern Planters and Plain Republicans of the North: Martin Van Buren's Formula for National Politics" (Ph.D. diss., Yale University, 1955); W. Dean Burnham, *Presidential Ballots, 1836-1892* (Baltimore, 1955); E. Malcolm Carroll, *Origins of the Whig Party* (Durham, N.C., 1925); Carl R. Fish, *The Civil Service and the Patronage* (New York, 1905); Samuel R. Gammon, Jr., "The Presidential Campaign of 1832," *Johns Hopkins University Studies in Historical and Political Science*, XL (Baltimore, 1932); Robert G. Gunderson, *The Log Cabin Campaign* (Lexington, Ky., 1957); Marquis James, *Andrew Jackson, Portrait of a President* (Indianapolis, 1937); O. D. Lambert, *Presidential Politics, 1841-1844* (Durham, N.C., 1936); Charles McCarthy, "The Antimasonic Party, A Study of Political Antimasonry ... 1827-1840," *Annual Report of the American Historical Association*, 1901, I; Eugene I. McCormac, *James K. Polk, A Biography* (Berkeley, 1922); Richard P. McCormick, "New Perspectives on Jacksonian Politics," *American Historical Review*, LXV (1960), 288-301; George R. Poage, *Henry Clay and the Whig Party* (Chapel Hill, N.C., 1936); John J. Reed, "The Emergence of the Whig Party in the North" (Ph.D. diss., University of Pennsylvania, 1953); Robert V. Remini, *Martin Van Buren and the Making of the Democratic Party* (New York, 1959); Frederick Jackson Turner, *Rise of the New West, 1818-1829* (New York, 1906); Florence Weston, *The Presidential Election of 1828* (Washington, 1938); and Leonard D.

White, *The Jacksonians: A Study in Administrative History, 1829-1861* (New York, 1954).

SOURCES FOR INDIVIDUAL STATES

NEW ENGLAND

Several of the works cited above, notably those of Cunningham, Livermore, Luetscher, McCarthy, and Reed, have been especially useful with respect to New England generally. I have also drawn extensively on William A. Robinson, *Jeffersonian Democracy in New England* (New Haven, 1916) and "Party Organization and Campaign Methods in New England in the Jeffersonian Era," *Washington University Studies*, III, Pt. II, #2 (1916).

Massachusetts

For my discussion of early party development in Massachusetts I used Samuel Eliot Morison, *The Life and Letters of Harrison Gray Otis, Federalist, 1765-1848* (2 vols.; Boston and New York, 1913); Anson Ely Morse, *The Federalist Party in Massachusetts to the Year 1800* (Princeton, 1909); and Charles Warren, *Jacobin and Junto* ... (Cambridge, Mass., 1931). J. R. Pole, "Suffrage and Representation in Massachusetts: A Statistical Note," *William and Mary Quarterly*, XIV (1957), 560-92, was helpful. The standard source on the Jacksonian era, Arthur B. Darling, *Political Changes in Massachusetts, 1824-1848* (New Haven, 1925) supplied basic background. *The Journal of the Proceedings of the* [Massachusetts] *National Republican Convention ... Worcester, October 11, 1832* reports one of the earliest state conventions in Massachusetts.

Because of the inadequacy of the secondary sources, I made extensive use of newspapers, including the (Boston) *Columbian Centinel*, 1823-30; *Boston Courier*, 1836-47; (Boston) *Independent Chronicle*, 1802-10; (Boston) *New England Palladium*, 1803-10; *Boston Patriot*, 1810; *Boston Statesman*, 1828-32; *Bridgewater Republican*, 1836; (Taunton) *Columbian Reporter*, 1825-26; (Taunton) *Old Colony Republican*, 1847-48; and (Windsor) *Vermont Republican*, 1810.

Maine

The political history of Maine after 1820 has received little attention. The only work of consequence is Louis C. Hatch, ed., *Maine, A History* (5 vols.; New York, 1919). A valuable local study is J. J. Stahl, *History of Old Broad Bay and Walboro* (2 vols.; Portland, Me., 1956).

Much of my understanding of party formation was obtained from the (Augusta) *Kennebec Journal*, 1828-29; (Portland) *American Patriot*, 1828; and (Portland) *Eastern Argus*, 1826-29.

New Hampshire

New Hampshire history has also been remarkably neglected. Two useful secondary works are Roy F. Nichols, *Franklin Pierce* (Philadelphia, 1931) and Lynn W. Turner, *William Plumer of New Hampshire, 1759-1850* (Chapel Hill, N.C. 1962). The *Proceedings and Address of the New Hampshire Republican State Convention* . . . [Concord, 1828] is the official report on the first state convention in New Hampshire.

I relied heavily on Isaac Hill's (Concord) *New Hampshire Patriot*, 1819, 1826-30, for the detailed account of the formation of the Jackson party. Also useful were the (Amherst) *Farmers Cabinet*, 1826; (Claremont) *National Eagle*, 1842; (Portsmouth) *New Hampshire Gazette*, 1809, 1832-33; and (Walpole) *Political Observatory*, 1804-5.

Connecticut

There are several excellent monographs dealing with the political history of Connecticut. Especially relevant for the first party system are Richard J. Purcell, *Connecticut in Transition, 1775-1818* (Washington, D.C., 1918); Norman L. Stamps, "Political Parties in Connecticut, 1789-1818" (Ph.D. diss., Yale University, 1952); and, for the colonial background, Oscar Zeichner, *Connecticut's Years of Controversy, 1750-1776* (Chapel Hill, N.C., 1949). The authoritative treatment of the later period is Jarvis M. Morse, *A Neglected Period of Connecticut's History, 1818-1850* (New Haven, 1933), to which I am particularly indebted. The *Address to the People of Connecticut Adopted at the* [Jackson] *State Convention* . . . (Hartford, 1828) reports the first state convention of that party in Connecticut.

Newspaper sources used were the *Hartford Times*, 1829; *New-Haven Advertiser*, 1829-30; and (New Haven) *Connecticut Journal*, 1828.

Vermont

Vermont has been neglected by political historians, although some information can be gleaned from T. D. Seymour Bassett, "The Rise of Cornelius Peter Van Ness, 1782-1826," *Proceedings of the Vermont Historical Society,* N.S., X (1942), 3-20; Hosea Beckley, *The History of Vermont* (Brattleboro, 1846); David M. Ludlum, *Social Ferment in Vermont, 1791-1850* (New York, 1939); Zadock Thompson, *History of Vermont, Natural, Civil, and Statistical* (Burlington, 1842); and Chilton Williamson, *Vermont in Quandary* (Montpelier, 1949).

My newspaper sources were the (Brattleboro) *Vermont Phoenix,* 1835-37; (Middlebury) *National Standard,* 1829-30; (Windsor) *Post Boy,* 1805; and (Windsor) *Vermont Republican,* 1810.

Rhode Island

Like Maine, New Hampshire, and Vermont, Rhode Island affords the student paltry secondary materials. David S. Lovejoy, *Rhode Island Politics and the American Revolution, 1760-1776* (Providence, R.I., 1958) is admirable on the colonial background. Thereafter the best general guide is Charles Carroll, *Rhode Island: Three Centuries of Democracy* (4 vols.; New York, 1932). Also useful are Samuel Greene Arnold, *History of the State of Rhode Island and Providence Plantations* (2 vols.; New York, 1860); H. M. Bishop, "Why Rhode Island Opposed the Federal Constitution," *Rhode Island History,* VIII (1949), 115-26; and Marcus W. Jernegan, *The Tammany Societies of Rhode Island* (Providence, 1897). Garbled and unreliable is Neil Andrews, *The Development of the Nominating Convention in Rhode Island* (Providence, R.I., 1894).

Much of my account of Rhode Island politics is derived from the *Newport Mercury,* 1828; (Newport) *Rhode Island Republican,* 1829-30; (Providence) *American and Gazette,* 1828; *The Providence Gazette,* 1815, 1816, 1818, 1820, 1821; *Providence Patriot and Columbian Phenix,* 1818, 1829-32, and (Providence) *Republican Herald,* 1836-37.

THE MIDDLE STATES

Many of the titles cited under previous categories provided detailed information on the Middle States, but I am especially indebted to Cunningham, Livermore, Leutscher, and Reed.

New York

Excellent secondary works are available in abundance on the political history of New York. On the colonial background some relevant studies are Carl Becker, "Growth of Revolutionary Parties and Methods in New York Province, 1765-1774," *American Historical Review,* VII (1901), 56-76; *The History of Political Parties in the Province of New York, 1760-1776* (Madison, Wis., 1909) ; and "Nominations in Colonial New York," *American Historical Review*, VI (1901), 260-75; as well as L. H. Leder, *Robert Livingston, 1654-1728, and the Politics of Colonial New York* (Chapel Hill, N.C., 1961) ; and M. M. Klein, "Democracy and Politics in Colonial New York," *New York History*, XL (1959), 221-46. For my purposes the best general guide to politics in the state in the early national period is Jabez D. Hammond, *The History of Political Parties in the State of New York* (4th ed., 2 vols.; Syracuse, 1852). Other indispensable works are Lee Benson, *The Concept of Jacksonian Democracy: New York as a Test Case* (Princeton, N.J., 1960) ; H. D. A. Donovan, *The Barnburners* (New York, 1925) ; Dixon Ryan Fox, "The Decline of Aristocracy in the Politics of New York," *Columbia University Studies in History, Economics and Public Law*, LXXXVI (New York, 1919) ; J. S. Jenkins, *History of Political Parties in the State of New York* (Auburn, N.Y., 1846) ; Howard L. McBain, "De Witt Clinton and the Origin of the Spoils System in New York," *Columbia University Studies in History, Economics and Public Law*, XXVIII (New York, 1907) ; Richard P. McCormick, "Suffrage Classes and Party Alignments: A Study in Voter Behavior," *Mississippi Valley Historical Review*, XLVI (1959), 397-410; and Glyndon G. Van Deusen, *Thurlow Weed* (Boston, 1947).

New Jersey

My chief reliance in treating New Jersey was on Carl E. Prince, "New Jersey's Democratic-Republicans, 1790-1817" (Ph.D. diss., Rutgers University, 1963) and on the research embodied in my article "Party Formation in New Jersey in the Jackson Era," *Proceedings of the New Jersey Historical Society*, LXXXIII (1965), 161-73. Also relevant are Walter R. Fee, *The Transition from Aristocracy to Democracy in New Jersey* (Somerville, N.J., 1933) and my *Experiment in Independence: New Jersey in the Critical Period, 1781-1789* (New Brunswick, N.J., 1950) and *The History of Voting in New Jersey* (New Brunswick, N.J., 1953). I also examined most of the extant New Jersey newspapers for the period.

Pennsylvania

Chiefly because of the impetus given to such studies by Roy F. Nichols of the University of Pennsylvania, there are a number of authoritative monographs treating the political history of that state. The major studies, in chronological sequence, are Theodore Thayer, *Pennsylvania Politics and the Growth of Democracy, 1740-*

1776 (Harrisburg, Pa., 1953); Harry M. Tinkcom, *The Republicans and Federalists in Pennsylvania, 1790-1801* (Harrisburg, 1950); Sanford W. Higginbotham, *The Keystone in the Democratic Arch: Pennsylvania Politics, 1800-1816* (Harrisburg, 1952); Philip S. Klein, *Pennsylvania Politics 1817-1832: A Game Without Rules* (Philadelphia, 1940); and Charles McC. Snyder, *The Jacksonian Heritage: Pennsylvania Politics; 1833-1848* (Harrisburg, 1958). Also important are James A. Kehl, *Ill Feeling in the Era of Good Feelings* (Pittsburgh, Pa., 1956), Henry R. Mueller, "The Whig Party in Pennsylvania," *Columbia University Studies in History, Economics and Public Law*, CI, No. 2 (New York, 1922); and Raymond Walters, Jr., *Alexander James Dallas* (Philadelphia, 1943).

Delaware

For my knowledge of the Delaware scene I have been able to rely upon the work of my brother-in-law, John A. Munroe, most particularly on his *Federalist Delaware, 1775-1815* (New Brunswick, N.J., 1954); "Party Battles, 1789-1850," in H. Clay Reed, ed., *Delaware: A History of the First State* (2 vols.; New York, 1947); and the manuscript of his definitive biography of Louis McLane.

Maryland

Like certain New England states, Maryland has not received adequate treatment by historians. There are distinguished works on the pre-national period, such as Charles A. Barker, *The Background of the Revolution in Maryland* (New Haven, Conn., 1940) and Philip A. Crowl, "Maryland During and After the Revolution," *Johns Hopkins University Studies in Historical and Political Science*, LXI, No. 1 (Baltimore, 1943), but after that the coverage is very poor. M. H. Haller's able article, "The Rise of the Jackson Party in Maryland, 1820-1829," *Journal of Southern History*, XXVIII (1962), 307-26, appeared too late to be useful to me, but it accords with my own understanding of events. Some information was obtained from J. V. L. McMahon, *An Historical View of the Government of Maryland* (Baltimore, 1831); J. R. Pole's two articles, "Constitutional Reform and Election Statistics in Maryland, 1790-1821," *Maryland Historical Magazine* LV (1960), 275-92, and "Suffrage and Representation in Maryland from 1776 to 1810: A Statistical Note and Some Reflections," *Journal of Southern History*, XXIV (1958), 218-25; J. H. Schauinger, "Alexander Contee Hanson, Federalist Partisan," *Maryland Historical Magazine*, XXXV (1940), 354-64; and Carl Brent Swisher, *Roger*

Brent Taney (New York, 1936). The *Address of the Jackson State Convention to the People of Maryland* . . . (Baltimore, 1827) is the product of the first state convention in Maryland.

Of necessity I have derived much of my knowledge of political practices and party organization from the (Annapolis) *Maryland Gazette*, 1798-1832; *Frederick-Town Herald*, 1802-3; and (Washington, D.C.) *National Intelligencer*, 1827, 1834-35.

THE OLD SOUTH

General works relating to the Old South upon which I have drawn are Thomas P. Abernethy, *The South in the New Nation, 1789-1819* (Baton Rouge, La., 1961); Arthur C. Cole, *The Whig Party in the South* (Washington, D.C., 1913); Fletcher M. Green, *Constitutional Development in the South Atlantic States, 1776-1860* (Chapel Hill, N.C., 1930); and—most helpful of all—Charles S. Sydnor, *The Development of Southern Sectionalism, 1819-1848* (Baton Rouge, La., 1948).

Virginia

For the pre-party background Lucille B. Griffith, *The Virginia House of Burgesses, 1750-1774* (Northport, Ala., 1963) and Charles S. Sydnor, *Gentlemen Freeholders* (Chapel Hill, N.C., 1952) are outstanding. On the first party system two articles by Harry Ammon, "The Formation of the Republican Party in Virginia, 1789-1796," *Journal of Southern History*, XIX (1953), 283-310, and "The Richmond Junto, 1800-1824," *The Virginia Magazine of History and Biography*, LXI (1953), 395-418, are indispensable. Also useful were J. R. Pole, "Representation and Authority in Virginia from the Revolution to Reform," *Journal of Southern History*, XXIV (1958), 16-50, and Anthony F. Upton, "The Road to Power in Virginia in the Early Nineteenth Century," *The Virginia Magazine of History and Biography*, LXII (1954), 259-80. The best authorities on the period of the second party system are Dice R. Anderson, *William Branch Giles: A Study in the Politics of Virginia and the Nation from 1790 to 1830* (Menasha, Wis., 1914); Charles H. Ambler, *Sectionalism in Virginia from 1776 to 1851* (Chicago, 1910) and *Thomas Ritchie: A Study in Virginia Politics* (Richmond, Va., 1913); Howard Braverman, "The Economic and Political Background of the Conservative Revolt in Virginia," *The Virginia Magazine of History and Biography*, XL (1952), 266-87; and H. H. Simms, *The Rise of the Whigs in Virginia, 1824-1840* (Richmond, Va., 1929).

Newspapers consulted included the (Raleigh, N.C.) *Star*, 1812; *Richmond Enquirer*, 1804-8; (Washington, D.C.) *National Intelligencer*, 1827.

North Carolina

There is a wealth of excellent secondary accounts related to the political history of North Carolina. William S. Hoffmann has produced one of the best histories of the Jackson era for any state, *Andrew Jackson and North Carolina Politics* (Chapel Hill, N.C., 1958). Earlier studies covering much the same ground are J. G. de R. Hamilton, "Party Politics in North Carolina, 1835-1860," *The James Sprunt Historical Publications*, XV, Nos. 1 and 2 (Chapel Hill, N.C., 1916) and C. C. Norton, *The Democratic Party in Ante-Bellum North Carolina, 1835-1861* (Chapel Hill, N.C., 1930). Other important items are Walker Barnette, "The Beginnings of Party Organization in North Carolina: A Documentary History of the Campaign of 1836" (M.A. thesis, University of North Carolina, 1925); John S. Bassett, "Suffrage in the State of North Carolina (1776-1861)," *Annual Report of the American Historical Association*, 1895 (Washington, D.C., 1896), 271-85; John W. Carr, Jr., "The Manhood Suffrage Movement in North Carolina," *Historical Papers Published by the Trinity College Historical Society*, XI (1915), 47-48; D. H. Gilpatrick, *Jeffersonian Democracy in North Carolina, 1789-1816* (New York, 1931); Fletcher M. Green, "Electioneering 1802 Style," *North Carolina Historical Review*, XX (1943), 238-46; William S. Hoffmann, "The Downfall of the Democrats: The Reaction of North Carolina to Jacksonian Land Policy," *ibid.*, XXXIII (1956), 166-80, and "The Election of 1836 in North Carolina," *ibid.*, XXXII (1955), 31-51, and "John Branch and the Origins of the Whig Party in North Carolina," *ibid.*, XXXV (1958), 299-315; Richard P. McCormick, "Suffrage Classes and Party Alignments: A Study in Voter Behavior," *Mississippi Valley Historical Review*, XLVI (1959), 397-410; A. R. Newsome, *The Presidential Election of 1824 in North Carolina* (Chapel Hill, N.C., 1939); J. R. Pole, "Election Statistics in North Carolina to 1861," *Journal of Southern History*, XXIV (1958), 225-28; John C. Vinson, "Electioneering in North Carolina, 1800-1835," *North Carolina Historical Review*, XXIX (1952), 171-88; and Henry M. Wagstaff, "State Rights and Political Parties in North Carolina, 1776-1861," *Johns Hopkins University Studies in Historical and Political Science*, XXIV (Baltimore, 1906).

Newspapers consulted included the (Raleigh) *Minerva*, 1808, 1812; (Raleigh) *North Carolina Standard*, 1836, 1838, 1848; *Raleigh Register*, 1813, 1840; *Raleigh Register and North Carolina Gazette*, 1820; and (Salisbury) *Western Carolinian*, 1824.

Kentucky

There are no adequate accounts of Kentucky politics in the early nineteenth century. Leonard P. Curry, "Election Year— Kentucky, 1828," *Register of the Kentucky Historical Society*, LV (1957), 196-212, is thorough on this limited topic. Also useful are O. W. Baylor, *John Pope: Kentuckian* (Cynthiana, Ky., 1943); Lewis Collins, *History of Kentucky* ... (Louisville, Ky., 1877); William G. Leger, "The Public Life of John Adair" (Ph.D. diss., University of Kentucky, 1953); A. M. Stickles, *The Critical Court Struggle in Kentucky* (Bloomington, Ind., 1929); and William Stickney, ed., *The Autobiography of Amos Kendall* (Boston, 1872).

Considerable detailed information was obtained from the (Frankfort) *Argus*, 1824; (Frankfort) *Argus of Western America*, 1827-28; (Frankfort) *Commentator*, 1827-28; (Lexington) *Kentucky Gazette*, 1800, 1804; (Lexington) *Kentucky Reporter*, 1830; and (Lexington) *Reporter* (1812).

Tennessee

My two basic references were Thomas P. Abernethy, *From Frontier to Plantation in Tennessee* (Memphis, Tenn., 1955) and Charles G. Sellers, *James K. Polk, Jacksonian, 1795-1843* (Princeton, 1957), supplemented by Thomas P. Abernethy, "The Origin of the Whig Party in Tennessee," *Mississippi Valley Historical Review*, XII (1925-26), 504-22; Thomas B. Alexander, "The Political Campaign of 1840 in Tennessee," *Tennessee Historical Quarterly*, I (1942), 21-43; Robert Cassell, "Newton Cannon and State Politics, 1835-1839," *ibid.*, XV (1956), 306-21; Powell Moore, "James K. Polk, Tennessee Politician," *Journal of Southern History*, XVII (1951), 493-516, and "The Revolt Against Jackson in Tennessee, 1835-1836," *ibid.*, II (1936), 335-59; Eastin Morris, *The Tennessee Gazetteer, or Topographical Dictionary* (Nashville, 1834); Charles G. Sellers, "Jackson Men with Feet of Clay," *American Historical Review*, LXII (1957), 537-51; and Robert H. White, ed., *Messages of the Governor of Tennessee* (6 vols.; Nashville, Tenn., 1952-63).

For party activities in 1840 I consulted *The Nashville Union*, 1840, and *The Nashville Whig*, 1840-41.

Georgia

The best account of Georgia politics in the Jackson era is Paul Murray, *The Whig Party in Georgia, 1825-1853* (Chapel Hill, N.C., 1948). Other useful sources of information are E. M. Coulter, *Georgia: A Short History* (Chapel Hill, N.C., 1947); A. L. Duckett, *John Forsyth, Political Tactician* (Athens, Ga., 1962); Thomas P. Govan, "John M. Berrien and the Administration of Andrew Jackson," *Journal of Southern History*, V (1939), 447-67; Stephen F. Miller, *The Bench and Bar of Georgia* (2 vols.; Philadelphia, 1858); H. Montgomery, ed., *Georgians in Profile* (Athens, Ga., 1958); Albert B. Saye, *A Constitutional History of Georgia, 1732-1945* (Athens, Ga., 1948); and Richard H. Shryock, *Georgia and the Union in 1850* (Philadelphia, 1926).

THE NEW STATES

For my discussion of the states of the Old Northwest I have made extensive use of three invaluable studies: John D. Barnhart, *Valley of Democracy: the Frontier versus the Plantation in the Ohio Valley, 1775-1818* (Bloomington, Ind., 1953); R. Carlyle Buley, *The Old Northwest: Pioneer Period, 1815-1840* (2 vols.; Bloomington, Ind., 1951); and Homer J. Webster, "History of Democratic Party Organization in the Northwest, 1820-1840," *Ohio Archaeological and Historical Quarterly*, XXIV, No. 1 (1915).

Ohio

Harry R. Stevens, *The Early Jackson Party in Ohio* (Durham, N.C., 1957) is definitive. Also relevant are Helen P. Dorn, "Samuel Medary—Journalist and Politician, 1801-1864," *Ohio State Archaeological and Historical Quarterly*, LIII (1944), 14-38; Edgar Allan Holt, *Party Politics in Ohio, 1840-1850* (Columbus, Ohio, 1931); and William T. Utter, "Saint Tammany in Ohio: A Study in Frontier Politics," *Mississippi Valley Historical Review*, XV (1928-29), 321-40. The *Proceedings and Address of the Convention of Delegates, That met at Columbus, Ohio, Dec. 28, 1827* [Columbus, Ohio, 1828] reports on the first state convention.

Indiana

The basic reference is Logan Esarey, *History of Indiana . . . to 1922* (3 vols.; Dayton, Ohio, 1923). Also indispensable are Esarey's two articles, "The Organization of the Jacksonian Party in Indiana," *Proceedings of the Mississippi Valley Historical Association*, VII (1913-14), 220-43, and "Pioneer Politics in Indiana,"

Indiana Magazine of History, XII (1917), 99-127, and Adam A. Leonard, "Personal Politics in Indiana, 1816 to 1840," *Indiana Magazine of History*, XIX (1923), 1-56, 132-68, 241-81; Dorothy Riker and Gayle Thornborough, "Indiana Election Returns, 1816-1851," *Indiana Historical Collections*, XL (n.p., 1960); and Gayle Thornborough and Dorothy Riker, "Readings in Indiana History," *ibid.*, XXXVI (Indianapolis, Ind., 1956).

Illinois

The standard account, which is highly satisfactory, is Theodore C. Pease, *The Frontier State, 1818-1840* (The Centennial History of Illinois, II, Chicago, 1919). Other sources used were Robert W. Johannsen, *Letters of Stephen A. Douglas* (Urbana, Ill., 1961); Theodore C. Pease, ed., *Illinois Election Returns* (Springfield, Ill., 1923); James W. Sheahan, *The Life of Stephen A. Douglas* (New York, 1860); C. M. Thompson, "Attitude of the Western Whigs Toward the Convention System," *Proceedings of the Mississippi Valley Historical Association*, V (1911-12); 167-89; and "The Illinois Whigs before 1846," *University of Illinois Studies in the Social Sciences*, IV (Urbana, Ill., 1915), 1-165.

Alabama

The outlines of party development in Alabama are traced by Theodore H. Jack, *Sectionalism and Party Politics in Alabama, 1819-1842* (Menasha, Wis., 1919). Other important sources are Hugh C. Bailey, "John W. Walker and the 'Georgia Machine' in Early Alabama Politics," *Alabama Review*, VIII (1955), 179-95; J. W. DuBose, *The Life and Times of William L. Yancey* (2 vols., New York, 1942); Grady McWhiney, "Were the Whigs a Class Party in Alabama?" *Journal of Southern History*, XXIII (1957), 510-22; Albert B. Moore, *History of Alabama* (University, Ala., 1934); Ruth K. Nuermberger, "The Royal Party in Early Alabama Politics," *Alabama Review*, VI (1953), 81-98; C. W. Williams, "Early Ante-Bellum Montgomery: A Black-Belt Constituency," *Journal of Southern History*, VII (1941), 495-525, and "Presidential Election Returns and Related Data for Ante-Bellum Alabama," *Alabama Review*, I (1948), 279-98.

For the critical years of party formation I consulted the (Huntsville) *Southern Advocate*, 1835-36.

Mississippi

The political history of the Jackson period in Mississippi has been thoroughly covered by Edwin A. Miles in his *Jacksonian*

Democracy in Mississippi (Chapel Hill, N.C., 1960) and two articles, "Andrew Jackson and Senator George Poindexter," *Journal
of Southern History,* XXIV (1958), 51-66, and "Franklin E. Plummer, Piney Woods Spokesman of the Jackson Era," *Journal of
Mississippi History,* XIV (1952), 2-34. Some additional information was obtained from J. F. H. Claiborne, *Mississippi as a Province, Territory and State* (2 vols.; Jackson, Miss., 1880); Cleo
Hearon, "Nullification in Mississippi," *Publications of the Mississippi Historical Society,* XII (1912), 37-71; J. P. Shenton, *Robert
John Walker: A Politician from Jackson to Lincoln* (New York,
1961); R. H. Thompson, "Suffrage in Mississippi," *Publications of
the Mississippi Historical Society,* I (1898), 25-49; and J. E. Walms-
ley, "The Presidential Campaign of 1844 in Mississippi," *ibid.,* IX
(1906), 179-97.

I also followed the course of party formation in the (Jackson)
Mississippian, 1834-38.

Louisiana

The definitive study is Joseph G. Tregle, "Louisiana in the
Age of Jackson: A Study in Ego Politics" (Ph.D. diss., University
of Pennsylvania, 1954), upon which I have relied heavily. There
is supplementary information in Leslie M. Norton, "A History of
the Whig Party in Louisiana" (Ph.D. diss., Louisiana State University, 1940); Roger W. Shugg, *Origins of Class Struggle in
Louisiana . . . 1840-1875* (University, La., 1939); and *Proceedings
of the Delegates of the Friends of the Administration of John
Quincy Adams, Assembled in Convention at Baton Rouge* (New
Orleans, 1827).

Missouri

The secondary sources for Missouri are less than adequate, but
some crude estimate of the situation can be obtained from William
N. Chambers, *Old Bullion Benton: Senator from the New West*
(Boston, 1956); P. McCandless, "The Rise of Thomas Hart Benton
in Missouri Politics," *Missouri Historical Review,* L (1955), 16-29;
Leota Newhard, "The Beginning of the Whig Party in Missouri,
1824-1840," *ibid.,* XXV (1931), 254-280; and Floyd C. Shoemaker,
Missouri and Missourians (5 vols.; Chicago, 1943).

SOURCES OF STATE ELECTION DATA

ALABAMA

Governor:

1819-1839, 1847-1859—*House Journal.*
1845—*Whig Almanac.*

President:

1824-1832—*The Alabama Review,* I (1948) , 284-88.
1836-1860—W. Dean Burham, *Presidential Ballots, 1836-1892* (Baltimore, 1955) .

CONNECTICUT

Governor:

1796-1818— (Hartford) *Connecticut Courant.*
1819-1840, 1842-1843—MSS, Secretary of State, Votes for Governor and Lieutenant-Governor, Connecticut State Library, Hartford, Connecticut.
1841—Niles' *Register,* LX, 131.
1844-1854—*Whig Almanac.*
1855-1860—*Tribune Almanac.*

President:

1820-1832—MSS, Secretary of State, Votes for Electors of President and Vice-President, Connecticut State Library, Hartford, Connecticut.
1836-1860—Burnham, *Presidential Ballots.*

Congress:

1820-1830—MSS, Secretary of State, Votes for Congress of the United States, 1821-1841, Connecticut State Library, Hartford, Connecticut.

DELAWARE

Governor:

1793-1858—*House Journal.*
1820, 1823 (special elections) —Niles' *Register,* XXVII, 121.

President:

1832—*Governor's Register, State of Delaware,* I (Wilmington, Del., 1926) , 301-2.
1836-1860—Burnham, *Presidential Ballots.*

Congress:

1812-1850—*Governor's Register,* I.

GEORGIA

Governor:

1825-1839—Stephen F. Miller, *The Bench and Bar of Georgia,* I (Philadelphia, 1858) , 267-8.
1841-1853—*Whig Almanac.*
1855-1859—*Tribune Almanac.*

President:

1828— (Milledgeville) *Georgia Journal,* Nov. 24, 1828.
1832—*Ibid.,* Dec. 10, 1832.
1836-1860—Burnham, *Presidential Ballots.*

Congress:

1790-1834—MSS, Executive Minutes, 1791-1838, Georgia Department of Archives and History, Atlanta, Georgia.
1836—Niles' *Register,* LI, 132.
1838—*Ibid.,* LV, 129.

ILLINOIS

Governor:

1822-1846—Theodore C. Pease, *Illinois Election Returns, 1818-1848* (Springfield, 1923) .
1848-1860—*Blue Book of the State of Illinois, 1925-1926* (Springfield, Ill., 1925) .

President:

1820-1844—Pease, *Illinois Election Returns.*
1848-1860—Burnham, *Presidential Ballots.*

Congress:

1819-1846—Pease, *Illinois Election Returns.*

INDIANA

Governor:

1816-1837—*House Journal.*
1840-1852—*Whig Almanac.*
1856-1860—*Tribune Almanac.*

President:

1824-1832—*Year Book of the State of Indiana . . . 1917* (Indianapolis, Ind., 1918) .
1836-1860—Burnham, *Presidential Ballots.*

Kentucky

Governor:

1800-1859—G. Glenn Clift, *Governors of Kentucky, 1792-1942* (Cynthiana, Ky., 1942).

President:

1824-1860—J. Shannon and R. McQuown, *Presidential Politics in Kentucky, 1824-1948* (Lexington, Ky., 1950).

Louisiana

Governor:

1812-1846, 1853—*House Journal.*
1849—*Whig Almanac.*
1855-1859—*Tribune Almanac.*

President:

1828-1832—J. G. Tregle, "Louisiana in the Age of Jackson" (Ph.D. diss., University of Pennsylvania, 1954), 356, 414.
1836-1860—Burnham, *Presidential Ballots.*

Maine

Governor:

1820-1846, 1848-1860—*Maine Register . . . 1957* (Portland, Me., 1957).
1847—Niles' *Register*, LXIV, 206.

President:

1824—Niles' *Register*, XXVII, 215.
1828-1832—*Maine Register . . . 1957.*
1836-1860—Burnham, *Presidential Ballots.*

Maryland

Governor:

1838-1853—*Whig Almanac.*
1857—*Tribune Almanac.*

President:

1788-1832—MSS, returns, Maryland State Archives, Annapolis, Maryland.
1836-1860—Burnham, *Presidential Ballots.*

MASSACHUSETTS

Governor:

1790-1815, 1817-1840—MSS, Secretary of Commonwealth, Abstracts of Votes for Governor and Lieutenant-Governor, 8 vols., 1790-1841, Archives Division, State House, Boston, Massachusetts.

1816—MSS, Secretary of Commonwealth, Court Records, 1815-1816, Archives Division, State House, Boston, Massachusetts.

1841-1848—Arthur B. Darling, *Political Changes in Massachusetts, 1824-1848* (New Haven, 1925).

1849-1854—*Whig Almanac.*

1855-1860—*Tribune Almanac.*

President:

1788-1832—MSS, Secretary of Commonwealth, Abstract of the Returns of Votes for President and Vice President of the United States, Archives Division, State House, Boston, Massachusetts.

1836-1860—Burnham, *Presidential Ballots.*

MISSISSIPPI

Governor:

1817-1859—*Official and Statistical Register of the State of Mississippi, 1908* (Nashville, Tenn., 1908).

President:

1824-1832—*Official and Statistical Register . . . 1908.*

1836-1860—Burnham, *Presidential Ballots.*

MISSOURI

Governor:

1820-1825—F. C. Shoemaker, *Missouri and Missourians* (5 vols.; Chicago, Ill., 1943), I, 410-11.

1828-1860—*Official Manual of the State of Missouri . . . 1889-1890* (Carson City, Mo., 1889).

President:

1824-1832—Shoemaker, *Missouri and Missourians,* I, 410-411.

1836-1860—Burnham, *Presidential Ballots.*

NEW HAMPSHIRE

Governor:

1800-1860—*New Hampshire Manual . . . 1891* (Concord, N.H., 1891).

President:

1788-1832—*New Hampshire Manual ... 1891.*
1836-1860—Burnham, *Presidential Ballots.*

NEW JERSEY

Governor:

1844-1860—*Manual of the Legislature of New Jersey ... 1956* (Trenton, N.J., 1956).

President:

1808—MSS, Minutes New Jersey Privy Council, II, State Library, Trenton, New Jersey.
1804, 1816-1832—Contemporary New Jersey Newspapers.
1836-1860—Burnham, *Presidential Ballots.*

Congress:

1791, 1792, 1803, 1806-1810, 1814—MSS, Minutes New Jersey Privy Council, I-II, State Library, Trenton, New Jersey.
1794, 1796, 1798, 1800, 1804, 1812, 1816-1840—Contemporary New Jersey Newspapers.

NEW YORK

Governor:

1801-1860—E. A. Werner, ed., *Civil List and Constitutional History of the Colony and State of New York* (2nd ed.; Albany, N.Y., 1886).

President:

1828—Niles' *Register,* XXXIX, 62.
1832—*Whig Almanac, 1838.*
1836-1860—Burnham, *Presidential Ballots.*

NORTH CAROLINA

Governor:

1836, 1838—*Whig Almanac.*
1840-1860— (Raleigh) *Weekly Standard,* Aug. 1, 29, 1860.

President:

1816-1832, 1840-1844, 1852-1856—MSS, Abstracts of Vote for Presidential Electors, Department of Archives and History, Raleigh, North Carolina.
1836, 1848, 1860—Burnham, *Presidential Ballots.*

OHIO

Governor:

1802-1859—*Ohio Election Statistics...1938* (n.p., 1939).

President:

1804-1808, 1816-1832—*Ohio Election Statistics...1938.*

1812—Wm. T. Utter, "Saint Tammany in Ohio...," *Mississippi Valley Historical Review,* XV (1928-1929), 339.

1836-1860—Burnham, *Presidential Ballots.*

PENNSYLVANIA

Governor:

1790-1829, 1835-1860—*The Pennsylvania Manual, 1935-1936* (Harrisburg, Pa., 1936).

1832—Niles' *Register,* XLIII, 199.

President:

1789-1832—*Pennsylvania Manual, 1935-1936.*

1836-1860—Burnham, *Presidential Ballots.*

RHODE ISLAND

Governor:

1797-1860—*Manual...of the State of Rhode Island, 1937-1938* (n.p., n.d.).

President:

1800-1832—*Rhode Island Manual, 1937-1938.*

1836-1860—Burnham, *Presidential Ballots.*

Congress:

1794-1851—*Rhode Island Manual, 1937-1938.*

TENNESSEE

Governor:

1801-1805, 1815, 1819, 1823-1833—*House Journal* and/or *Senate Journal.*

1807—(Nashville) *Impartial Review and Cumberland Repository,* Sept. 20, 1807.

1817—*The Official and Political Manual* (Nashville, Tenn., 1890).

1821—*Nashville Clarion,* Aug. 28, 1821.

1835-1860—*The Official and Political Manual.*

President:

1824-1832—*The Official and Political Manual.*
1836-1860—Burnham, *Presidential Ballots.*

VERMONT

Governor:

1812-1860—*Vermont Legislative Directory and State Manual,
1953* (n.p., n.d.) .

President:

1828-1832—*Ibid.*
1836-1860—Burnham, *Presidential Ballots.*

VIRGINIA

Governor:

1851—*Whig Almanac.*
1855-1859—*Tribune Almanac.*

President:

1800-1832—Tabulations of Manuscript returns, Virginia State
Library, Richmond, Virginia.
1836-1860—Burnham, *Presidential Ballots.*

Note: In computing the percentage of adult white males voting in
elections, I calculated from the federal decennial censuses the
numbers of adult white males for each state in each census year
and then, by interpolation, estimated the figures for the specific
years in which elections were held.   Several states, notably
Ohio, New York, Louisiana, and Kentucky conducted periodic
censuses of electors, but I did not use these figures because it
seemed proper to adhere consistently to the federal data.

INDEX

———•———

DATE DUE

NOV 2 '67			
RESERVE			
MAY 14 '68			
OCT 22 '68			
MAY 1 '69			
SEP 23 '69			
OCT 20 '69			
OCT 27 '69			
NOV 10 '69			
MAR 31 '71			
OCT 5 78			
OCT 19			
NOV 3 70			
NO 4 '80			